Economics in a
Business Context

Business in Context Series

Editors:

David Needle
Head of Undergraduate Studies, East London Business School,
University of East London

Professor Eugene McKenna
Chartered Psychologist and Emeritus Professor, University of London

Accounting in a Business Context (3rd edition)
Aidan Berry and Robin Jarvis
ISBN 1 86152 090 5

Business in Context (3rd edition)
David Needle
ISBN 1 86152 358 0

Economics in a Business Context (3rd edition)
Colin Haslam, Alan Neale and Sukhdev Johal
ISBN 1 86152 400 5

Human Resource Management in a Business Context
Alan Price
ISBN 1 86152 182 0

Economics in a Business Context

Third Edition

Colin Haslam
Alan Neale
Sukhdev Johal

THOMSON

Australia • Canada • Mexico • Singapore • Spain • United Kingdom • United States

THOMSON

Economics in a Business Context: 3rd Edition

Copyright © 2000 Colin Haslam, Alan Neale and Sukhedev Johal

The Thomson logo is a registered trademark used herein under licence.

For more information, contact Thomson, High Holborn House, 50-51 Bedford Row, London, WC1R 4LR or visit us on the World Wide Web at: http://www.thomsonlearning.co.uk

British Library Cataloguing-in-Publication Data
A catalogue record for this book is available from the British Library

ISBN 1-86152-400-5

Third edition published 2000 by Thomson Learning
Reprinted 2002 by Thomson

Typeset by LaserScript, Mitcham, Surrey
Printed in the UK by TJ International, Padstow, Cornwall

Contents

About the authors

Colin Haslam is Professor of Accounting and Business Strategy and Associate Director in the Management School, Royal Holloway University of London. He has researched and published extensively on subjects as diverse as the car industry, the European single market, Japanese management practices and British manufacturing decline.

Alan Neale is a visiting research fellow at the University of East London and teaches business studies students on undergraduate and postgraduate courses. He has published and researched in the areas of labour market economics and management of the environment and environmental policy.

Sukhdev Johal is a lecturer in accounting in the Management School, Royal Holloway University of London. He has researched and published extensively in accounting and particularly the importance of accounting for the household and more recently how shareholder value metrics influence management strategy.

Series foreword

This book is part of the 'Business in Context' series. The books in this series are written by lecturers, all with several years' experience of teaching on undergraduate business studies programmes. When the series first appeared in 1989, the original rationale was to place the various disciplines found in the business studies curriculum firmly in a business context. This is still our aim. Business studies attracted a growing band of students throughout the 1980s, a popularity that has been maintained in the 1990s. If anything, that appeal has broadened, and business studies, as well as being a specialism in its own right, is now taken with a range of other subjects, particularly as universities move towards modular degree structures. We feel that the books in this series provide an important focus for the student seeking some meaning in the range of subjects currently offered under the umbrella of business studies.

With the exception of the text, *Business in Context*, which takes the series title as its theme, all the original texts in our series took the approach of a particular discipline traditionally associated with business studies and taught widely on business studies and related programmes. These first books in our series examined business from the perspectives of economics, behavioural science, law, mathematics and accounting. The popularity of the series across a range of courses has meant that the second editions of many of the original texts are about to be published and there are plans to extend the series by examining information technology, operations management, human resource management and marketing.

Whereas in traditional texts it is the subject itself that is the focus, our texts make business the focus. All the texts are based upon the same specific model of business illustrated below. We have called our model 'Business in Context', and the text of the same name is an expansion and explanation of that model.

The model comprises four distinct levels. At the core are found the activities which make up what we know as business, including innovation, operations and production, purchasing, marketing, personnel and finance and accounting. We see these activities operating irrespective of the type of business involved; they are found in both the manufacturing and service industry, as well as in the public and private sectors. The second level of our model is concerned with strategy and management decision-making. It is here that decisions are made which influence the direction of the business activities at our core. The third level of our model is concerned with organizational factors within which business activities and management

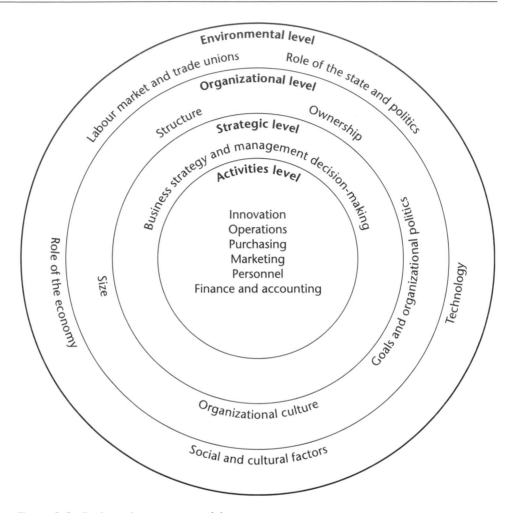

Figure **0.1:** Business in context model

decisions take place. The organizational issues we examine are structure, size, goals and organizational politics, patterns of ownership, and organizational culture. Clear links can be forged between this and other levels of our model, especially between structure and strategy, goals and management decision-making, and how all aspects both contribute to and are influenced by the organizational culture. The fourth level concerns itself with the environment in which businesses operate. The issues here involve social and cultural factors, the role of the state and politics, the role of the economy, and issues relating to both technology and labour. An important feature of this fourth level of our model is that such elements not only operate as opportunities and constraints for business, but also that they are shaped by the three other levels of our model.

This brief description of the 'Business in Context' model illustrates the key features of our series. We see business as dynamic. It is constantly being shaped by and in turn is shaping those managerial, organizational, and environmental contexts within which it operates. Influences go backwards and forwards across the various levels. Moreover, the aspects identified within each level are in constant interaction with one another. Thus the role of the economy cannot be understood without reference to the role of the state; size and structure are inextricably linked; innovation is inseparable from issues of operations, marketing and finance. Understanding how this model works is what business studies is all about, and forms the basis for our series.

In proposing this model we are proposing a framework for analysis and we hope that it will encourage readers to add to and refine the model, and so broaden our understanding of business. Each writer in this series has been encouraged to present a personal interpretation of the model. In this way we hope to build up a more complete picture of business.

Our series therefore aims for a more integrated and realistic approach to business than has hitherto been the case. The issues are complex, but the authors' treatment of them is not. Each book in the series is built around the 'Business in Context' model, and each displays a number of common features that mark out this series. Firstly, we aim to present our ideas in a way that students will find easy to understand and we relate those ideas wherever possible to real business situations. Secondly, we hope to stimulate further study, both by referencing our material and by pointing students towards further reading at the end of each chapter. Thirdly, we use the notion of 'key concepts' to highlight the most significant aspects of the subject presented in each chapter. Fourthly, we use case studies to illustrate our material and stimulate further discussion. Fifthly, we present at the end of each chapter a series of questions, exercises, and discussion topics. To sum up, we feel it most important that each book will stimulate thought and further study and assist the student in developing powers of analysis, a critical awareness, and ultimately a point of view about business issues.

We have already indicated that the series has been devised with the undergraduate business studies student uppermost in our minds. We also maintain that these books are of value wherever there is a need to understand business issues and may therefore be used across a range of different courses including some BTEC Higher programmes and some postgraduate and professional courses.

David Needle and Eugene McKenna

Preface to third edition

In this the third edition of this text readers will notice that the structure and content has changed considerably since the first edition. We have reacted to suggestions provided by users of the text and have also incorporated many new developments arising from our own research efforts. At the end of each chapter we develop an extensive case study designed to bring together the themes and issues arising from that chapter.

We have restructured the materials and make central to the text an accounting approach that uses a value added accounting framework to describe the context within which modern international business operates. To understand how a changing business environment impacts upon the competitiveness of international business we utilize our accounting framework to review the micro, meso and macro-economic context.

At a macro level the changing structure of economies presents firms with opportunities to migrate from operations where growth is slow and price competition is intensive into new economic spaces in services that offer more favourable growth and profit conditions. We note that, at a micro level, companies are dynamically adjusting their business activity mix to exploit the financial opportunities of operating outside a traditional industry sector. At a meso-economic level firms like Ford lead the way and find opportunity by consolidating financial results from a range of business segments such as car repairs and financial services.

We introduce the student to a number of key concepts that help to contextualize business policy. In relation to market conditions we outline the concept of trajectory and competitor interaction observing that dynamically sales revenues follow an arc-like trajectory as volumes and prices come under pressure. We describe operating architecture as that relating to the internal cost structure of a business. As revenue percolates down through the business to satisfy the various stakeholders a residual of cash and profit is available to cover the cost of capital in the balance sheet. Using the accounting framework outlined in this text we expect students to understand that between firms operating within sectors, across sectors and national economies the relationship between market conditions, operating architecture and capitalization is variable and contingent.

Firms continually exploit new market opportunities or face the prospect of restructuring and downsizing their activities. In an increasingly financialized world the interests of the shareholder-owner rub up against market maturity and relatively fixed internal operating ratios. It has often been argued that firms can transform their financial performance through the adoption of international world-class production management systems. We have argued in our previous editions and again here that emulation of systems without being able to replicate the context within which that so-called world-class business operates is likely to frustrate outcomes. When we consider these world-class benchmarks like Toyota, MicroSoft, Intel, etc. we often find that the context within which these firms operate are peculiar and rather specific. With MicroSoft it is the licence over the software, with Toyota low international labour costs and exceptional growth in output that underwrite financial success.

Mergers and acquisitions, management buy-ins, buy-outs, restructuring, outsourcing, share buy-backs and financial engineering are policies employed by managers to maintain the lump of cash and profit and return on capital. Many once-revered Japanese firms like Toyota, Nissan and Mazda are either being taken over or are restructuring – even Toyota is buying backs its shares. When it is no longer possible to sustain growth, operating ratios and return on capital firms must reorganize their resource configuration(s).

We are also sensitive to the fact that business operates in a political context where government policy(s) can directly or indirectly impact positively and negatively against the interest of business in the pursuit of cash and profit. It is often argued that the role of government is to stand back from the economy only ensuring that macro variables like inflation, interest rates and exchange rates are favourable. In an increasingly integrated world economy with free capital movement traditional policy instruments no longer have the impact on the domestic economy they might once have had. Even so governments still have influence through employment and wages on national demand and output. Privatization of public sector industry and services progressively removes government from influencing the circuits of consumption and production.

We are also, as with previous editions of this text, concerned to introduce the student to an understanding of environmental policy and how this impacts upon the context within which business must operate. To what extent are business calculation(s) shaped by the environment and to what extent can such sensitivities to the environment and use of resources sustain business advantage? Under what circumstances and to what extent can environmental concerns be made to align with the interests of business?

As with previous editions of this text we are mindful of the fact that many students using this text will embark on careers in business. They need tools of analysis that can contextualize the business environment within which their organization operates. They need to make sense of and rank factors that constrain or promote performance. We hope that students will find this text stimulating and that its framework of analysis provides a practical basis for revealing business in its context.

Colin Haslam
Royal Holloway June 1999

Acknowledgements

We would like to thank our families for their support over the past year. In addition we would also like to acknowledge the important contribution of: Julie Froud School of Accounting, University of Manchester, Professor Karel Williams (Director of Graduate Studies at the University of Manchester) and John Williams (emeritus Professor of Aberystwyth University) who have all developed many of the ideas contained in the text. Also Karen Ferrari for her help with proof-reading and correcting text and the library staff at Flemings Asset Management for their assistance with materials for research.

Figures

Tables

Key concepts

CHAPTER 1

Competitive advantage, cost reduction and cost recovery

In this chapter we explore how the role of management in business has become increasingly important. As organizations have evolved we observe a separation of ownership and control where management have day-to-day responsibility for the organization and control of resources with ownership residing with shareholders.

Economic texts provide a range of theories that attempt to explain how the motivations and objectives of a firm will differ when management is given day-to-day control. These theories argue that management objectives will differ from the owner-entrepreneur type business where profit maximization is the general rule.

Historically management's role is to look after operational detail and efficiency to ensure that profits will be made. In the post-war period management texts stress the importance of management strategy. Porter and Drucker stress the importance of strategy and develop models for management decision making and analysis. Porter's industry-structure analysis can be used to evaluate the competitive landscape and inform the choice of generic strategy. There are today many models that can be used to assess an organization's strengths and weaknesses.

There has also been a long tradition of emulation or copying best managerial practice. In the post-war period managers are informed about American best practice and in a later period Japanese best practice. Using a process of benchmarking to identify best practice management the weaker firm is informed about the systems and practices that are present in the successful firm and absent in the failing firm.

Whether or not management is about operational details, strategy or emulation of international best practice it is clear that throughout the post-war period the struggle is to enhance 'cost recovery' and economize on costs 'cost reduction'. The cost recovery/cost reduction couplet is a powerful determinant of financial success or failure.

Introduction

In this first chapter we review the historical development of business analysis. We observe that from an American perspective the development of business analysis is one which is characterized as a gradual shift from analysis at an operational level to analysis which is concerned with strategic management at a national and international level.

In *The Practice of Management* (1961) Peter Drucker suggests that economists do not take seriously the role of management and how management calculations and business analysis can improve decision making. The strategic imperative motivating management action is generally assumed to be that of utilizing business resources in a way that improves competitiveness and sustains competitive advantage. The general objective of the business policy text is one of equipping the manager with strategic framework(s) that inform business analysis in ways which are relevant for managing the modern international business. Any model or framework of business analysis should encourage the manager to critically assess the possibilities and limitations of particular strategic action(s) that are directed at maintaining competitive advantage.

When Drucker referred to the **Economists' Model of the Firm** he refers specifically to the theory of perfect competition. In this model of the firm, all the owner needs to do is adjust output in relation to price because the assumption is that all factor inputs (land, labour, capital and materials) are already combined in a technically and economically efficient way to meet the required market price.

In Figure 1.1 we describe the model of behaviour which constructs the economist's model of the perfectly competitive firm. In this model the firm is said to be unable to influence price and price is the single factor which

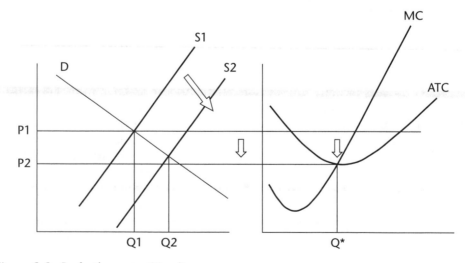

Figure **1.1:** Perfectly competitive firm

determines consumer behaviour and firm action. If price is originally at P1 then the perfectly competitive firm can sell quantity Q1 at a price P1 which exceeds the firm's average costs of production and so revenues exceed average total costs (ATC) and abnormal profit is being made.

If other firms observe there are abnormal profits being made they will enter this product market, so shifting (increasing) supply in this product market. When the supply curve shifts down to the right, price falls to P2 because market competition forces down prices until they settle at a level P2 which is just equivalent to the average total unit cost of production.

Within this framework of analysis the firm and the owner-manager are passive agents reacting to market prices in order to stay in business but are not able to influence market prices or the competitive position of the business. In practice a firm or business is not simply a passive actor in its relevant market, but rather it will attempt to influence consumer behaviour and its fortunes within a particular product market or economic space within which it operates.

The economist's 'business man' or entrepreneur, that underwrites the prevailing economic theory of the firm and the theorem of maximization of profits essentially reacts to economic developments in a passive rather than active way. Basically the manager is still the 'investor' or 'financier' rather than that of the professional manager (Drucker, 1961).

The point Drucker makes is that within the discourse of economics, management action is passive not active. In the 1960s and 1970s economic theory takes on board the fact there has been a separation of ownership and control and that the objectives of the 'manager' may differ from the shareholder who takes an ownership stake in the business. Economists such as Baumol and Marris do consider the fact that the objectives of management may interfere with the single overriding objective of profit maximization. At a general level, economic theory has accepted the role of management in shaping overall goals and objectives and manipulating consumer behaviour through advertising, marketing and differentiation of output. However, the detail of business analysis and calculation(s) which shape the combination of factor resources of land, labour, capital and materials in relation to output are often underdeveloped in the economist's text and this gap has been filled by the business policy/strategy text.

In Figure 1.2 we describe a number of possibilities which are at variance with the profit maximizing assumption (PM). Economists accept that the separation of ownership (shareholder) and control (management) establishes the possibility that firms may take on board objectives that reflect the interests of management. Marris (1964) presents an argument that management pursue policies and objectives that maximize organization growth. That is, growth in sales, assets and the size of the business will secure the interests of the owner for profits and the managerial interest is that of sustaining their employment and status. Baumol (1959) suggests that management(s) seek to generate maximum sales growth subject to a profit constraint. That is, management will push output and sales up to the point *Sm* where sales revenue is maximized but sufficient profits are available for dividend distribution to shareholders. These theories do take us some way from the model of the perfectly competitive firm but the economist's production function survives

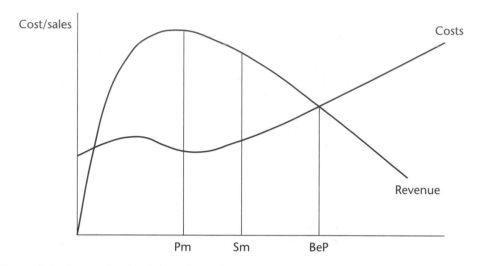

Figure **1.2:** Output levels of the sales and profit maximizing firm

these twists and turns. The production function represents the business as a black box within which an optimum mix of resources will be applied to meet a particular price set by the market or managerial objective specified.

In practice an organization needs to react to a complex set of internal and external factors which are determined by economic, political social and institutional factors. The role of senior management in the organization is elevated precisely because control is delegated by the owner(s) to make and shape corporate objectives. Management uses information at its disposal to dynamically reconfigure resources, both operationally and strategically, in the interests of sustaining corporate competitive advantage. The traditional concept of the entrepreneur as both owner and controller of the business abstracts from a number of legal and structural changes which impact on the performance of an organization. Simon (1955) and Cyert and March (1963) observe that organizational behaviour is to some extent influenced by the 'actors' within the organization. According to Simon the goals set and established are often not 'maximized' but are rather set at a satisfactory level so as to accommodate for the fact that it is often not possible to identify the maximum outcome nor motivate actors to achieve maximum results. Cyert and March further elaborate the fact that business goals and objectives are set by the interaction of various actors for a variety of technical and functional backgrounds.

The separation of ownership and control ensures that the unitary objective of profit maximization cannot be satisfied because other interests will shape business policy and behaviour. Technically the condition of maximized profit requires that organizations identify marginal cost, marginal revenues and production output up to a point where marginal cost of the last unit produced just equates to the marginal revenue received from its sale. In practice accounting rules and regulations and standards are used to determine cost and price per unit and signal whether a business has improved performance from one period to the next. Financial budgets are employed to estimate cost structure of a product or service provided and annual report and accounts present an organization's profit and loss, balance sheet and cash flow position year on year. These accounting figures reflect a complex relation between market conditions, the productive organization of resources and form(s) of capitalization of a business. That is, financial outcome(s) (value added, cash generation or profit generated) are conditioned by a complex variable set of relations between the market, resource mix and capitalization (sources of capital) of the business.

Total Revenue — Total Costs = Profit

In accounting terms the profit recorded in a set of company annual report and accounts is the difference between total revenues (or cost recovered from the market) minus total costs of materials, labour and capital costs, etc. The question as to how management goes about trying to improve the financial performance of the organization is often bounded by a series of structural and institutional constraints that can either promote or frustrate financial performance. For example, market conditions will vary over time, volume sales may stagnate, prices per unit fall or export markets expand because the exchange rate is favourable. Cost, recovery, or revenue generated, is therefore the outcome of a complex series of interactions and relations. Costs incurred in production (materials, labour costs and capital costs, etc.) are also subject to a complex series of influences. Labour costs will be affected by the part-time/full-time split, conventions over hours worked, social welfare mark up, age distribution and gender mix. Cost comparisons and benchmarking between businesses producing the same product are fraught with difficulties in comparing like with like. In circumstances where many of the revenue and costs variables are determined by factors outside the organization's control we should be wary of theories and statements that suggest that management 'controls' the business or that management strategy 'turned the business around'. In this respect the idea that management action is constrained by macro-economic variables beyond the control of a particular business would take us back somewhat towards the economic assumption that scope of managerial agency is bounded by a series of constraints.

Drucker in *The Practice of Management* critically engages with the economist's view that management has only a passive role to play in determining the fortunes of a business in perfect competition. Drucker takes the view that in the modern corporation management has an active role both in determining the organization of resources and strategic objectives.

> Managing goes a long way beyond passive reaction and adaptation. It implies responsibility for attempting to shape the economic environment, for planning, initiating and carrying through changes in that economic environment, for constantly pushing back the limitations of economic circumstances on the enterprise's freedom of action – it is management's specific task to make what is desirable first possible and then actual.
>
> *(Drucker, 1955)*

Good management is therefore an important weapon in the fight against external competitive market forces because it is capable of pro-actively shaping the economic environment, not merely being a passive agent. Michael Porter argues much the same about the application of management knowledge and the importance of using business analysis to evaluate competitive possibilities. According to Porter, industry structure analysis provides useful knowledge as to the sources of competitive advantage. With this particular model managers can run through a checklist of the strengths, weaknesses, opportunities and threats facing the business. Porter's framework for business analysis is grounded in micro-economic theory and concepts such as economies of scale, barriers to entry, differentiation and price competition can then be used to inform and direct strategic management and the choice of generic strategy.

> Knowledge of these underlying sources of competitive pressure provides the groundwork for a strategic agenda of action. They highlight the critical strengths and weaknesses of the company, animate the positioning of the company in its industry, clarify the areas where strategic changes may yield the greatest payoff, and highlight the places where industry trends promise to hold the greatest significance as either opportunities or threats.

(Porter, 1979)

Business analysis is therefore a process of collecting information which can be used to inform management action and this management knowledge can, according to Porter, be systematized using a classification process in which information is collected under different headings, often known as Porter's Five Forces Model:

1 What your competitors are doing.
2 The relationship your firm has with its suppliers.
3 The bargaining power of buyers.
4 The threat of new entrants.
5 The threat of substitute products.

Once this knowledge has been collected and assessed then opportunities emerge which, according to Porter, are related to an assessment of the strengths and weaknesses of your own business and the strengths and weaknesses of your rival competitors. For Porter business analysis provides 'the groundwork for a strategic agenda of action'.

There is no doubt that modern management texts one way or another stress management's ability to positively change the strategic direction of the business. These texts generally reinforce strategic concepts with a case study to demonstrate the positive application or the inappropriate use of the strategic concept by management. Successful management applies management knowledge to improve internal resource use and react to external competitive forces strategically and positively in a way that underwrites the competitiveness of the business.

The role of business analysis should be, as Porter observes, to critically interrogate the environment within which the business operates and to seek out ways of sustaining competitive advantage. Articulating and understanding operating context within which national and international business operates is an important objective of this text.

The internationalization of best practice

Strategic management texts and consultancies have often uncritically recommended emulating world-class management systems but the results, for those who copy, are often disappointing. In each successive era we observe that a dominant country-based model of world-class business emerges and is usually associated with that country's strong performance internationally. The strong successful country acts as the role model to be copied by those countries and economies where performance is weak.

American management practices have served as a powerful role model for emulation at least up until the 1980s. It is not possible to capture all that is American management practice and so we must consider the major themes that emerge from a consideration of management practice in key large American firms, reports published by semi-official government institutions and academic/practitioner texts.

The period 1879 to 1929 represents a golden age for American business because year-on-year output growth across a whole range of manufacturing enterprise ran into double figures. Growth in output of steel, textiles, industrial equipment and commercial goods was extremely rapid. Growth was such that in the period 1879 to 1929 the output of American manufacturing increased by a factor of ten (Table 1.1). Over this same period annual output growth averaged five per cent per annum, which was double the rate of growth per annum, achieved after 1929 and up to 1990.

Henry Ford's manufacture of the Model T at Highland Park in the period 1909 to 1916 is a case that illustrates well how the emergent auto industry in America in the early part of the twentieth century was established. From 1909 to 1916 Ford increased output fifty-fold starting with the production of 10,000 Model Ts. Seven years later the company was producing 500,000 Model Ts at the Highland Park plant in Detroit. As output expanded so Ford

Table **1.1:** Output increase in American manufacturing 1879–1929

Period	Output Index 1929 = 100	Average growth per annum %
1869–1879	10.2	3.9
1879–1889	18.3	7.2
1889–1899	27.5	4.6
1899–1909	43.4	5.3
1909–1919	61.0	3.7
1919–1929	100	5.8

(Source: S. Fabricant (1940) *Output of Manufacturing Industries*, National Bureau of Economic Research)

managed to take cost out of the product. The concept of economies of scale is often used to simplify our understanding of Henry Ford's achievements at Highland Park. In Figure 1.3 we describe the economies of scale or long-run average cost curve as the downward sloping curve which tangentially connects each short-run cost curve. That is, as we build larger plants or factories the unit cost profile described by successive short-run average cost curves falls. The long-run average cost curve therefore describes a relationship between output expansion and unit costs such that as output expands so total units costs fall.

At Ford cost reduction did not reveal itself simply as the result of building larger and larger factories, rather unit costs were reduced through a judicious and continuous process of productive reorganization. The reorganization of physical space enabled the firm to produce more of the Model T in-house at lower cost. Ford also paid attention to the design characteristics of the Model T – it had to be light but strong for driving on the dirt tracks that led out of Detroit. Cost and price reductions coupled with reliability fed the latent demand for personal transportation and this expanded at such a rate that Ford was unable at times to satisfy the demand. The overriding management problem at Ford Highland Park was how to satisfy demand against the constraint of materials flow within factory (Williams *et al.*, 1993).

The management of operations at Ford was dynamic and subject to constant change in the struggle to reduce costs. The company employed sophisticated costing system even though Henry Ford was known to despise accountants. Ford methods are excellently described in Arnold and Faurote's (1914) study *Ford's Methods and Fords Shops* (see also Tolliday 1998).

Concern with the management of operational detail in the early part of this century was reflected in the work of F.W. Taylor and consultants such as C. Knoeppel. F.W. Taylor's contribution to operational management is best summarized under the generic title 'scientific management' and specifically

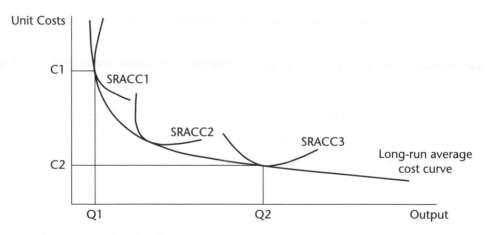

Figure **1.3:** Economies of scale curve

outlined in the publication *The Principles of Scientific Management* (1929). In this work Taylor outlines the principles of time and motion study in addition to his work on the variables affecting the cutting of metals and the functional organization.

Taylor's approach to business analysis required an understanding of 'how work should be done'. In particular it was first necessary to understand existing operational details before improvements to the method of work could be implemented to reduce costs. As we shall see later in this book, it is still the case that nationally or internationally, the most important internal costs to manage are labour cost. Placing a great deal of attention on how work should be done makes sense in the light of the fact that most conversion cost is labour cost. The objective of measuring the time for a task or set of tasks was to establish the standard time for accomplishing the work to be done.

Establishing a measurement of the standard was important because as Taylor saw it:

> Both sides (the workforce and management) must recognise as essential the substitution of exact scientific investigation and knowledge for the old individual judgement or opinion.
>
> *(Taylor, 1929)*

The importance of time measurement and use of labour time cannot be underestimated and it was a factor central to the management of costs at Highland Park where minute costs for all operations had been constructed as early as 1909. Once this information was made available to management it could then be used to plan and schedule the work to be done in the day or week. After carrying out the time and motion study at Bethlehem Steel in the materials yard, Taylor introduced a planning department which issued instructions to the foremen as to what work was to be done at what time during the day. At this early stage in the development of management practices we can already observe that the collection of and measurement of standard work times was a particular form of business analysis which was appropriated by management. The analysis could be used to determine what was to be done in the working day and the best way to meet demand at the lowest cost.

The preoccupation is with measurement and its presentation, in various forms, to management for the purposes of exercising control of operations. We have noted that at Ford Highland Park the time taken for particular operations was of great importance to management in establishing the labour costs for a particular operation and was recorded in great detail in Ford's cost books. Attention to operational detail was not just employee centred but consideration was also given to factory layout and the use of machinery. Ford engineers were concerned to combine operations performed at one machine so that a bundle of tasks could be completed at one workstation. They also paid particular attention to the layout of machines according to their sequence of use so that the flow of materials could be enhanced. As Bornholt observed, the company's practice was to arrange machines regardless of function according to 'sequences of use' (Bornholt, 1913) because this improved the flow of materials through the factor and reduced unnecessary indirect labour costs involved in trucking.

In order to co-ordinate, plan, and control, management needs to be provided with knowledge describing the detail of operations. American Journals such as *Industrial Management* reflected the desire to improve the functioning of management through the use of 'management information systems'. In 1919 Charles Knoeppel, founder of the consultancy firm C.E. Knoeppel and Co Inc, presented a series of articles on 'Graphic production control'. His purpose was to explain how graphical charts could be used to visually represent the manufacturing activity as a relationship between revenues (volume times price per unit) and cost incurred in production. The two purposes for which these calculations were carried were: firstly to undertake 'Analysis' which according to Knoeppel was

> The determination of what is to be done, the manner of doing and what it should cost in time and money – the standard to work to.

and secondly to achieve 'Control' which was

> the means provided for enabling the shops to either measure up to the standard determined upon, or to investigate variations in such a way as will result in a constructive attempt to subsequently attain it. With *Analysis* and *Control* utilised to the fullest – the manufacturing world can be assured that it will secure the maximum operating efficiency.

The importance of Knoeppel's work is that it combines the measurement of standard times to do the work with the labour rate per hour so as to determine the cost of performing a particular operation. According to Knoeppel, his business analysis using graphic production control not only 'controls production but leads indirectly to better strategic organisation' (Knoeppel, 1919).

There is no doubt that up to a point the focus of management, academics and consultants in the early part of this century was, with internal resource management, what might generally be termed 'cost consciousness'. As American firms reaped the benefits of output expansion co-ordination and control become important concerns. Co-ordination of the large corporation and control required a more sophisticated organization structure and systems of management accounting.

Charles Knoeppel was already presenting possible solutions to the problem, as he saw it, to the issue of large-scale business co-ordination and management. He observed that no business can be as successful as it is possible to be with two or three heads running things. There must be a single co-ordinating and directing function.

Whereas Ford is credited with introducing the moving assembly line, General Motors is the company often credited with establishing the organization structure designed to control and administer large-scale business. In the next section we consider the importance attached to the divisional structure and how structure contributed to the development of organization strategy.

Organization structure and control

In 1962 and 1964 two influential texts were published: Chandler's *Strategy and Structure* and Alfred Sloan's *My Years With General Motors*. Both these texts describe the strategic benefits of the divisional form of organization structure.

In 1927, Sloan presented a paper to the Automobile Editors of American Newspapers:

> A few words about our organisation itself. We operate on the principle of what I might term a decentralised organisation. I mean by that, each one of our operations is self-contained, is headed up by an executive who has full authority and is responsible for his individual operations.

> *(GM Archive, USA)*

Divisions were located somewhere between the Head Office and the functional departments in the functional form of organization structure (see Key Concept 1.1).

According to Chandler,

> The executives in charge of these divisions, in turn, have under their command most of the functions necessary for handling one major line of products or set of services over a wide geographical area, and each of these executives is responsible for the financial results of his division and for its success in the market place. This administrative form, often known in business parlance as the *decentralised* structure.

> *(Chandler, 1962)*

The decentralized form of organization (for which read divisional form) is an organization structure in which the divisions take responsibility for operational day-to-day administrative functions. The head office is then free to concentrate on more long-term business planning and regulating the outcomes of these longer term policies. The planning and co-ordination function is the basis for creating a business strategy according to Chandler.

> The departmental and divisional offices may make some long-term decisions, but because their executives work within a comparable framework determined by the general office, their primary administrative activities also tend to be tactical or operational. The general office makes the broad strategic or entrepreneurial decisions as to policy and procedures and can do so largely because it has the final say in the allocation of the firm's resources, men, money and materials.

> *(Chandler, 1962)*

A divisional structure was an important development because it sealed the separation of operational management and its associated calculations from strategic business analysis which would be undertaken in the head office. Accounting techniques such as budgeting and the development of strategic management accounting inform business analysis and influence corporate

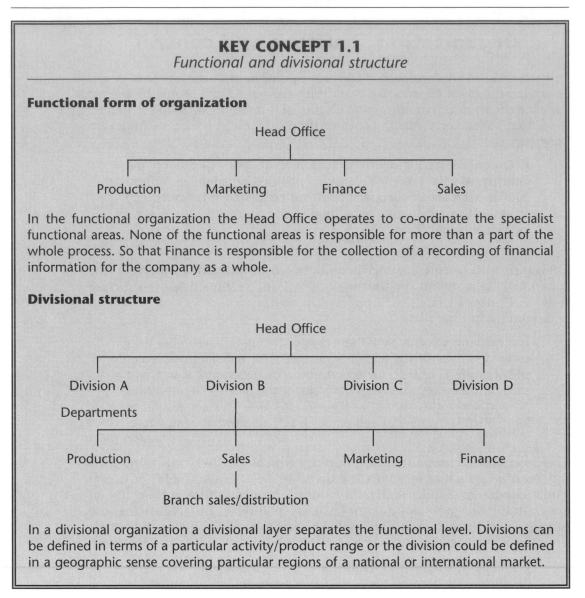

KEY CONCEPT 1.1
Functional and divisional structure

Functional form of organization

Head Office

Production   Marketing   Finance   Sales

In the functional organization the Head Office operates to co-ordinate the specialist functional areas. None of the functional areas is responsible for more than a part of the whole process. So that Finance is responsible for the collection of a recording of financial information for the company as a whole.

Divisional structure

Head Office

Division A   Division B   Division C   Division D

Departments

Production   Sales   Marketing   Finance

Branch sales/distribution

In a divisional organization a divisional layer separates the functional level. Divisions can be defined in terms of a particular activity/product range or the division could be defined in a geographic sense covering particular regions of a national or international market.

decisions. Apart from day-to-day financial control, Joel Dean elaborates on the strategic use by the early 1950s of the financial investment appraisal technique Discounted Cash Flow (DCF). This accounting calculation was at the time presented as a form of financial analysis that could be used to predict and prioritize capital allocation towards the most profitable of investment projects (Dean, 1953). At a strategic level the tools of corporate financial planning suggested that management could strategically select the most profitable of investment options and so secure the competitive position of the business.

The 1929 Great Crash in America resulted in massive write down in the value of shares, and shareholders questioned the nature of firms' cost control and profit reporting. In his 1933 text *Profit Engineering* Charles Knoeppel observes that

> a post depression text or business should be motivated by profit mindedness. Apart from this there is the requirement to satisfy the interests of the shareholders and protecting their return on investment.

Financial and especially management accounting become the staple tools of business analysis at a strategic level within American business from the 1930s onwards. The health warning was now:

> Profits being vital and necessary if business is to render the service it should, should never be left to accident, hope and blind chance. They should be planned on in advance and so controlled, all of the time as to assure that they will be made. In other words profit should be the first deduction from the dollar on income, and the business should be budgeted to operate off the balance.
>
> *(Knoeppel, 1933)*

The emphasis placed in Knoeppel's text is that the head office should utilize accounting knowledge in the form of business analysis because this would ensure that resources will be best directed towards maintaining profitability and an efficient use of capital.

In Dent's (1935) publication *Management Planning and Control* a British audience is introduced to the detail of financial business analysis and how this can enhance co-ordination, planning and strategic control by management. The management practices and forms of business analysis undertaken in large American Corporations had a major impact on the international business community in the post-war period. Corporations such as General Motors and Sears Roebuck were, in the 1960s, presented as role models of best modern management practice and the key elements of their systems should be emulated. In particular the success of General Motors over Ford in the 1920s is generally linked to the efficacy of General Motors' policy of directed financially managed business.

The diffusion of American management practices was also made possible by the multinationalization of American business, the development of business schools and international consultancy services. At the start of this chapter we emphasized the point that Drucker, and later Porter, consider the role of senior management in formulating strategy for the business and establish that business analysis and its associated techniques can inform strategic action(s). Sensibly used business analysis can support strategic advantage and maintain above average profit performance. The corporate executive needs to employ business analysis to shape management calculations and roll back competitive forces and create strategic opportunity for the business.

In the 1970s and 1980s Michael Porter presents a framework of business analysis in a series of articles. This framework could, he argued, be used to inform strategic decision making in a way that would ensure sustained competitive advantage (Porter, 1979, 1980). Porter combines a framework of business analysis namely industry structure analysis with the concept of generic strategy.

Porter's framework of business analysis 'industry structure analysis' describes what he considers are the 'underlying economics' of the business (Key Concept 1.2). The elements which make up Porter's framework of analysis to a great extent are borrowed from the discourse of economics and can be used to classify the relation of your own business to its competitors, suppliers, and distribution network. The framework of analysis thus becomes a checklist against which a manager can position a business against those in the industry generally. Porter's framework for business analysis can then be used to describe the competitive forces giving rise to the shape of the industry structure in which your business operates. According to Porter:

> The strategist, wanting to position his company to cope best with its industry environment and to influence that environment in the company's favour, must learn what makes the environment tick.

Porter's model of business analysis is summarized in Key Concept 1.2. This model of analysis can be used to evaluate the ways in which an organization could be situated, not just in a particular industry structure, but also a series of power relations. For example analysis of the supplier relation could establish the point that large-scale suppliers are able to exert their economic power in a way which could undermine your own organization objectives. Suppliers of new cars for example, are known to exert a strong control over dealership margins because they can restrict prices and/or volumes. Pharmaceutical companies have for a long period of time recovered revenues on the basis that their product patents are protected. Organizations like Glaxo-Wellcome are increasingly subject to the threat of low-cost generic substitutes as drugs go ex patent. The expiry of the patent could then undermine price structures for the product or service, so damaging profits.

Industry structure analysis provides a checklist of the strengths, weaknesses, opportunities and threats facing an organization. The challenge facing the organization is then one of sustaining competitive advantage (profitability) relative to competitors in the long run and the route to this end is prescribed by the so-called 'generic strategy' followed by the business. The choice of generic strategy is one that is informed by the business analysis undertaken.

Porter classifies possible 'generic strategies' into four distinct categories in a simple but effective two-by-two matrix (see Figure 1.4).

A generic strategy is a route towards competitive advantage. A generic strategy of low-cost leadership implies that the firm will set out to be a cost leader. Industry analysis may have identified that a market leadership position is one that can only be sustained where the output is sold at the lowest cost. An organization's strategic response may then be one of seeking to produce a product or service at the lowest cost and price within the industry or commercial sector within which it operates.

According to Porter 'A low cost producer must find and exploit all sources of cost advantage'. To exploit all sources of cost advantage, the firm must obtain the benefits of economies of scale across all areas of the business. The promise is that low-cost leadership will sustain competitive advantage for the

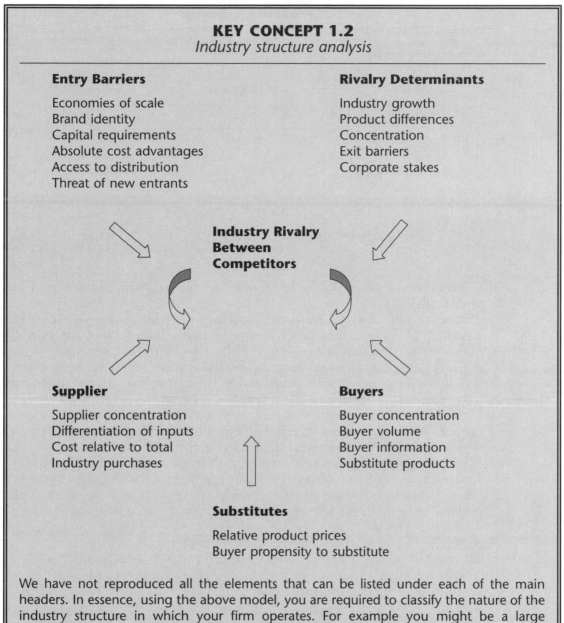

KEY CONCEPT 1.2
Industry structure analysis

Entry Barriers

Economies of scale
Brand identity
Capital requirements
Absolute cost advantages
Access to distribution
Threat of new entrants

Rivalry Determinants

Industry growth
Product differences
Concentration
Exit barriers
Corporate stakes

Industry Rivalry Between Competitors

Supplier

Supplier concentration
Differentiation of inputs
Cost relative to total
Industry purchases

Buyers

Buyer concentration
Buyer volume
Buyer information
Substitute products

Substitutes

Relative product prices
Buyer propensity to substitute

We have not reproduced all the elements that can be listed under each of the main headers. In essence, using the above model, you are required to classify the nature of the industry structure in which your firm operates. For example you might be a large organization producing car components and your suppliers of materials are tied into you because they supply 80 per cent of their sales to you alone. The substitute product range cannot compete on cost but new entrants are possible from overseas suppliers. You sell to a major car assembler and this contract represents 45 per cent of your sales so you are tied into a strong buyer relationship.

Further Reading: Porter (1980) *Competitive Strategy* Free Press.

Competitive Advantage

Competitive Scope	Lower Costs	Differentiation
Broad Target	Cost Leadership	Differentiation
Narrow Target	Cost Focus	Differentiation Focus

Figure **1.4:** Porter's generic strategies

organization and establish an above-average performance in terms of profitability.

Rather than choose a low-cost leadership generic strategy it is possible, according to Porter, to choose a strategy of differentiation. These are generally non-price factors that have been identified from the demand side of the industry structure analysis. Product design, quality and after sales service should be the focus of strategic attention if the firm can charge a premium price and secure higher profit. Using the concept of value-chain analysis, Porter (1985) argues that a company is profitable when the value it creates exceeds the cost of performing the value-chain functions. The choice is either that you produce at a lower cost than your competitors or construct the value-chain function in such a way that you can charge a premium price because the service or product provided is in some way differentiated from competitor products/services. Differentiation generic strategies focus on a particular product segment or market segment and are sometimes referred to as a 'niche marketing strategy'. Often it entails obtaining competitive advantage from a particular segment of a market rather than overall competitive market advantage. For example, producing small cars rather than medium and luxury cars or off-road vehicles or specific specialist computer software that is specifically designed for the client. For Porter, business analysis informs strategic choice because it facilitates the choice of generic strategy. Organizations which choose a generic strategy sensitive to the industry structure analysis undertaken will increase their chances of securing superior performance and competitiveness (see Key Concept 1.3 and Figure 1.5).

In the 1970s and 1980s a range of strategic business analysis techniques were introduced and included SWOT and PEST (see Key Concept 1.4) analysis, the Boston Consulting Group matrix and portfolio analysis. These forms of analysis are like Porter's industry-structure analysis, concerned with establishing the extent to which the environment in which the organization operates offers opportunities or threats. The objective is to seize upon the opportunities and avoid strategic pitfalls.

KEY CONCEPT 1.3
Value-chain analysis

The value chain describes how a series of sequential activities add value to input. That is, inbound raw materials flow through internal operations, are then distributed, marketed and provided with an after-sales service. At each stage in the sequence human, technical and financial resources are applied at add value (cost) to the product or service being provided.

Value-chain analysis is used to identify where value is added (costs incurred) within the sequence of operations. In a broad sense this financial information can form the basis of identifying where most value is added making broad comparisons with competitors producing similar products and services.

This analysis converts into useful strategic knowledge when the information is used to adjust the articulation and use of resources so as to meet benchmark cost reduction targets.

(See also R. Lynch (1997) *Corporate Strategy*, pp. 246–248, Pitman)

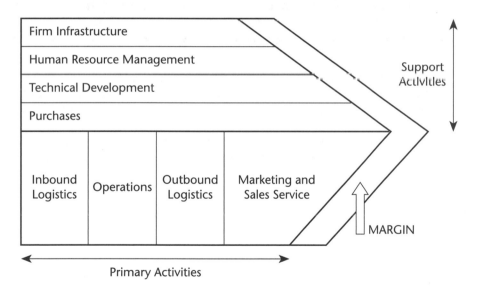

Figure **1.5**: The value chain

SWOT analysis produces an analysis or checklist of the organization's internal strengths and weaknesses – for example an internal strength may be your low-cost position and cash generation based on market dominance and financial operating architecture. Weaknesses would be the opposite, for example falling market share and weak financial performance. Opportunities and threats are defined as being external to the organization. An opportunity might be related to competitor weakness or political and economic changes

KEY CONCEPT 1.4
PEST analysis

PEST analysis is a tick-the-box checklist approach which evaluates the impact of Political, Economic, Socio-cultural and Technological aspects of an organization's environment. The list of factors to be considered can be continually extended but broadly it is concerned to evaluate issues such as:

P : Political stability, legislation, relations to government, etc.

E : GDP trends, inflation, the exchange rate, investment costs, employment and wages, commodity prices, etc.

S : Changes in cultural values, environmental issues, education and health, changes in the distribution of income, population changes, etc.

T : R&D breakthrough, speed of technical change, R&D spending in competitor organizations, patents and licensing.

Many factors are of great significance when evaluating the direction to take with regards to an organization's business strategy. The health warning is that we need to attach a hierarchy of importance to these variables and understand that this ordering of priorities will dynamically change over time.

which directly or indirectly support your firm's goals and objectives. On the other hand threats come from new entrants, low market growth or political and technological change which undermines your market and financial position.

The Boston Consulting Group (BCG) two-by-two matrix (Figure 1.6) is concerned with the classifying of an organization's product portfolio.

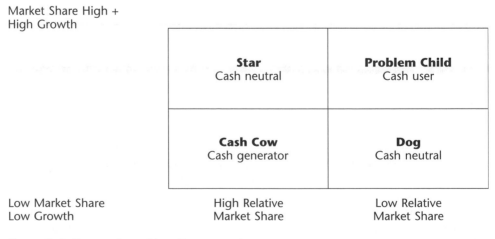

Market Share High +
High Growth

	Star Cash neutral	**Problem Child** Cash user
	Cash Cow Cash generator	**Dog** Cash neutral

Low Market Share
Low Growth

High Relative
Market Share

Low Relative
Market Share

Figure **1.6**: Boston Consulting Group matrix

A star product is one on a growth trajectory and is winning a high market share relative to similar products or services. Whilst the model assumes that such products will be cash neutral it is often the case that businesses operating in a strong market with a dominate market share tend to have cash generative operations.

A cash cow is a product or service able to generate the lion's share of a mature market and is at a stage in the product life cycle where it requires fewer costs and so can be used to generate cash flow. A business with a portfolio of cash generative products is able to invest the financial surplus in new product development and the marketing of new possible star products.

The form of business analysis suggested by the previously outlined models are generally concerned with directing management action towards improving the organization of internal resources so that costs are progressively taken out of the product or service provided and that market opportunities are fully exploited. At a strategic level business analysis should be concerned with informing management as to the strategic business opportunity(s) available within a domestic economy and across international markets.

The internal-operational and external-strategic forms of business analysis should complement each other because business analysis is concerned with cost reduction and strategic business analysis is concerned with extending the revenue base of the business.

As national home markets are increasingly saturated by domestic firms, cost recovery intentions shift towards overseas markets as a means to expand revenues and profits. Globalization is often a rather abused concept because it is difficult to establish the argument that the world is becoming a global market place. It is the case that many firms do consolidate a large proportion of their sales and profits from sales made overseas. Internationalization of business and globalization are popular concepts within the mainstream business strategy texts. It is generally assumed that the world is becoming one large trading block where exports and capital flows between economies diminish the importance of the national economy for a business. There is no doubt that world trade through exports has expanded dramatically in the last 30 years and that capital flows in the form of foreign direct investment have increased.

Direct exports from a home production base is still is the main lever by which organisations expand cost recovery beyond the confines of their home market. Whilst Foreign Direct Investment (FDI) (see Key Concept 1.5) often involves setting up production and distribution operations overseas through subsidiaries. It is also possible to establish an overseas market presence through a joint venture or merger/take-over.

Growth in international trade has led some commentators to argue that we are moving away from economic systems where national markets are distinctive entities isolated from each other by trade barriers, geographic distance and time. It is argued that markets are merging into one huge global market place. The impression this creates is that all businesses are global and have their strategic sights on exporting and manufacturing overseas. The likes of Coca-Cola, Reebok and Microsoft spring to mind as examples of the new

---

KEY CONCEPT 1.5
Foreign Direct Investment (FDI)

Foreign Direct Investment (FDI) involves an investor in one country purchasing and/or acquiring a controlling interest in assets in another country. Direct investment is usually undertaken to establish overseas branch operations by multinational corporations. Dunning (1979) suggests that a firm will be interested in expanding overseas where analysis suggests that:

1 The firm is able to gain ownership advantages such as access to technologies and so exclude competitors.
2 The firm may prefer to have a direct control over the technology or protect its interest in R&D.
3 There may be production cost and distribution cost advantages because you are able to get around trade barriers or access low labour costs.

The main sources of international FDI flows are the USA, Europe and Japan. In 1960 these regions accounted for over 80 per cent of world FDI flows and still currently account for roughly 80 per cent of total world FDI.

---

form of global business. Hirst and Thompson (1996) have critically engaged with the business policy literature on globalization.

The authors argue that transnational corporations tend to concentrate their operations within a home base, observing that some 70 per cent of output is on average produced at home. Another measure, more specific to manufacturing, reinforces the general impression that in 1992 the production overseas by Japanese firms represented just 6.6 per cent of total (domestic and overseas) production whereas the proportion of the US was 27.1 per cent. In Germany, generally not keen on moving production capacity out of the country, the proportion had been 20 per cent in 1989 (MITI, 1992).

It is therefore possible to employ analysis to engage with the assumptions that Japanese manufacturers are globalizing their activities. We can get an idea as to the scale of direct investment abroad by the major international FDI donor countries and put this into some general perspective. American, Japanese and European FDI overseas has been of less significance than investment at home. This can be briefly indicated from a general measure of FDI as a proportion of gross fixed capital formation in the domestic economy.

Only the UK stands out as being a major investor overseas in terms of the ratio of FDI to domestic capital formation and even here the magnitudes are not large. The USA and Japan invest even less than Germany and France the two main European FDI donor countries. Apart from the UK most of the major industrialized economies invest over 95 per cent of their investment funds in domestic capital formation rather than in overseas capital formation (see Table 1.2).

Looking at Table 1.2, as far as FDI is concerned, international business prefers to invest more at home than it does overseas. Globalization is not just

Table **1.2:** Ratio of foreign direct investment to domestic fixed capital formation (in nominal terms) by main investing country (average)

	1980–1985	1986–1990	1991–1993
UK	11.93	18.30	13.27
Germany	2.80	5.49	4.90
France	2.38	6.54	6.81
US	1.67	3.11	5.43
Japan	1.39	3.72	1.83

(Source: JETRO White Paper on Foreign Direct Investment 1995, summary, March 1995, p. 6 Table 1–5, Tokyo)

about capital investment and FDI but is more broadly about exports and international trade. Here again it would be difficult to argue that trade represents are large proportion of national GDP and even within the major trading blocks the balance of trade in 20 years rarely exceeds +/– 4 per cent of the national income of these countries.

In aggregate at the level of the national economy it is easy to establish the point that the relative magnitudes of FDI and exports are low in comparison to domestic investment and output. But this may not be so at the micro firm level and here it is true that many organizations operate with a high export to home sales ratio, overseas production to domestic production ratio and capital formation overseas compared to home market investment. Where an organization is faced with a limited expansion of its home market, a globalization of business activity makes sense if cost recovery is to expand further. An organization's home market may have become saturated and cyclical and overseas market expansion offers the possibility of extending the limits of cost recovery. Investment overseas may facilitate distribution and market access to a less mature market which is still on a trajectory of expansion or where price structures are more favourable than that within the home based economy. Investment overseas may facilitate cost reduction possibilities because the organization gains access to lower wage cost structures and longer working hours.

It is generally argued that the motivation of a company to expand globally is that of increasing the scale of profits because these are increasingly limited for a domestic home-based enterprise. In this respect we can explain business behaviour by extending Porter's value chain to include an international perspective. Organizations will exploit overseas markets in order to expand cost recovery and access low-cost resources in a global supply chain. Accessing a market in which a premium price can be recovered requires price structures of that host economy be more favourable than the home market. Locating a particular portion of the value chain overseas could facilitate access to lower production costs. In this way globalization is still driven by the imperatives of enhanced cost recovery and cost reduction. To remain competitive cost recovery and cost reduction go hand in hand with the generation of more secure financial results. As we shall see in the next section cost recovery and cost reduction are the essential ingredients of a cash generative business.

We have already observed that the logic underlying the globalization of the business is financial. The promise is that exceptional financial performance will accrue to firms that extend the international scope of their operations. We will use a case study on Japanese manufacturing FDI to illustrate how analysis can used to establish the strategic motivations of Japanese FDI and the rewards of such strategies.

Case study: Japanese foreign direct investment

By the early 1980s Japanese firms, through their Foreign Direct Investment (FDI), had already established substantial overseas production capacity in sectors such as consumer electronics and car manufacture. We can infer the underlying motivations of Japanese corporations from the geographic patterns of this FDI strategy. Up until the early 1980s most of this overseas foreign direct investment (54 per cent in 1980) had been directed into Asia and Latin America.

At this stage there were relatively large differences in labour costs between Japan and the Asian recipients of this investment. The underlying motivation of Japanese firms was to look for opportunities to reduce costs. In the mid and late 1980s there was a shift to Europe and, especially, the US which received on average 77 per cent of total Japanese FDI by 1990. In this second stage of overseas direct investment the strategic focus of Japanese firms was on cost recovery. Overseas transplant operations can facilitate access to affluent markets where income (gross domestic product) per head is high and price structures are favourable. Transplants were also used to defuse political opposition to imports from Japan which had, in the US and Europe, taken an increasing share of their domestic durable goods markets. During the 1990s we have seen a gradual shift back to investment in Asia (which took one-third of Japanese FDI in 1993) as cost reduction again becomes increasingly important for Japanese parent firms. This has been particularly the case as the yen to $ exchange rate has appreciated in recent years (see Table 1.3). In general Japanese firms have globalized

Table **1.3:** Changing factors behind Japanese FDI

1950s and 1960s	1970s	1980s	Early 1990s
Resource development	Market expansion	Market expansion	Cost reduction yen appreciation
Industrialization and import substitution	Trade friction in TVs and machine tools	Appreciation of yen	
		Cost competitiveness	Increase international procurement
		Trade friction in Autos and VTRs	Access liberalized trading zones NAFTA, EU, AFTA

(Source: JETRO White Paper on FDI, 1996)

their operations in order to access stronger market and hence cost recovery conditions and reduce costs by locating production in offshore low labour cost regions (see Table 1.4).

The pressure of yen appreciation has been of particular importance to manufacturers who are export exposed. For example, Toyota like many other Japanese car assemblers is highly dependent on its export markets and 25 per cent of total sales revenue is derived from exports to the USA.

In a recent Toyota Report and Accounts, the Chairman and President observe:

> We'd been planning for plants outside Japan to make about one-third of the six million cars and trucks we expect to be selling annually by the turn of the century. That compares with 25% now. But faster-than-expected appreci- ation of the yen is prompting us to pick up the pace in globalizing our operations. In that sense, the strong yen is causing pain and disruption for us and our suppliers in Japan. From a global perspective, the measures we are taking to deal with the strong yen are making Toyota a stronger competitor: a more innovative developer, a more cost-competitive manufacturer, a more aggressive marketer.

(Annual Report, 1995 p. 1)

The two generic strategies of cost reduction and cost recovery are a strong couplet which can interact positively (or negatively) to establish the financial precondition for a strong (or weak) cash generative business (see the next section on the calculation of value added and cash from operations). We can observe that in the operations of their overseas affiliates Japanese corporations skilfully manage their cost recovery and cost reduction operations on a global scale. This can be observed from an analysis of Japanese sourcing and procurement arrangements internationally.

In the case of the USA and Asia some 50 per cent of procurement is obtained from local sources and the rest predominantly comes from Japan. Local procurement is undertaken to ensure that materials and services are purchased at the lowest cost but still a large percentage of procurement is from the home-based manufacturing operation which underwrites their cost recovery.

Table **1.4:** Japanese FDI (US Dollars) 1981–91 (cumulative)

Area	Manufacturing %	Non-Manufacturing %	Total US $ Mill
Pacific Rim			
Asia	44.2	55.8	52,300
North America	29.8	70.2	171,424
Latin America	10.0	90.0	42,547
Rest of the World			
Europe	24.1	75.9	76,111
Residual	11.8	88.2	29,634
Total			372,016

(Source: JETRO (Ministry of Finance))

Japanese transplants in the EU, like those in Asia and USA, import around 40 per cent of their procurement requirement from the parent companies in Japan. The EU transplant operations are however different from those in Asia or America, because their level of local procurement from within the region is unusually low. In the EU case, local procurement is low because a significant part of their component requirements come from Asian affiliates. Of the EU Japanese parents 29 per cent of the value of Japan's EU transplant purchases is locally sourced against something like half the value of purchases in the American and Asian cases. As a result, the import content of purchases is materially higher in the EU case where two-thirds of purchases are imported from outside the EU. It is hard to see this changing because European electronic parts are an expensive substitute for low wage Asian output and the capacity of the automotive transplants to source within the EU is limited by the fragmented, low-volume nature of their operations. Low local procurement is a structural fact of life for Japanese European transplants (see Table 1.5).

We have already noted that a major motivating force behind the process of globalization of business activity is the pursuit of maximum profit and return on capital invested. In Europe and the USA, Japanese affiliates have found it difficult to make profit from their overseas operations. According to a 1994 JETRO survey, 51.2 per cent of Japanese transplant affiliates in the EU were making operating losses by 1992.

National and international business policy is driven by two overriding generic strategies: cost recovery and cost reduction. Strong cost recovery and effective cost reduction are an important strategic couplet that can underwrite the financial performance of an organization. The bottom line is an expansion of cash generated from operations. Sustained cash generation is needed to ensure that competitive advantage is sustained. However as we shall also observe many factors outside of the control of management can frustrate this general objective and the skill of management is to anticipate these variables and take action to limit damage.

A value-added accounting framework for business analysis in the next section will explore the generic strategies of cost recovery and cost reduction. We will use this

Table **1.5**: Breakdown of procurement source for Japanese manufacturing affiliates (by region as of financial year 1992)

Location of Japanese Manufacturing Affiliates by Region	Local Procurement %	Imported From Third Country Other Than Japan %	Imported From Japan %	Total Import Content of Japanese Affiliates
Asia	48.5	8.9	37.9	46.80
US	51.7	6.2	42.1	48.30
EU	29.0	21.8	44.4	66.20
World	46.5	12.6	40.9	53.50

Notes: Imported from third countries indicates mainly imports from low wage Asia.
(Source: Japanese Ministry of International Trade and Industry (1992) *Overseas Business Activities of Japanese Corporations*)

framework of international business analysis to consider the extent to which, and under what, conditions competitive advantage is sustainable.

In the Japanese case a major lesson is that the decision to globalize operations through direct exports and/or overseas distribution and manufacture was taken strategically at a time when the exchange rate was much more favourable than it is now. The appreciation of the yen after the Plaza agreement in 1985 rapidly turned Japanese producers into high cost exporters and profits made in $, for example, are translated back into fewer yen (see Figure 1.7).

The generic strategy of cost reduction fervently pursued by Japanese firms within their domestic market is proving difficult to sustain against market maturity and yen appreciation. Many firms are now shifting production capacity overseas to access lower labour costs. Japanese firms are also redefining their marketing strategies positioning product in premium price segments and selling on the basis of non-price characteristics e.g. Toyota Lexus brand.

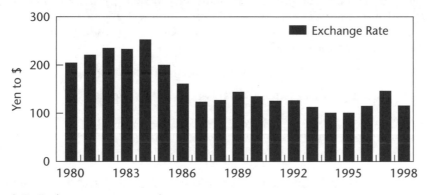

Figure **1.7:** Exchange rate yen to $

Global emulation: Americanization or Japanization?

The internationalization of business systems and globalization of business are popular concepts within the mainstream business strategy texts and they come into their own when it is combined with 'productivity analysis' and 'benchmarking'. In these studies productivity analysis identifies the weak firm, sector or national economy. The strong firm, sector or national economy becomes the defining benchmark. The benchmark(s) differ depending on the particular study undertaken but they often include: education levels, R&D capability, managerial system, infrastructure, innovation, institutional practices and regulatory frameworks.

KEY CONCEPT 1.6
Productivity and benchmarking

Productivity analysis

This generally utilizes the economist's concept of total factor productivity. Output levels are determined by two factors: the level of labour and capital and the efficiency with which these resources are deployed; and the productivity of the firm, sector and national economy. Total factor productivity (the productivity of capital and labour) is calculated as:

Total Output/Inputs of Labour and Capital

Total factor productivity combines the results of both labour and capital productivity.

Labour productivity at the firm or sector level can be measured simply as the total employment divided into total physical output. Often a physical output numerator is not easy to identify and so a financial proxy for the physical measure of output is used namely value added or net output per employee (see Chapter 2 for calculation of value added). It is possible to refine the labour productivity calculation by dividing the total number of labour hours worked into the value added to obtain a financial index of value added generated per labour hour. Economists often use GDP (Gross Domestic Product in real terms) per capita to define national productivity.

Net Output or Value Added/Physical Units of Labour

Net Output or Value Added/Total Labour Hours Worked

Capital productivity is often calculated as capital stock (total gross fixed assets before depreciation or capital consumption) divided into the net output or value added figure. This is used to establish the value of output generated from a quantum of capital employed.

In general greater weight and significance is attached to the trend and level of labour productivity because it accounts for the greater share of total factor input costs or costs in value added (again see Chapter 2).

Benchmarking

This is where firm, sector or national productivity comparisons are made. This analysis establishes rank order relations between firms, sectors or national economies. Once the gaps between firms or national economies are identified, the reasons for the gap are explained and firms, sectors and national economies are recommended to emulate best national or international practices.

There is also a strong element of recurrence in the various productivity studies undertaken historically, and to demonstrate this we review the major UK national efficiency studies. In 1908 the Board of Trade compared Britain with Germany and to a lesser extent with the US and concluded that technical education and the health of the workforce centrally explained the gap in productivity between the UK and the other two.

In the late 1940s and early 1950s the Anglo American Council on Productivity Reports (AACP) asked the question of the time 'How could

Europe live with superior American productivity?' These reports emphasized the scale of American operations, design standardization and the management of operations as well as differences in managerial control, for example the divisional organization structure and financial control. On the management of operations the AACP drew attention to the layout of American factories to improve flow and the use of multifunction machines to reduce production cycle time.

In the 1980s and 1990s our attention is drawn to Japanese productive superiority defined in the Oliver and Wilkinson (1988) study of Japanese-UK transplants and their assumed superiority over domestic UK firms in the same industrial sector. The MIT studies – *The Future of the Automobile* (1984) and *The Machine that Changed the World* (1990) identify a productivity gap between Japanese car producers and their counterparts in the US and Europe. In the later MIT study the concept of the lean production is used to encapsulate the Japanese 2:1 productivity advantage over American and Europe car producers. That is, Japanese firms use on average half the labour hours to produce an average saloon car and the point is driven home with a example comparing GM's Framingham assembly plant with Toyota's Takaoka assembly plant. Management Consultants Arthur Andersen (1992, 1994) produce a series of 'Lean Enterprise' benchmarking reports that confirm the 2:1 productivity gap in car component suppliers. Williams *et al.* (1994, 1995) have argued that differences in productivity between Japanese car assemblers and their American counterparts are exaggerated. Using a value added to sales correction factor (to adjust for differences in vertical integration see also Chapter 2) they find that the value added per employee at a company level in US dollars is roughly 20 per cent higher in Toyota compared to Ford. At a sectoral level the total build hours per vehicle is roughly equivalent, with the Japanese motor vehicle sector taking 130–140 hours to produce a vehicle compared to 150 hours in the US. If we take all the hours worked in the sector that go into producing an average car the difference is not 2:1.

In a recent productivity study, McKinsey and Co. (1998) national and sector comparisons are made and as with earlier studies a productivity gap between the UK its benchmark countries/industry sectors are found and explanations sought.

> Our study reveals that the United Kingdom currently lies bottom of the G7 league table in a representative sample of key market sectors. The study explores what UK companies are doing differently at an operational level and why, and how these differences contribute to the productivity gap.
>
> *(McKinsey, 1998, p. 2)*

The explanation for the productivity difference between the UK and its competitors has 'four root causes':

1 It is argued that UK firms are subjected to low levels of competitive intensity from externally located overseas competitors. Exposing UK firms to intensified competition would force complacent management to improve the management of resources.

2 Product market and land use regulations prevent the most productive firms from expanding and gaining from economies of scale. Small fragmented firms remain intact when rationalization of capacity would improve efficiencies.

3 So-called spillover effects mean that low productivity in one sector flows over into other related sectors because they too can become complacent.

4 Managerial practices can dictate how companies compete. Managers must energetically pursue, adopt and implement international world-class management practices.

In aggregate, the McKinsey productivity study finds that there is a 26 per cent difference between UK market sector performance and that for the USA and a 13 and 14 per cent difference between the UK and France and Germany. Most of the total factor productivity (TFP) difference is explained as a deficiency of labour productivity in the UK relative to its major competitors (see Figure 1.8).

Achieving higher productivity one year to the next is always, and everywhere, a beneficial objective. In 1945 Fabricant observed that in the case of US industry 'Doing with less labour per unit of output in these industries means that that labour is released to augment their output, to provide additional or better products of other industries, or to lengthen leisure' (Fabricant, 1945, p. 26). Where organizations can increase productivity economy in the use of labour establishes lower unit costs and the precondition for further output expansion. Baumol (1985) notes that:

> Above all productivity growth provides the most obvious benefit – it contributes to the general standard of living of a society. When each worker produces more with a given outlay of effort, that person's family can generally expect (albeit with some time lag) to have more real income to spend on behalf of its members. This benefit of productivity growth is so self-evident and well-known that any fuller discussion of the relationship itself would be otiose.

(Baumol, 1985, p. 10)

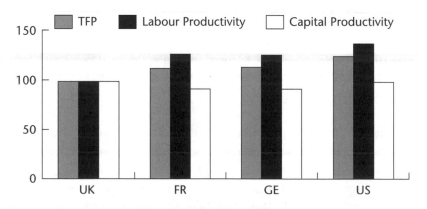

Figure **1.8:** Market sector total factor productivity 1994–96
(Source: McKinsey and Co. 1998)

The general promise is that action and effort directed towards improving productivity will then, unproblematically, improve performance at all levels within the firm, sector or national economy. However the context within which managerial action takes place is of great importance. Physical improvements in process and plant performance may not translate into financial gain at the consolidated company level. For example a business that saves costs may pass all of this on to the customer in the price, or lower costs expand output requiring an increase in the distribution and marketing labour force. Physical productivity improvement does not necessarily translate into higher profit margins and financial value added per employee.

At a sector level the translation from physical into financial results is also affected by external variables that are beyond influence and control of the firm. For example, the rate of growth of sector value added will be determined by consumer expenditure patterns and the distribution of household income. In motor vehicle sector market maturity combines with a skewed distribution of household income to restrict demand even though prices in real terms fall year on year. Or in the case of food retailing where the product becomes so cheap that spend per person in the household regardless of household income is relatively flat.

Cost reduction and cost recovery do go hand in hand because an expansion in sales volume driven by a lower cost per unit is a necessary condition for improving financial performance but it is not a sufficient condition. Business policy is a constant struggle between what it is possible to manage and that which is structurally determined and limiting. This text will explore the possibilities and limitations of management action within a variable economic context.

Workshop questions/exercises

Q1 What do you understand by the term 'divisional organization structure'? In what ways could this organization structure improve co-ordination and control of business resources?

Q2 How can Porter's 'industry-structure analysis' be used to inform strategic decision making and the strategic positioning of a business?

Q3 To what extent is the globalization of business an accomplished reality?

Q4 What do you understand by the term 'benchmarking'? Illustrate your answer with any relevant case examples.

Q5 To what extent can the emulation of world-class business practices transform an organization's performance?

Q6 What do you understand by the terms 'cost recovery' and 'cost reduction'?

Exercise

Table **1.6:** Toyota domestic and export sales and overseas production

	1988	1990	1992	1994	1996	1997	1998
Total sales bill yen	7,216	9,193	10,163	9,263	10,828	12,244	11,678
Sales in Japan	4,450	5,400	5,880	5,296	6,417	6,449	5,024
Sales Outside Japan	2,766	3,793	4,283	3,967	4,411	5,795	6,654
Ratio of Sales inside to outside Japan	1.60:1	1.42:1	1.37:1	1.33	1.45:1	1.11:1	0.75:1
Exchange Rate yen to $	126	134.4	124.8	99.8	116	129.9	130.9
Exports units	1.837	1.706	1.701	1.472	1.311	1.538	2.549
Overseas Production	0.244	0.677	0.764	1.052	1.35	1.378	in above
Total Overseas Units mill	2.081	2.383	2.465	2.524	2.661	2.916	2.549
Domestic Sales mill units	2.194	2.425	2.331	2.010	2.191	2.216	1.907

Note: in 1985 before the Plaza agreement the yen to dollar rate was 238 yen to the $

1   Is Toyota operating in a mature home market in terms of volume sales?
2   In 1985 the Plaza agreement resulted in an appreciation of the yen to the $ with the rate falling from 238 yen progressively to 120–130 yen in the late 1980s and early 1990s. What would be the impact this currency appreciation on the value of Toyota's exports?
3   Has Toyota's overseas production strategy been a success in maintaining the sales revenue base of the business?

Table **1.7:** Sales and distribution networks in Japan

	Toyota			Nissan		
	Employees	Showrooms	Domestic car sales mill units	Employees	Showrooms	Domestic car sales mill units
1985	103400	3843	1.69	74173	3007	1.028
1986	108296	3972	1.777	74740	2914	1.006
1987	109589	4056	1.955	75907	3004	1.055
1988	108626	4265	2.096	72844	2927	1.173
1989	114727	4529	2.436	71878	2977	1.385
1990	119468	4755	2.471	74578	3066	1.378
1991	119468	4755	2.337	78294	3176	1.318
1992	127140	4901	2.2	77847	3176	1.178
1993	130142	4936	2.016	75396	3099	1.062
1994	128095	4966	2.051	74961	3090	1.05
1995	122683	4977	2.02	71773	3971	1.111
1996	122683	4977	2.191	69949	3048	1.111

1 Calculate the cars sold per employee productivity figure for each company in the respective showrooms in Japan for Toyota and Nissan. Which is the more productive of the two companies?
2 Calculate the cars sold per showroom for each company. Which is the more productive of the two companies?
3 What other information would be needed in order to assess which of the two companies had the most effective distribution system for selling cars in Japan?

References

Altstuler, A. et al (1985) *The Future of the Automobile Industry*, Cambridge, Mass.:

Anglo American Council on Productivity Report on Internal Combustion Engines (June 1950) and report on Management Accounting (Nov. 1950).

Arnold, H. and Faurote, F. (1915) *Ford's Methods and the Ford Shops*, New York: Engineering Magazine Co.

Arthur Andersen Consultants (1992, 1994) *Lean Enterprise Benchmark Survey*, London.

Baumol, W. J. (1959) *Business Behaviour, Value and Growth*, London: Macmillan.

Baumol, W. J. and McLennan, K. (1985) *Productivity Growth and US Competitiveness*, Oxford, OUP.

Board of Trade (1908).

Bornholt, A. (1913) 'Placing machines for sequence of use: the trucking involved when machines are grouped by classes', *Iron Age*, December.

Boston Consulting Group, The (1996) *Shareholder Value Management*, Booklet 2, London.

Chandler, A. (1962) *Strategy and Structure*, Cambridge, Mass.: MIT Press.

Cyert, R.M. and March, J. (1963) *A Behavioural Theory of the Firm*, Hemel Hempstead: Prentice Hall.

Dean, J. (1953) 'Measuring the productivity of capital', *Harvard Business Review*, Jan/Feb.

Dent, A. (1935) *Management Planning and Control*, London: Gee.

Drucker, P. (1961) *The Practice of Management*, Mercury: London.

Fabricant, S. (1945) *Labor Savings in American Industry*, US National Bureau of Economic Research (NBER), November.

Hirst, P. and Thompson, G. (1996) *Globalization in Question*, Polity Press.

JETRO (1995) White Paper on Foreign Direct Investment, Japan External Trade Organisation, March, Tokyo.

JETRO (1996) White Paper on Foreign Direct Investment, Japan External Trade Organisation, March, Tokyo.

Knoeppel, C. (1919) 'Graphic production control', *Industrial Management*, Feb.

Knoeppel, C. (1933) *Profit Engineering: Applied Economics in Making Business Profitable*, London: McGraw-Hill.

Lynch, R. (1997) *Corporate Strategy*, London: Pitman.

Marris, R. (1964) *Theory of Managerial Capitalism*, London: Macmillan.

McKinsey & Co Consultants (1998) *Driving Productivity and Growth in the UK Economy*, London.

MITI (1992) *22nd Survey of Overseas Activities of Japanese Corporations*, Tokyo.

Oliver, N. and Wilkinson, B. (1988) *The Japanisation of British Industry*, Oxford: Blackwell.

Porter, M. (1979) 'How competitive forces shape strategy', *Harvard Business Review*, March/April, pp. 136–45.

Porter, M. (1980) *Competitive Strategy*, New York: Free Press.

Porter, M. (1985) *Competitive Advantage*, Boston MA: Free Press.

Simon, C.H. (1955) 'A behavioural model of rational choice', *Quarterly Journal of Economics*, Vol. 69.

Sloan, A. (1927) *The Principles and Policies behind General Motors*, Sept, GM Archives, Flint Michigan (Sloan, A.P. Jnr, C.2 83 – 12.16.).

Sloan, A. (1964) *My Years with General Motors*, New York: Doubleday.

Taylor, F.W. (1929) *Principles of Scientific Management*, New York: Harper and Bros.

Tolliday, S. (1998) *The Rise and Fall of Mass Production*, Vol. 1 and Vol. 2, Cheltenham: Edward Elgar.

Williams, K., Haslam, C., Johal, S. and Williams, J. (1994) *Cars: Analysis, History, Cases*, Oxford: Berghahn Books.

Williams, K., Haslam, C., Johal, S. and Williams, J. (1995) 'The Crisis of Cost Recovery and the Waste of the Industrialised Nations', *Journal of Global Competition and Change*. Vol. 1, pp. 67–93.

Williams, K., Haslam, C.,Williams, J. (1993) 'The myth of the line: Ford's production of the Model T at Highland Park 1909–1916', *Business History*, Vol. 35, no. 3, pp. 67–85.

Womack, J., Jones, D. and Roos, D. (1990) *The Machine that Changed the World*, New York: Rawson Associates.

CHAPTER 2

A competitive business analysis: A value-added framework

In this chapter we introduce an accounting framework that can be used for business analysis. This framework is what we term a value-added accounting framework but is a calculation that would be familiar to economists and also accountants. In this chapter we outline how it is possible to calculate value added from a set of company accounts from both the subtractive and additive perspective.

We use this framework to establish connections between market conditions, internal operating architecture and financial results. Value added is determined by market conditions and the trajectory upon which the organization is operating. Market conditions are often variable as between firms within the same economy and sector.

The internal operating architecture of a firm is best described as a series of ratios that show how sales revenue is netted off to cover internal operating costs. Purchases received from suppliers of external products or services are netted off the gross sales to obtain the value added. The ratio of purchases to sales is also variable between firms. Deducting labour costs from value added derives the cash from operations. Financial ratios such as profit earned per unit of sales is the combined result of the variable relation between market conditions and internal operating ratios. Return on capital employed (ROCE) is an important financial performance indicator and it too results from the variable relation between market conditions, internal operating ratios and the capital employed in the balance sheet.

The value added accounting framework can also usefully be used to compare and contrast performance as between firms nationally or internationally. We show in the case study how two companies Caterpillar and Komatsu can be benchmarked against each other. Value added analysis is also used to question whether or not Komatsu was the stronger of the two firms.

Introduction

According to Wood (1978), value added is a measure of wealth created by a business or an activity.

> It differs fundamentally from sales revenue because it excludes the wealth created by the suppliers of the businesses. Thus value added is a measure of the net rather than the gross output of a factory, company, industry, or even country.

Gilchrist (1971) notes that:

> The creation of Added Value is an object which ought constantly to be in the minds of company executives. Whenever decisions are made, the acid test of their effectiveness will be whether they have resulted in an improvement in the Value Added per unit of resource input.

This chapter will explore how a value-added accounting framework can be used to:

1 Describe the financial operating architecture of a business.
2 Understand the relationship between market conditions, operating architecture and cash generation.
3 Benchmark the firm against competitors.

The calculation of value added

The calculation of value added is outlined by Bernard Cox in his text *Value Added*. In this management accounting text Cox describes the various managerial applications of the value added accounting calculation. He illustrates how a set of consolidated annual report and accounts can be used to calculate value-added and observes that:

> Value added can be thought of from two stand-points: the subtractive, which is sales less purchases, and the additive, which is the sum of profits, depreciation, interest, payroll costs, dividends and taxation. The subtractive viewpoint represents the creation of value added, while the additive is the way in which wealth created is distributed.

(Cox, 1979)

The calculation of value added at the level of the firm is similar to that which we find in the national accounts for the economy as whole. The concept is not new; Pigou in the 1920s had formulated the calculation of value added (or net output) as sales revenue minus bought-in materials. This, he argued, avoided including the output of others as your own by deducting the value of inputs. Cox illustrates the link between company level value added and national accounting for value added (see Figure 2.1).

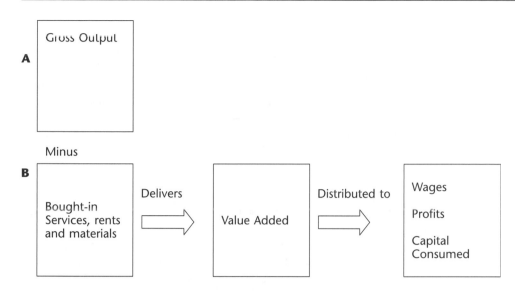

Figure **2.1:** The constituents of value added (Adapted from B. Cox, 1979)

He observes that blocks A and B in the national accounts represent total or gross income for all industries. By deducting all that is purchased (Block B) we have the calculation of value added. This figure can also be found by adding together: income from employment (including social costs); gross trading profits and an imputed charge for capital consumed (a depreciation charge)

To illustrate how we calculate value added we use accounting information taken from the Ford Motor Corporation annual report and accounts (see Table 2.1). Each year companies produce an annual report and accounts and it is possible to reconstruct a value-added accounting statement. Subtractively, value added is calculated by deducting all expenses relating to the supply of materials and services from the total sales revenue for a given year. Value added is the value (or costs) that is added to all purchases made by the business in order to bring a product or service to a finished saleable state. Additively, value added can be calculated by adding together labour costs

Table **2.1:** Ford: Value added calculated using subtractive and additive method

Figures all in million of $	199Y	199X
Sales Revenue	146,991	137,137
Minus: Purchase of materials and services	(101,720)	(94,955)
Value Added	45,271	42,182
Labour costs including social charges	25,687	23,758
Depreciation	12,791	11,719
Operating Profit	6,793	6,705
Value Added	45,271	42,182

(Source: Ford Consolidated Annual Report and Accounts)

(including social costs) to depreciation and operating profit or net income before interest and tax.

In this particular example 70 per cent of the total sales revenue earned by the Ford Motor Company is paid out to suppliers of materials, components and services. What is left over after these payments are made is the value added generated from operations. Value added therefore represents the value of work undertaken by Ford in its own organization as a per cent of total market sales. Value added as a percentage of sales revenue is a financial proxy for the degree of vertical integration of a business (see Key Concept 2.1). If we were to undertake the same calculations for other car manufacturers we would establish the degree to which Ford is internationally more or less vertically integrated than its competitors. In this way the value added accounting calculation becomes a useful tool for benchmarking one firm against another in a similar line of business.

The company would then need to apply the fund of value added to cover internal conversion costs. Value added will be used to pay labour costs in the form of wages and salaries (including social costs of pensions and healthcare), depreciation (the provision for capital replacement) and operating profit which covers payments to government (taxes), banks (interest payments) and shareholders (dividends).

At Ford the value added is appropriated to cover the cost of employment and in this example labour costs account for 57 per cent of the value added. After covering labour costs, what remains is used to cover depreciation and profits share in value added. By far the largest cost to a business like Ford is

KEY CONCEPT 2.1
Vertical integration

Vertical integration can be understood as the degree to which value added is generated within a business or outside the boundaries of the organization in the supply chain. It is an important calculation because it allows us to establish the degree to which costs are internalized or externalized.

Calculated as: Value added/Sales × 100
Ratio of 100   = Total vertical integration
Ratio of 0   = Total vertical disintegration

Where a business is perfectly integrated all costs are internally generated and subject to internal managerial control systems. As a business progressively increases outsourcing it becomes more vertically disintegrated and a larger proportion of overall costs are located in the supply chain. Porter's (1985) value chain analysis is concerned with the management of costs within the business defining these as support or primary activities.

Our concern is that for Ford, as with many other businesses, a large percentage of total cost is outside of the immediate management and control systems. It is therefore necessary to understand the balance between internal and external costs and so identify strategic initiatives to reduce cost.

the cost of labour and this generally takes up to two-thirds of total value added.

According to Bernard Cox '... payrolls normally account for a large proportion of value added – the average is about 70 per cent in UK manufacturing industries' (Cox, 1979).

The value-added calculation therefore deducts externally determined costs for the purchase of materials and services and what remains (the value added) are the internal costs of manufacture or the cost of providing a service. It has become fashionable to argue that labour costs no longer matter and it is true that direct labour costs only account for a small proportion of overall total costs. However the calculation of labour's share of value added gives an altogether different perspective on the importance of labour costs. In the next section we will observe that nationally labour costs account for 60 to 70 per cent of total internal organization value added. The management and control of labour costs is therefore of great importance.

What remains after the labour costs have been subtracted from the value added is, in economics, technically termed the gross operating surplus (GOS). This residual, after labour costs have been covered, can be used as a proxy for cash generated from operations (depreciation plus operating or trading profit). This definition of cash from operations can be substantially reconciled with a company source and application of funds as cash flow from internal operations (see Key Concept 2.2). Subtracting labour costs from value added generates a rather crude definition of cash flow from operations that will not reconcile perfectly with a firm's cash flow or funds flow statement which includes funds from financing and funds released (or not, as the case may be) from working capital adjustments.

KEY CONCEPT 2.2
Cash flow

A set of annual report and accounts will normally produce a source of funds or cash flow statement, the format of which varies nationally and internationally but normally contains the following key financial information.

	$	
Net Income/loss for Year	X	Positive or negative
Depreciation + Amortization	X	
Working Capital Adjustments		
Increase/Decrease in Inventory	X	Positive or negative
Increase/Decrease Accounts Receivable	X	Positive or negative
Increase/Decrease in Accounts Payable	X	Positive or negative
Cash Flows From Operations	Y	Positive or negative

The lessons we draw from the value-added accounting framework are: first we should not be complacent about the importance of labour costs; and second we should not underestimate the importance of cash flow. Cash flow is a precarious (and precious) residual financial variable. Cash flow generated from operations is a powerful indicator of corporate vitality and financial health because it is an index of an organisation's financial ability to sustain corporate competitiveness. The standard business policy texts suggest that profit is the essential index of competitive advantage. For example, Porter (1985) argues that firms who correctly analyse their environment and choose the 'correct' generic strategy will achieve above average profitability in the industry in which they operate. Porter's index of competitiveness is therefore profit and whilst he observes that profit is of importance he does not clearly specify how we should calculate profit. In contrast Kay, in his text *Foundations of Corporate Success* (1993), works within a value-added accounting framework to establish his index of competitive strength. Kay deducts labour, capital, and raw material costs from sales to determine value added. Kay's derivation of value added is equivalent to the accounting calculation of operating profit rather than gross value added which includes labour costs, depreciation and operating profit.

Value added: John Kay (1993)
Foundations of Corporate Success

Kay calculates what he defines as the value added for a range of international organizations. His calculation deducts from sales revenue: raw material costs, wages and salaries, capital costs. So for Glaxo the pharmaceuticals company we have:

		£ million
		1994
Sales		8,701
Wages and Salaries	(2,000)	
Capital Costs	(978)	
Raw Materials	(3,526)	
Value Added		2,197

This measure of value added is approximately equivalent to gross profit from operations. The definition of value added used in the value-added accounting framework adds back labour costs which is the traditional accounting and economist calculation of value added. Including labour costs in value added also highlights how the value added is distributed within particular organizations and dramatizes the importance of labour costs.

Kay's analytical framework operates within accounting to derive an index of profit or net operating surplus and uses this measure as an indicator of corporate strength. The value-added accounting framework in this text privileges cash generation over profit. Cash generation from operations is important because it is from this financial resource that the business is able to reproduce itself into the future and sustain growth. Cash generated from operations is applied to cover the following main expenses of the business: capital expenditures on new plant and equipment; the purchase of financial investments; the payment of dividends; repayments on debt financing; finance adjustments in working capital; and cover the effect of exchange rate fluctuations. If cash generated from operations deteriorates, a business will find it more difficult to maintain the reproduction of the business into the future. For example, the business may cut back on much needed capital expenditure programmes or struggle to maintain repayments on debt or sustain growth in dividends paid. In these circumstances competitiveness will be damaged either because vital capital expenditure programmes slow down the rate of product and process renewal, or banks foreclose on loans and request immediate repayment. In a broad sense cash flow is a financial fund that operates to renew the organization into the future and strategically underwrite competitive advantage.

In recent years it has become fashionable to talk of 'stakeholder capitalism'. A value-added accounting framework can be used to understand how the various stakeholders are affected by changes in market conditions, etc. The value-added accounting framework makes visible the external stakeholders (suppliers of materials and services) and the interest(s) of internal stakeholders: employees, shareholders, banks and other providers of funds. However, we must be clear to differentiate the calculation of value added described above from the rather more recent forms of calculation promoted by fund managers and consultancy companies such as Stern Stuart and Boston Consultants. We briefly outline these rather more narrowly defined calculations of 'value added' or 'shareholder value'.

EVA™ (Economic Value Added), MVA (Market Value Added) and TSR (Total Shareholder Return)

Creating shareholder value has become an urgent concern. To respond to investor and board pressures, executives are seeking tools to manage value creation better at all organisational levels. Accepted financial theory offers little aid. To align tools and processes with value creation, managers require new metrics that quantify and track relevant performance.

(The Boston Consulting Group (1996) (Shareholder Value Management (Booklet 2)).

Some argue that business analysis and strategic calculation(s) should be geared towards the maintenance of all stakeholder interests. Financial calculations such as EVA™, MVA and TSR are accounting calculations presented as forms of business analysis/calculation which stress the primacy of maintaining shareholder interests and shareholder value and that creating and extending shareholder value can alone underwrite the long-term competitiveness of a business.

The general business rule is that value has only been created for the shareholders when the return on investment from capital projects exceeds the return that investors could obtain from investing in other securities with the same risk profile. Internal 'hurdle' rates which are used in Discounted Cash Flow (DCF) and Net Present Value (NPV) calculations (see Key Concept 2.3) should be set with these investor expectations in mind and used to judge whether individual projects meet this basic return on capital test.

EVA™ (Economic Value Added)

The calculation of EVA™ requires that managers deduct from a firm's net operating profit the 'true' charge for the capital it employs. If the result, after making this deduction for the cost of capital, is positive the firm has created surplus shareholder value but if the result is negative then shareholder value is being eroded or destroyed. The objective of management strategy is therefore to ensure that a growing surplus value is created over time. (Stern, J. and Stewart, B., 1998)

To execute an EVA™ calculation we first need to calculate a firm's capital employed (economic capital) by adding together equity plus debt plus adjustments for goodwill (associated with acquisitions). To calculate the required rate of return on this capital base we then need to establish the weighted average cost of capital which represents the average rate of interest paid out to holders of debt and equity within the business. If an organization has $500 million of capital employed and its weighted average cost of capital (WACC) is 20 per cent and if net operating profit after tax is $400 million then

---

KEY CONCEPT 2.3
Net present value

Net Present Value (NPV) is a form of strategic capital appraisal that is used to assess the future profitability of investment projects. Future net cash flows from the project are estimated and their present value calculated using a discount factor based on the company weighted average cost of capital. This is the discounted cash flow of the project.

Once the discounted future net cash flows have been calculated and summed a project is deemed to be profitable where: the summation of future discounted cash flows exceeds the initial capital cost of the project, or the NPV (Net Present Value is positive).

economic value added (EVA^{TM}) is a positive $300 million. That is the EVA^{TM} is $400 million minus (0.20 × 500) $100 million = $300 million.

Cash flow return on investment (CFROI) unlike EVA^{TM} is a profit-adjusted return which relates cash flow to an inflation-adjusted capital base. The problem, it is argued, with both these measures is that they are based on backward-looking profit figures and balance-sheet valuations of capital employed. Two calculations which relate performance to the external value of market capital are MVA (Market Value Added) and TSR (Total Shareholder Return). (See Myers, R., 1996)

MVA^{TM} (Market Value Added) and TSR (Total Shareholder Return)

Market value added deducts the balance sheet value of equity, loans and retained earnings from the market value of share capital and debt. TSR by way of contrast calculates the change in market capitalization including dividends paid out of a business from one year to the next expressing this change as a percentage of the start of year market value of equity and dividends. In both cases the managerial objective becomes one of securing a growth in market value of shareholder funds.

Many shareholders (for which read fund managers in pension funds, insurance companies and unit trusts) are looking closely at these measures because they offer the possibility of generating a higher return on capital on their funds. This requires that the corporate governance system of an organization be aligned with the financial calculations of shareholders. Management is encouraged to take the new metrics seriously. They should only invest in capital projects that secure a rate of return on capital that exceeds the cost of capital employed. Or put another way, where projects generate a positive Economic Value Added (EVA^{TM}) or increase shareholder value.

> The idea that management's primary responsibility is to increase value has gained widespread acceptance in the United States since the publication of *Creating Shareholder Value* in 1986. With the globalisation of competition and capital markets and a tidal wave of privatisations, shareholder value rapidly is capturing the attention of executives in the United Kingdom, continental Europe, Australia, and even Japan. Over the next ten years shareholder value will more than likely become the global standard for measuring business performance.
>
> *(Rappaport, 1998)*

These new forms of business/shareholder value analysis are internalized through the corporate governance system so, for example, you might link executive share options and performance-related pay to the shareholder-value-based models. This would modify managerial behaviour especially that relating to the investment of capital funds to particular investment projects. Management would need to be more keenly aware of the need to take into account the cost of capital when assessing the financial costs and benefits of their investment plans or merger and acquisition strategy. A take-over bidder for example would need to take into account the degree to which the acquired firm adds positively to shareholder value and an improved return on capital employed.

In a recent debate in *Fortune* magazine Gary Hamel has argued that the efficient use of capital is not the single most important determinant of competitive advantage and that the objectives of business strategy should be more broadly defined to include innovation. More broadly other academics argue that business analysis should take into account a range of financial and non-financial objectives as part of a balanced scorecard approach to strategic business management.

Operating architecture

Returning to the value-added accounting framework we start with the observation that businesses can be more or less cash generative even when they operate in the same industrial or commercial sector. This is because there is a variable and dynamic relation between, on the one hand, the operating architecture of a business and on the other the trajectory of the market(s) in which the business operates.

We will first explore the concept of operating architecture. To do this we should remind ourselves as to how value added is calculated.

The calculation of value added:

Sales	XXX
Minus Purchases	(YYY)
= Value Added	ZZZ
Distributed to:	
Labour Costs including social costs	AAA
Plus Depreciation	BBB
Plus Operating Profits	CCC
= Value Added	ZZZ

The first deduction against sales revenue is that for purchases of materials and services bought in by a business. This figure can be by far the largest deduction against sales revenue and so affects the retention of value added within the business. It is the case that between business sectors the percentage of purchases deducted from sales is variable. It is even the case that firms operating in the same business sector have variable purchase to sales ratios. It is also possible for an individual firm to dynamically adjust the purchase to sales ratio by making more in-house or increase the level of contracting out. In grocery retailing it is the case that over an extended period of time more value is being added within the retail store because activities such as baking and general food preparation are being brought on site and undertaken in-house.

The immediate impact of a high purchase to sales ratio is that it reduces the percentage of sales revenue retained internally by the business. The purchase to sales ratio is an important first step in the process of calculating internal organization value added.

In Table 2.2 we calculate the purchase to sales ratio for the main international auto assemblers and it is immediately apparent that a large series of differences emerge between Japanese and American/European firms. In general Japanese firms such as Toyota and Nissan are vertically disintegrated and so buy-in a larger percentage of turnover as purchases, on average 80 to 85 per cent. In contrast American and European firms deduct 60 to 65 per cent of their sales revenue to cover the cost of purchases. The result is that Japanese firms retain 15 to 20 per cent of sales revenue as value added and American and European firms 30 to 40 per cent of sales revenue as value added.

In order to establish cash generated from operations we still need to deduct labour costs including social costs (pension provisions and healthcare costs) from value added. Here again a variable deduction of labour costs will be made against value added. This is because the share of labour costs in value added is also variable as between industry sectors and firms operating in the same sector. Labour's share in value added can also change over time for the individual firm. To illustrate these points we again return to the car assembler example to calculate labour's share of value added in Table 2.3

We observe that cash generation is variable between firms to the extent that even when they are operating in the same line of business cash generated per unit of sales revenue varies markedly. For BMW, Ford and Volkswagen-Audi-Golf, cash generation as a percentage of sales was strong in the 1980s and 1990s. This interpretation is somewhat at odds with the common assumption that Japanese performance was superior in the 1980s. Japanese firms are not generally highly cash generative and only Toyota comes close to

Table **2.2:** Purchase to sales ratios for major car assemblers

Purchase to sales ratios: International cars business (Average for 1980s and early 1990s)	
	% Purchases deducted from Sales
Toyota	86
Nissan	81
Ford	62
General Motors	66
BMW	65
Peugeot-Citroen	66
Volkswagen-Audi-Golf	62

(Source: Company Annual Report and Accounts)

Table **2.3:** Labour's share of value added and cash generation in major international car assemblers

Cash to sales ratios: International cars business (Average for 1980s and early 1990s)		
	Value Added as a % of Sales	Labour's share of Value Added %	Cash as a % of Sales revenue
Toyota	14	42	8.1
Nissan	19	68	6.1
Ford	38	71	11.0
General Motors	34	74	8.8
BMW	35	63	13.0
Peugeot-Citroen	34	72	9.5
Volkswagen-Audi-Golf	38	72	10.6

(Source: Company Annual Report and Accounts)

matching the second tier of cash generative international car assemblers. (Williams *et al.*, 1994). It is not always the case that superior productive performance translates into a clear financial advantage. As Wood (1978) notes it is possible to have two identical companies generating the same level of value added and value added per employee. However profit depends on whether these two companies pay the same wages and if one pays lower wages its profits will he higher. The shareholders might believe that the more profitable firm is more efficient.

> The two companies are equally efficient in generating wealth. They differ only in the way the wealth is shared out between employees and investors. The difference is important but it has nothing to do with the efficiency in the use of resources.
>
> *(Wood, 1978, p. 35)*

To summarize: a highly cash-generative business is one which combines a low purchase to sales ratio with a low labour's share of value added. A low purchase to sales ratio results in a high retention of value added for distribution within the business. A low labour's share of value added leaves a high residuum of cash per unit of value added and sales revenue.

A value-added accounting framework applied in this way allows us to classify businesses as being strongly or weakly cash generative. It is generally well known that grocery food retailers have a high purchase to sales ratio because these shops buy-in grocery foodstuffs which are stacked high on the shelves. Much of the value added is located within the manufacturing and food processing supply chain. A purchase to sales ratio of over 80 per cent is common in many grocery retailers and so this leaves just 20 per cent of sales revenue retained within the supermarket retailer as value added. From the value added as much as 50 per cent of the value added could be appropriated to wages and salaries leaving just 10 per cent of sales revenue as cash. Utilities like water companies tend to have a low purchase to sales ratio and also a low labour's share of value added which generates strong cash generative businesses. Pharmaceutical companies have a low purchase to sales ratio and relatively low labour's share of value added and are also highly cash generative (see Table 2.4).

In Table 2.5 we calculate cash generation as a percentage of sales for a few American corporations. These calculations again establish the fact that cash generation is variable between firms in different sectors. Intel and Microsoft operate within a business sector where patents and licensing arrangements ensure that the competition does not undermine margins on their computer processor chips and software products. Cash generation in these two companies is between 30 to 35 per cent of sales revenue. This compares with companies like Ford and Boeing where price competition drives down margins and limits cash generation on sales. Sears, Roebuck and Co, a retailer, generates a low cash to sales ratio because price competition is intensive and, as we have already noted, retailing also has a high purchase to sales ratio which limits value added and cash generated as a per cent of sales.

Table **2.4:** High and low cash-generative businesses

	Activity	Purchases to Sales Ratio %	Labour's Share of Value Added	Internally generated cash as a percentage of Sales
High Cash Generative	Water Utilities	25	30	53.0
High Cash Generative	Pharmaceuticals	30	40	42.0
High Cash Generative	Telecommunications	33	60	26.80
Low Cash Generative	Grocery Retailing	80	55	9.00

(Source: Annual Report and Accounts)

Table **2.5:** Cash generation as percentage of sales for US firms

Company	Sales Revenue $ mill 1996	Cash Flow $ mill 1996	Cash Flow as % of Sales 1996	Comment
Intel Corp	20,847	7,045	33.79	Producer of computer micro-processors
Microsoft Corp	8,671	2,675	30.85	Operating systems software
Boeing Co	22,681	2,086	9.20	Commercial jet airline producer
Ford Motor Co.	146,991	11,321	7.70	Car assembler and financial services
Sears, Roebuck and Co	38,236	1,943	5.08	Retailer of clothing and home appliances etc.

Notes: Cash flow is defined as net income before extraordinary items and discontinued operations and after preferred dividends but including depreciation and amortization.
(Source: Standard and Poor's: 500 Guide 1998, McGraw-Hill, USA)

We can use the value-added accounting framework to undertake financial benchmarking analysis as between close competitors in a similar line of business. This financial framework can also be used to inform management about why cash generation is strong or weak and therefore help support alternative strategic business policy response(s).

We have illustrated how the structure of costs determines the residuum of cash and that the operating architecture and cost structure of organizations is variably determined. In a business where cash generation is low, management action might be directed towards reducing the purchase to sales ratio or lowering labour's share of value added. If we look at grocery retailing, the calculations of large grocery stores is to bring in-house goods which were traditionally bought-in from suppliers. Supermarkets now operate their own bakeries, food preparation and finishing activities to reduce purchases as a percentage of sales and increase the lump of value added and cash retained (so long as price competition does not pass on the benefits to the consumer). The introduction of self-service and automatic tilling can also reduce labour costs in value added. All the above management actions are directed towards squeezing more cash out of sales revenue.

The balance of intervention between reducing purchase cost or internal labour cost would depend on the structure of costs because this determines the leverage on cash extraction. In telecommunications the major proportion of cost is internal labour cost rather than purchases. Management attention should therefore be directed towards the reduction of labour costs in value added within the telecommunications industry.

Whilst it is possible for the operating architecture of a business to remain relatively stable over a period of time this is not so true of the economic context within which the business operates. Market conditions can change for the better or worse rapidly and competitor interaction can result in a loss of market share. The structural context within which a business operates can operate to sustain strong financial performance or it can undermine the financial condition of the business. For example, fluctuations in the exchange rate can promote competitiveness on home or overseas markets and at the same time rapidly undermine financial results.

Market conditions and trajectory

The operating architecture of a business describes the relationship between revenues, costs and cash generation. A favourable operating architecture will result in a high percentage of cash generated from sales. However in addition to the operating ratios it is also important to take into account the level (or lump) of cash generated from operations and this is determined by market conditions (volume sales and price structure). Growth in sales volume is by far the most important determinant of the lump of value added and cash generated by a business. A virtuous relationship between the market(s) within which a business functions and its operating architecture establishes the preconditions for an expansion of the lump of value added and cash generated from operations.

Intel in the mid-1980s already generated a high level of cash per $ of sales revenue because the operating architecture of the business was inherently favourable. Intel's real sales revenue has also increased by a factor of seven over the last ten years. A trajectory of uninterrupted growth has combined with a favourable operating architecture to ensure that Intel is now even more cash generative. Intel has increased cash generated per $ of sales from 18.1 per cent in 1987 to 33.8 per cent in 1996 (see Table 2.6). To sustain a high level of cash generation per unit of sales Intel must maintain a favourable set of operating ratios in combination with strong volume sales and favourable prices for its microprocessors.

A classic example of the virtuous relationship established between operating architecture and market trajectory is that experienced by the Ford Motor Company (FMC) at Highland Park in the early part of this century. Rapid market expansion combined with a favourable operating architecture to generate strong cash generation (see Table 2.7).

Ford managed to maintain a favourable series of operating ratios as price cuts established the precondition for a trajectory of rapid market expansion. An exceptional trajectory of market expansion resulted in a twenty-five-fold increase in the lump of cash generated from operations. We can contrast this with another notable car assembler Toyota that moved off a trajectory of output expansion in the late 1980s. This shift from favourable to

Table **2.6:** Intel Corporation: real sales and cash generation as a percentage of sales

Year	Sales $ mill	Consumer Price Index	Real Sales	Cash as a % of Sales
1987	1,907	0.87	100.00	18.1
1988	2,876	0.91	144.18	23.1
1989	3,127	0.95	150.17	20.0
1990	3,921	1.00	178.88	24.0
1991	4,779	1.042	209.24	25.8
1992	5,844	1.074	248.24	27.1
1993	8,782	1.106	362.25	34.3
1994	11,521	1.134	463.50	28.8
1995	16,202	1.166	633.93	30.5
1996	20,847	1.200	792.56	33.8

Note: To review how we convert financial data into real figures see Key Concept 4.3.
(Source: Standard and Poor's Stock Report)

Table **2.7:** Ford at Highland Park 1909–16

	Purchases as a % of Sales	Labour's Share of Value Added	Cents per $ of Sales Revenue	Total cash $ mill	Units sold
1909	68.2	27.7	26.2	3.0	13,941
1916	55.5	39.1	27.1	75.5	585,400

(Source: Annual Report and Accounts)

unfavourable growth trajectory led to a deterioration in the financial operating ratios of the business and severely damaged cash generation from operations (see Table 2.8).

As sales growth slows, labour's share of value added at Toyota increased to 60 per cent and cash generation from operations dropped by approximately 20 per cent by 1996. Toyota's response has been to cut capital expenditure by roughly 50 per cent from the 1991 peak level of 1,000 billion yen to 471 billion yen by 1996.

It is generally accepted that macro-economic conditions for manufacturers have deteriorated in the past 20 years since the long post-war boom for consumer durables slowed after the first oil crisis in 1973. The recent history of the international car market is a good illustration of a more generalized problem of market maturity. Cars are an interesting case because the product is complex and expensive and is globally produced and internationally traded.

The American car market is highly saturated with three cars for every two economically active persons. The American car market has not shown any sustained volume growth in the last 20 years and the sales peak of 11.35 million cars in 1973 has not yet been surpassed. Replacement demand is highly volatile and the market is prone to cyclical downturns where year on year sales can be as much as 25–30 per cent lower or higher depending on market circumstances (see Key Concept 2.4).

Table **2.8:** Toyota in the 1990s

	Value added mill yen	Labour's share of value added	Cash flow mill yen	Units sold mill
1984	814.5	41	480	3.293
1991	1,447	44	815	4.538
1996	1,660	60	662	4.335

(Source: Annual Report and Accounts)

KEY CONCEPT 2.4
Replacement demand cycle/Cyclical markets

A market reaches a state of maturity where demand is determined by replacement of the existing product. Some products such as washing machines have a relatively long replacement cycle, maybe up to ten years before a consumer needs to replace the product in their kitchen. Other products have a relatively short replacement cycle because they deteriorate more rapidly through frequent use and are a relatively small expenditure for the household.

A cyclical market is generally a mature market in which volume fluctuates at or around a steady pattern of demand. A fall in retail sales may be the result of consumers deciding to postpone their replacement purchase for a period of time. The effect of this postponement is to create a cyclical trend in sales.

Market volatility and market maturity impacts on the flow of production and capacity utilization for the major car assemblers such as GM, Ford and Chrysler. These car assemblers experience volatile switchback movements in market demand and year by year fluctuation of plus or minus 30 per cent or more is not unknown. This cyclical pattern of demand impacts financially on US car assemblers such that their cash flow is unpredictably strong one year and weak the next (see Figure 2.2). From the 1960s US car manufacturers have adapted to this pattern of intermittent cash flow. Business techniques used to determine the allocation of capital funds stress the importance of capital rationing because cash flow is such a precarious resource.

The European experience over the past 20 years has been much more favourable. The European car market has a history of volume growth so that each cycle has historically taken volume sales to a higher level. But the position from 1994 onwards is of flat EU demand with intermittent cyclical collapse. The European Union countries in 1996 had a stock of 156 million cars and the 'big four' national economies have a park of 122 million cars; this represents 1.4 cars for every economically active person. The industry's efforts to produce a durable, long-life product may even reduce sales in the medium term now that the market is also maturing and saturated (see Table 2.9).

In consumer electricals and electronics, the market problems are different but equally threatening to cash flow. In electronics at least there is the possibility of stimulating consumer demand by developing new products for the mass market. The industry has, however, found it increasingly difficult to develop new 'must have' products to replace old products like colour televisions which are now available in the relatively high-income economy markets at next-to-nothing prices. The VCR of the mid-1980s was the industry's last winner; fewer than 40 per cent of European households have CD players, microwaves or video cameras because the current generation of new products either requires expensive software or performs supplementary functions which many can live without.

	Mill Units	% Movement Peak to Trough
1960	6.7	
1961	5.5	−17.9
1965	9.3	+69.0
1967	7.4	−20.4
1968	8.9	+20.2
1970	6.6	−25.8
1973	9.7	+46.9
1975	6.7	−30.9
1977	9.2	+34.3
1982	5.1	−44.6
1985	8.2	+60.8
1991	5.5	−33.0
1994	6.6	+20.0
1996	6.1	−7.6

Figure **2.2:** Car production in the USA 1960 to 1996: peak and trough production (Source: Society of Motor Manufacturers and Traders, London)

Table **2.9:** Park of cars in use in EU (12), 1967–96

	Vehicles in use 000	Cars in use 000	Cars per economically active person	Cars per square kilometre
1967	53,326	45,953	0.37	20.5
1971	70,322	62,415	0.49	27.8
1975	86,171	77,007	0.65	34.3
1979	103,319	91,446	0.65	40.7
1987	131,838	116,005	0.67	52.1
1991	153,002	134,791	0.94	60.1
1996	178,519	156,350	1.35	69.7

(Source: *Yearbook of Labour Statistics*, International Labour Office, *Motor Vehicle Statistics of Great Britain*, SMMT, various years)

Table 2.10 illustrates the problems by considering the price, volume and real market value trends over the decade from 1983 to 1993 in the markets for ten old and new products across the four major European national markets. These markets account for 65 to 75 per cent of EC sales in these product lines. Market trends for new and existing product lines are profoundly discouraging because the electrical and electronics firms have been cutting prices without realizing the benefits of increased demand.

Price cuts are nearly universal; the unit price has been falling in old products such as colour televisions as well as in new products like microwaves and video cameras and in mechanical products such as cookers and washing machines as well as in electronic products like VCRs. The impact on volume has been generally disappointing; only four relatively new products (microwaves, VCRs, video cameras and home computers) manage volume increases of more than 50 per cent and only the two newest products (microwaves and video cameras) manage spectacular volume increases of

Table **2.10:** Percentage change in market volume, price and value (in 1983 prices) for 10 electrical products in the four largest EC national markets

Product	Market price % change	Market volume % change	Market value % change
Electric cookers	−55	+49	−37
Colour televisions	−47	+55	−18
Washing machines	−27	+6	−23
Refrigerators	−35	+25	−19
Electric toasters	−37	+41	−12
Vacuum cleaners	−14	+52	+27
Microwave ovens	−72	+634	+205
VCRs	−67	+113	−30
Video cameras	−69	+1,905	+225
Home computers	−30	+78	+25

(Source: *Consumer Europe*, Euromonitor, various years)

more than 500 per cent. Declining prices and weak volume increases combine arithmetically to reduce the overall value of the market in real 1983 prices. In six of the ten product lines market value declines and only two of the remaining four cases (microwaves and video cameras) show large increases in the value of the market. One interpretation is that uncontrolled price cuts in saturated markets are not stimulating demand but undermining the conditions of cost recovery (see Williams *et al.* 1995).

These observations from two important sectors do not of course imply global market saturation in all sectors. But it is difficult to be optimistic about the positive development of product markets whose trajectories of price and volume are increasingly combining in an adverse way to undermine revenue growth and cash generation.

Figure 2.3 illustrates the cost recovery problem where mature and cyclical volume market sales combine with aggressive price competition to undermine the total real revenue base of the market. The aggregate market value for a particular product or service expands at a decreasing rate until market maturity and cyclicality becomes the norm. Where market maturity also combines with a sustained fall in unit costs, the overall revenue generated in this product market will fall. In a mature market aggressive price competition serves to undermine the cost recovery characteristics of the product market.

In domestic markets intensified competition segments and fragments product markets which further limits the volume base available to a particular firm. Segmentation is the process by which a particular product market is competed for by an increasing number of product variants (see Figure 2.4).

Fragmentation by way of contrast is the process by which a particular product segment is competed for by more than one competitor. The net result is that the process of product market segmentation and fragmentation combine with mature market conditions to limit the revenue one particular organization is able to generate from its home or overseas market (see Figure 2.5).

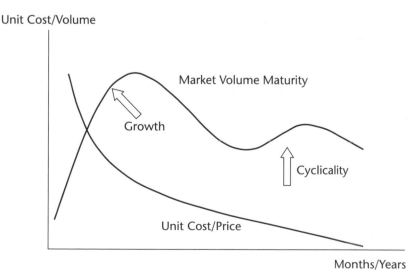

Figure **2.3:** Volume and unit cost/price relations in a mature market

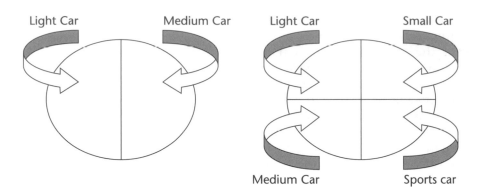

As the product market matures new segments emerge as product differentiation takes place

Figure **2.4:** Product market segmentation

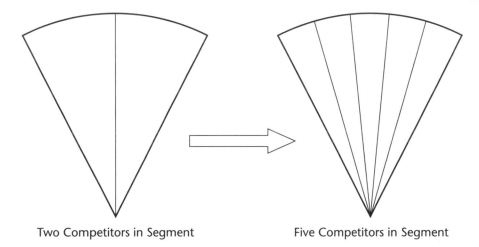

Figure **2.5:** Fragmentation of product segments

Benchmarking and competitor interaction

Benchmarking is the process through which an organization obtains information about best or world class management practice. Benchmarking can be used internally to learn from the organization's own best process, factory or department and it can also be applied to externally evaluate your own organization's performance with other competitor(s) in a similar line of business. It is argued that one of the best ways to enhance an organization's competitiveness is to identify world-class performance and then emulate the elements that make up this world-class performance. An example of case of benchmarking is given by the work of Arthur Andersen Management Consultants (1992, 1994) in their benchmarking world-wide competitiveness study on the car components industry. In this study world class business performance is identified and weak companies are then advised to close the gap between themselves and the world-class business. In the early 1980s Xerox used benchmarking techniques to identify how it could improve efficiency by comparing its internal functions which similar functions elsewhere. In this case Xerox compared its distribution procedures with L.L. Bean and Deere and Company for central computer operations and Procter and Gamble for marketing and Florida Light and Power for quality management processes.

In our case study on Caterpillar and Komatsu we utilize the value added accounting framework to evaluate the strengths and weaknesses of the two companies. A benchmark study carried out by Caterpillar in the early 1980s concluded that in order to close the competitive gap, Caterpillar should emulate the management practices of its main competitor Komatsu. Using a value added accounting analysis of the two companies we will establish whether Caterpillar's problems stemmed from weak management practices/ systems or were the result of a series of external factors which were to all intents and purposes beyond management control.

Case study: Caterpillar and Komatsu

The opening of the 'Assembly Highway' at Caterpillar Inc. in May 1989 completed the restructuring of Caterpillar's organization that built construction equipment such as motor graders and off-highway trucks. This was part of Caterpillar's 'Plant With A Future' (PWAF) programme of factory modernization introduced in 1984 under pressure of Japanese competition. The programme, implemented between 1984 and 1991, sought to improve competitiveness by adopting best practice of its major international rival Komatsu.

The PWAF programme combined out-sourcing of non-core operations with internal reorganization around the principles of cellular manufacturing, mixed model assembly and computer integration, which together would deliver improved flow and reduced costs. Materials flow would be ordered, integrated and monitored using new computer technologies while competitive benchmarking against Komatsu, Caterpillar's Japanese competitor highlighted differences in performance. The PWAF programme of 1984 aimed to make Caterpillar the lowest cost producer through the achievement of a 22 per cent cost reduction by 1986 on a 1981 base.

The assumption of the benchmarking study was that Caterpillar had inferior performance in terms of its productivity. Using our value added framework we can firstly question this assumption. Table 2.11 presents data for both companies on the trend of value added per employee which is effectively an indirect index of cost reduction because, if cost reduction is being achieved, then real value added per employee in the domestic currency should increase steadily. Second, it presents a comparative production flow measure for the two companies in the form of a value added/stocks ratio which partially corrects for the greater vertical disintegration at Komatsu which would otherwise distort the comparison of both companies.

Table **2.11**: Komatsu and Caterpillar value added per employee and value added stock turn 1985–95

	Komatsu value added per employee		Caterpillar value added per employee	Komatsu stock turns (stocks divided by value added)	Caterpillar stock turns (stocks divided by value added)
	yen mill.	$			
1980	6.297	30,867	48,609	1.26	2.07
1985	7.567	37,835	51,173	1.00	2.51
1986	7.237	45,804	50,222	1.06	2.30
1987	7.010	57,934	56,964	1.05	2.22
1988	7.826	63,113	63,727	1.09	1.86
1989	8.241	61,962	63,441	1.47	1.82
1990	9.009	57,019	62,979	1.40	1.79
1991	9.270	65,745	58,069	1.25	1.69
1992	8.549	64,278	70,061	1.30	1.93
1993	8.215	71,435	86,399	1.40	2.86
1994	7.944	77,882	90,625	1.30	3.61
1995	8.273	95,092	87,237	1.27	2.47

(Source: Caterpillar and Komatsu Report and Accounts, various years)

The table shows that the process Kaizen (see Key Concept 2.5) at Komatsu expressed in terms of value added per employee in yen does not show step-like improvements but rises in the later stages of the Hesei boom after 1987 before falling away after 1991. The 1994 level of 7.9 million yen per employee is less than 5 per cent ahead of the level achieved a decade earlier in 1985. This is the cyclical pattern of productivity gain and loss that is familiar to many Western companies like Caterpillar where the short-run trend of costs is determined by the trend of output.

The results on company-wide flow use the calculation of stocks divided into value added and this is a good indicator as to how well internal resources are being managed. The company with superior flow in every year from 1980 to 1995 is Caterpillar not Komatsu: over the years 1988–95 the Komatsu average is around 1.4 whereas the Caterpillar average is a very creditable 2.3. The conclusion must be that, when Komatsu threatened Caterpillar in the mid-1980s, its advantage did not rest on its superior ability to organize high flow, cost-reducing production in its factories.

The original benchmarking studies identified Caterpillar's problems as resulting from low productivity and the poor internal management of operations compared to their main competitor Komatsu. The value-added analysis (value added per employee and flow indicator) identifies that the problems were not all inside Caterpillar's factories.

It is possible to change the focus and provide an alternative account based on company financial analysis and market data. Information relating to market conditions, the exchange rate and competitor interaction can be used to construct a different analysis and explanation of Caterpillar's problems.

KEY CONCEPT 2.5
Kaizen

Kaizen is the Japanese word for 'continuous improvement' or 'steps towards improvement' across every aspect of the organization's operations. In Japanese organizations a number of management systems are combined to generate 'Kaizen'.

Kanban systems are designed to ensure that products or services are made to order rather than for stocks. Attention is paid to reducing wasted labour time through layout improvements and relations with suppliers ensure that raw material stocks are kept low when they are delivered Just-in-Time (JIT). The aggregation of these physical interventions is translated into the management and financial accounting systems of Japanese firms as a target cost reduction.

According to Cooper:

> Japanese managers have argued that target costing outperforms the conventional Western approach and the cost-plus approach because it provides a specified cost reduction target for everyone in the firm to work toward. Once cost reduction negotiations are complete, the target cost becomes the common focal point that all the departments must work together to achieve.

(Cooper, 1995)

Market trajectory

The analysis begins with an outline of the long-term trajectory of the firm based on company report and accounts. Market trajectory can be captured by considering the long-term trend of real sales and of cost recovery, by which we mean the ability to realize a surplus which meets the internal productive requirement for renewal of process and product and the external claims of lenders and shareholders.

The calculation of real sales requires the deflation of nominal sales with an appropriate producer or consumer price index (see Key Concept 2.6). Cost recovery and the generation of a surplus is best indexed by labour's share of value added (LSVA) which provides a snapshot of the surplus in percentage terms after labour (which usually accounts for the largest share of internal costs) has been paid for. Value added is calculated by subtracting the external cost of purchases from sales revenue. If the company does not make major acquisitions and divestments, the two indicators of real sales and LSVA provide a time series account that shows us the growth of revenue and its distribution to different stakeholders.

The graph of Caterpillar's real sales (see Figure 2.6) shows a sharp and decisive transition between two distinct periods when the trajectory was very different. The first period, after 1954, saw sustained growth with each downturn representing only a pause in growth before the next upturn took the company to a new peak: real sales doubled every ten years or so and increased no less than six times between 1950 and the late 1970s. The next period begins in 1973 although it only becomes obvious after 1981: the gains of the upswing after 1973 were not consolidated and an unprecedented downturn

KEY CONCEPT 2.6
Nominal and real financial information

At times we refer to the 'nominal' figures or the 'real' figures. The nominal figures are those which are taken straight from the annual report and accounts of a company or from national or sectoral statistics. Real financial information is that which relates to the nominal 'deflated' by the retail price index expressed as a decimal.

Nominal financial information from a set of company accounts includes the effect of price inflation passed on to the customer. In order to strip out the effects of price inflation we deflate the nominal financial information by the retail price index. A comprehensive international source for price inflation indices (consumer prices) is the *International Monetary Fund (IMF) Financial Statistics Yearbook*, 1997, Washington DC)

UK retail price index 1980 = 100

Year	Index
1980	100
1981	111.9
1982	121.4
1983	127.1
1984	133.4
1985	141.5
1986	146.4
1987	152.4
1988	159.8
1989	172.3
1990	188.6
1991	199.8
1992	207.1
1993	210.4
1994	215.7
1995	223.0
1996	228.5

In order to calculate the real sales from the nominal sales obtained from a set of accounts we divide the nominal sales by the retail price index expressed as a decimal. The retail or consumer price index measures the change in price for a basket of consumer products related to a particular base year of 100.

Real sales for a particular year (year n) is found by dividing nominal sales for a particular year by the retail price index for that year (year n).

Year	Nominal Sales Revenue £ mill	RPI	Real Sales £ mill	Real Sales Index 1980 = 100
1980	1,000	1.000	1,000	100
1985	1,680	1.415	1,187	118.7
1990	1,860	1.886	986	98.6
1996	1,940	2.285	850	85.0

Overall, in real terms, revenues have fallen by 15 per cent in the base year 1980.

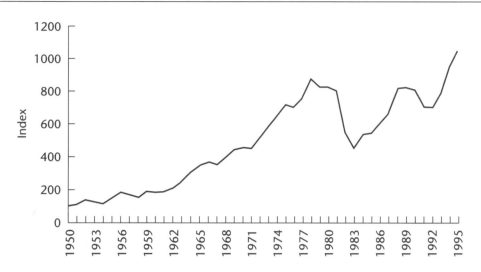

Figure **2.6:** Caterpillar: index of real sales 1950 = 100

after 1981 reduced sales by half compared to 1970 levels. The company trajectory since 1981 shows us a familiar pattern of saw tooth fluctuations without sustained growth, where the downturn after 1989 reduced real sales by 15 per cent and the upturn since 1993 brought gains which, on recent trends, are unlikely to be consolidated.

Firms which move from a trajectory of real output expansion to one of stagnation and cyclicality typically suffer deterioration in their capacity to generate cash surplus, though again the pattern will depend on the sector and the firm's position within the sector. Deterioration needs to be understood in the context of a normal range of variation. As a generalization, in a Western manufacturing firm, a labour share of value added (LSVA) of around 70 per cent (cash from operations share of 30 per cent) is required if the firm is to meet the internal requirement for productive renewal and satisfy the external financing claims. In cyclical activities the LSVA rises in downturns and falls on the upturn. In the earlier period Caterpillar was already operating at the upper end of the normal range of variation.

As Figure 2.7 shows, in the whole period 1954–81 the LSVA ranges from 67 per cent to 79 per cent; in 7 of the 28 years the share is uncomfortably high at 75 per cent or higher. The second period 1982–94 is separated from the first by two trends. The first trend is a step like shift upwards into a higher range of variation starting at the point where the earlier variation ended. From 1982–94 the LSVA varies between 74 and 92 per cent and in only 3 of those 13 years is the LSVA in the comfortable area below 75 per cent. The other notable trend is that the fluctuations in LSVA become much more extreme: for example, the relatively modest sales downturn after 1989 is associated with a serious rise in the LSVA from 72 per cent in 1988 to 94 per cent in 1991.

Company configuration

The sharp change in Caterpillar's trajectory after 1973 becomes explicable if it is related to a second contextual element, the company's configuration. The background here

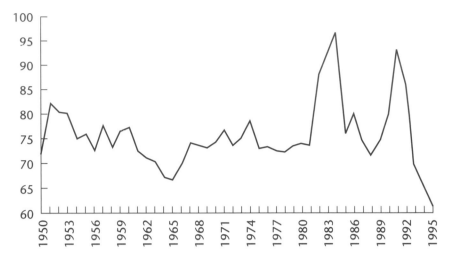

Figure **2.7:** Caterpillar: labour's share of value added (%)

can be obtained from the segment analysis in the company report and accounts which summarizes the broad distribution of the company's product lines and the geographic location of its production facilities and the markets where product is sold.

In terms of configuration, however, Caterpillar is unusual in one respect. Most American multinationals are heavily committed to overseas production as a way of accessing high wage markets and low wage production sites. In its reliance on American production as way of serving world markets, Caterpillar is more or less unique: its only peer is Boeing, another world-leading firm which produces expensive capital goods, albeit in Boeing's case with substantial assistance from Asian subcontractors. Caterpillar's US production accounts for nearly 80 per cent of the value of output and its US workers account for almost 75 per cent of employment in recent years.

Table 2.12 shows the US market has accounted for just under half of total sales since 1979, so that Caterpillar has been meeting a substantial part of the global demand for its products by exporting the output of its North American factories. Since 1979, direct exports from the US generally account for just over 30 per cent of Caterpillar's sales and 1 per cent of all US exports. Only in the European market does the sales value of local production exceed the value of imports from plants in the United States.

Competitor interaction

Analysis of trajectory and configuration can be made more valuable and illuminating when it is complemented with another form of analysis which deals with the dynamics of advantage and the scope and logic of management action to influence competitor interaction. This raises the issue of the Japanese firm Komatsu. Komatsu is important because it is the only serious broad line competitor in global construction equipment. Komatsu built a volume base and financial strength on its protected Japanese home market before moving out to threaten Caterpillar on its American home market with exports and local production.

Table **2.12:** Caterpillar domestic, exports and subsidiary sales 1978–95

	Total Sales	US Sales		Exports from US operations		Overseas Subsidiary Sales	
	$ mill.	$ mill.	%	$ mill.	%	$ mill.	%
1978	7,219	3,750	52	2,184	30	1,285	18
1979	7,613	3,510	46	2,500	33	1,603	21
1980	8,597	3,690	43	3,094	36	1,813	21
1993	11,615	5,710	49	3,743	32	2,162	19
1994	14,328	7,010	49	4,512	31	2,806	20
1995	16,072	7,420	46	5,126	32	3,526	22

(Source: Annual Report and Accounts, various years)

We must identify the changing basis of Komatsu's competitive advantage against Caterpillar and this requires a fresh analysis of company level statistics. At the time of the PWAF programme, Caterpillar management implied that Komatsu had an advantage based on superior manufacturing practice. This theme is echoed more generally in the subsequent literature on lean production and benchmarking more generally. (Despite the broader evidence of Japanese corporate under-performance since the end of the Hesei boom (see Haslam *et al.*, 1996).)

A broader consideration suggests that the most important variable to explain the competitive threat from Komatsu was exchange rate movements whose effects were magnified by the configuration of the two companies which made them both unusually vulnerable to such fluctuations. As we have noted, Caterpillar manufactured predominantly in the USA from where it exported to the rest of the world. The breakdown of the Bretton Woods fixed parity system, therefore, left the company in a very risky situation because it was routinely exposed to 20–30 per cent movements of major currencies against the dollar over a couple of years. For most American multinationals these fluctuations were manageable because they simply increased or diminished the amount of profit repatriated from their substantial overseas manufacturing operations. But for a firm with Caterpillar's configuration, they were threatening because one third of company sales were tied into exports from North America that could become unprofitable within the space of a year. Caterpillar responded as best it could by hedging against currency fluctuations to cover cost and profit positions up to three years ahead. Caterpillar's only consolation was that its Japanese competitor, Komatsu, was exposed to a corresponding exchange risk because 85 per cent of its production originated from Japanese factories.

From this point of view, the yen/dollar exchange rate is identifiable as the main influence on the changing balance of advantage between these two manufacturers. The threat from Komatsu depended on a favourable exchange rate between the yen and the dollar up to the mid-1980s when that rate shifted against the yen, Komatsu's advantage was rapidly removed. This point can be illustrated crudely but effectively by presenting the total dollar labour cost per worker at Caterpillar and Komatsu year by year alongside the average exchange rate (see Table 2.13).

Table **2.13:** Komatsu and Caterpillar employee labour cost including social charges

	Komatsu Employee Costs $	Caterpillar Employee Costs $	Ratio of Komatsu to Caterpillar Labour Costs	Exchange Rate yen to $[1]
1980	22,010	31,228	0.70	204
1981	20,901	34,874	0.60	222
1982	18,105	33,797	0.54	248
1983	20,504	36,678	0.56	238
1984	20,879	39,705	0.53	239
1985	22,383	38,942	0.57	235
1986	33,861	40,444	0.84	158
1987	45,124	42,453	1.06	121
1988	46,694	45,647	1.02	124
1989	46,992	47,500	0.99	133
1990	42,089	50,787	0.83	158
1991	47,376	54,579	0.87	141
1992	48,496	53,441	0.91	133
1993	57,739	60,277	0.96	115
1994	63,824	59,583	1.07	102

Note: The exchange rate used is taken from the Komatsu report and accounts for the purposes of converting yen into dollar figures.
(Source: Annual Report and Accounts, various years; Japan Development Bank: Handbook of Industrial Financial Data, various years)

As can be seen from Table 2.13, from 1981 to 1985, at 220–250 yen to the dollar, Komatsu's dollar labour costs per employee were 53–60 per cent of Caterpillar's. From 1986 onwards, however, at 120–155 yen to the dollar, Komatsu's dollar labour costs per employee were 79–106 per cent or close to parity with Caterpillar's. After the early 1990s, with endaka and the yen at 100 to the dollar, Komatsu's dollar labour costs were consistently higher than Caterpillar's.

The Caterpillar–Komatsu case informs us that the effects of factory improvement and productive reorganization in America or Japan were generally overwhelmed by the much stronger influence of exchange rate variation. Consider, for example, the position in 1990–91 when the weakening of the dollar against the yen was temporarily interrupted and reversed to the benefit of Komatsu. The PWAF programme had promised a 20 per cent cost reduction in seven years. In the 15 months from January 1989, the weak dollar rallied by 30 per cent against the yen so that the exchange rate alone slashed Komatsu's costs by a greater percentage than the reduction Caterpillar anticipated from its entire modernisation programme.

The structural source of advantage and disadvantage results from movements in the exchange rate, limited the capacity of Caterpillar and Komatsu to actively manage competitor interaction through marketing or productive intervention as envisaged in management texts. Caterpillar's management reaction to these difficulties took a variety of forms – the most shrewd and effective move was not reorganizing the factories in Peoria but lobbying the politicians in Washington. Under CEO Lee

C. Morgan the company ostentatiously distanced itself from other American firms and industries which lobbied for protection and import restraint against unfair Japanese competition. Caterpillar instead pressed for a lower dollar against the yen, which would make free trade work for American exporters by redressing the balance of disadvantage. Caterpillar's lobbying for a lower dollar helped lead towards the Plaza Accord of 1985 under which the industrialized nations agreed to drive the dollar down (*Wall Street Journal*, 6 April 1990).

This turned the tables on Komatsu's management because a weak dollar then made exporting to America very difficult while at the same time it strengthened Caterpillar as exporter to third markets outside the USA and Japan. Under this pressure Komatsu management needed an effective counter move but instead panicked into what the media at the time called a corporate 'marriage of desperation'. In 1988 Komatsu set up an American joint venture with Dresser Industries. In 1991, Komatsu announced a new policy of diversification that aimed to reduce the share of construction equipment in total sales from 63 to 51 per cent in the 1990s. The company slogan of 'catch up with Caterpillar and surpass it' was dropped as Komatsu management symbolically removed the bulldozer that had sat on top of their Tokyo headquarters building (*Wall Street Journal*, 13 May 1992).

Workshop questions/exercises

Q1 How would you calculate value added?

Q2 In what ways is it possible to understand the relationship between product market conditions and financial outcome using the value added accounting framework of business analysis.

Table **2.14**: Caterpillar financial data

Caterpillar Inc					
mill $	**1997**	**1996**	**1995**	**1994**	**1993**
Sales	18,925	16,522	16,072	14,328	11,615
Profit	1,665	1,361	1,136	955	652
Depreciation	738	696	682	683	668
Labour Costs	3,773	3,437	2,919	3,136	3,038
Average No of Employees	58,366	54,968	54,263	52,778	50,554
Caterpillar sales outside the USA					
	1997	**1996**	**1995**		
Sales Outside USA	9,180	8,140	8,030		

Q3 Using the information in Table 2.14 and relating this material to the Caterpillar/Komatsu case study in this chapter:

1 To what extent have Caterpillar's fortunes and strengthened in the last few years?

2 'Caterpillar Inc is rated "3". Our caution towards the stock stems from our belief that the demand for construction equipment is riding the crest of a near-term cyclical earnings peak. We continue to believe that the demand for construction equipment in North America is above normal and demand for construction equipment could falter as the domestic economy slows' (Industry Analyst). How would a slow-down in market demand affect the financial performance and cash generation of Caterpillar Inc?

Table **2.15:** Volvo financial data

			Volvo Group Consolidated **Nominal Values SEK mill**			
	Sales	**Purchases**	**Labour Costs**	**Depn.**	**Profit after Interest and before Tax**	**Employment**
1984	87,052	67,314	10,689	1,402	7,647	68,600
1985	86,196	65,347	11,522	1,725	7,602	67,850
1986	84,090	61,666	13,012	2,062	7,350	73,150
1987	92,520	67,190	14,106	2,213	9,011	75,350
1988	96,639	70,669	15,434	2,293	8,243	78,614
1989	90,972	64,445	16,875	2,685	6,967	78,690
1990	83,185	62,626	17,865	3,021	−327	68,797
1991	77,223	55,637	17,654	3,129	803	63,582
1992	83,002	67,775	16,857	3,119	−4,749	60,115
1993	111,155	90,531	19,489	3,777	−2,642	73,641
1994	155,866	110,225	24,156	5,107	16,378	75,549
1995	171,511	125,559	27,248	5,656	13,048	79,050
1996	156,060	110,509	25,997	5,351	14,203	70,330
1997	183,625	136,702	26,951	6,796	13,176	72,900

(Source: Volvo Report and Accounts and Fact Book)

Q4 From Table 2.15 calculate:

1 Value Added for each year (labour costs plus depreciation plus profit before interest and tax).

2 Cash from operations each year (as depreciation plus profit after interest and tax).

3 Cash as a percentage of sales.

4 Value added as a percentage of sales.

Using the inflation index deflate in Table 2.16 (that is take out inflation effects) the value added to obtain a real value added figure with a base year

Table **2.16:** Inflation/price index for Sweden

1984	100
1985	102
1986	104
1987	107
1988	110
1989	111
1990	115
1991	118
1992	122
1993	127
1994	131
1995	133
1996	140
1997	142

1984 = 100. That is in each year divide the value added in mill SEK by the price index expressed as a decimal.

Once you have calculated the real value added (or net output) for Volvo divide the real value added in mill SEK by the numbers employed to obtain a figure real value added per employee.

E.g. value added in 1984 = 19,738 mill SEK

Real value added in 1984 prices = 19,738/1.00 (base year index of 100 as a decimal)

Real value added per employee = 19,738/0.0686 (million employees)

Real value added per employee = 287,725 SEK

To what extent has labour productivity at Volvo increased during this period of time?

Q5 Using the information for the oil companies in Table 2.17 you need to calculate:

1 The EBIT (earnings before interest and tax) as a percentage of sales for each company for each year. Then compute an overall average for the period 1990 to 1998.

2 The ROCE (return on capital employed) as earnings before interest and tax (EBIT) as a percentage of total capital employed for each company for each year. Then compute an overall average for the period 1990 to 1998.

3 Calculate the ROCE (earnings after tax) as a percentage of capital employed for each company for each year. Then compute an overall average for the period 1990 to 1998.

In your opinion which of these companies is performing the stronger in terms of the ROCE as calculated in 2 and 3 above? Remember that the higher the percentage return on capital the stronger the earnings being generated per £ of capital employed in the business.

Table **2.17:** Oil integrated companies. All figures in £000s

	1990	1991	1992	1993	1994	1995	1996	1997	1998
BP Amoco (UK)									
Sales	41710992	41266992	43314000	47654992	46264992	50200000	59394000	56626000	41208000
EBIT	3439000	1926000	784000	1977000	2823000	2444000	4078000	3942000	3459000
After tax profit	1726000	383000	−453000	617000	1589000	1117000	2560000	2478000	2004000
Dividends	860000	904000	568000	457000	577000	849000	1101000	1261000	2486000
Total Capital Employed	20590992	22050992	23354000	22492000	22178000	22212000	20424992	21470000	39682000
Exxon (USA)									
Sales	105518992	102846992	103160000	97824992	99682992	107892992	116728000	120278992	100696992
EBIT	15455000	14761000	13753000	14116000	14230000	17232992	18612992	19586992	15152000
After tax profit	5282000	5767000	5057000	5530000	5333000	6771000	7894000	8866000	6625000
Dividends	3082000	3334000	3495000	3558000	3598000	3714000	3866000	4015000	3999000
Total Capital Employed	63682000	66706000	65367008	65554928	68368992	72560000	76022000	76410000	73218000
Royal Dutch Shell									
Sales	49568960	52737280	52192096	45994192	48122416	46874416	48129200	58742608	67844432
EBIT	7602659	7806921	5700704	5119410	4881538	5414686	5924689	8151386	8565552
Net Int Charges	−112028	16460	29968	−386485	67114	15156	−10619	−43427	35122
After tax profit	7038231	7209570	2359646	2753083	2442924	3288226	3266945	4470003	4376707
Dividends	1860926	1909571	1994745	2055552	2092035	2150573	2310940	2566418	3016431
Total Capital Employed	35884768	35037408	36579568	37384272	39689152	37720464	37682624	43257232	46907888
Elf Acquitaine (Fr)									
Sales	26751584	30592544	30575616	31964736	31659680	31753600	35475952	38768688	32250992
EBIT	3417297	3225821	2290089	1304964	1384085	2467082	3410285	3276892	1826000
Net Int Charges	712242	781606	767581	902041	852495	690746	501405	488447	191000
After tax profit	1781062	1629070	1088334	128363	185074	987717	1313653	1072631	776000
Dividends	467820	502380	510186	510262	523891	538297	584185	629614	630564
Total Capital Employed	23064048	26551216	27474560	29124736	27453536	25664464	25686576	26483584	25320432

References

Arthur Andersen Consultants (1992, 1994) *Lean Enterprise Benchmark Survey*, London.

Cooper, R. (1995) *When Lean Enterprises Collide*, Boston, Mass.: Harvard Business School Press.

Cox, B. (1979) *Value Added*, London: Heinemann.

Dunning, H. (1979) 'Explaining Changing Patterns of International Production', *Oxford Bulletin of Economics and Statistics*, Nov

Gilchrist, R.R. (1971) *Managing for Profit: The Added Value Concept*, London: George Allen.

Hamel, G. (1997) 'How Killers Count', *Fortune*, June 23.

Haslam, C. *et al.* (1996) 'A Fallen Idol? Japanese Management in the 1990s', *Asia Pacific Business Review*, Vol. 2, pp. 21–43.

Kaplan, R. and Norton, P. (1992) 'Using the Balanced Scorecard for a Strategic Management System', *Harvard Business Review* Jan/Feb, pp. 71–79.

Kay, J. (1993) *Foundations of Corporate Success*, Oxford: OUP.

Myers, R. (1996) 'Metric Wars', *CFO Magazine*, October, pp. 1–10.

Pigou, A.C. (1920) *Economics of Welfare*, London: Macmillan.

Porter, M. (1985) *Competitive Advantage*, New York: Free Press.

Rappaport, A. (1998) *Creating Shareholder Value*, New York: Free Press.

Stern, J. and Stewart, B. (1998) 'Stern Stewart EVA^{TM} Roundtable', in Stern, J. and Chew, D. (Eds) *The Revolution in Corporate Finance*, Third Edition, Malden MA: Blackwells.

Williams, K. *et al.* (1994) *Cars: Analysis, History, Cases*, Oxford: Berghahn Books.

Williams, K. *et al.* (1995) *The Crisis of Cost Recovery and the Waste of the Industrialised Nations, Competition and Change*, Vol. 1, pp. 67–93.

Wood, E.G. (1978) *Value Added: The Key to Prosperity*, London: Business Books.

CHAPTER 3

Competitive business: The macro-economic context

In this chapter we use the value-added accounting framework to understand how the composition of an economy's Gross Domestic Product (GDP) changes over time. If we look at the newly industrializing countries (NICs) we can observe a large shift from agricultural output into manufacturing and services.

We find that agriculture and manufacturing progressively make a smaller contribution to GDP growth in the mature advanced economies and even NICs like Taiwan. The trajectory of GDP growth in manufacturing slows down and the case study on Japanese manufacturing at the end of this chapter is used to illustrate this point.

In the major mature industrial economies such as Japan, USA, UK and Germany it is services that are making an increasingly large contribution to GDP growth. In the period 1970 to 1993 the contribution of services towards overall GDP growth was between 60 and 75 per cent in Japan, USA, UK and Germany. Our analysis suggests that in terms of trajectory business opportunity lies with the provision of services and less so within manufacturing.

Our analysis of labour's share of value added also suggests that services generally, and financial services specifically, are more cash generative than manufacturing activities. In terms of the macro-economic context the value-added accounting analysis can be used to discover opportunity for business even in economies that are growing slowly – overall there are still sectors of an economy that thrive.

We will also observe in this chapter that manufacturers and retailers are migrating into the provision of services and financial services because these moves promise to enhance cost recovery, profits and return on capital.

Introduction

Business analysis should inform the manager of a business enterprise about structural adjustments in the macro-economic environment. In the last 20 years the macro-economic context, within which international business operates has undergone substantial transformation. In the advanced economies a rapid growth in manufacturing output in the first 50 years of this century secured a structural shift from essentially agrarian to industrialized economy. This chapter describes the main changes in macro-economic structure. In general these are the increasing weight and significance of manufacturing in the economic development of the newly industrialized countries (NICs) and the increasing importance of services in the advanced economies.

Changes in the sectoral composition of national output suggests that some sectors are able to generate rates of growth which increase their contribution in national value added (Gross Domestic Product or GDP) in terms of profit, share in value added and cash.

Historically we observe a general shift in the composition of national output from:

Agriculture ⟶ Manufacturing ⟶ Services

Changes in the composition of Gross Domestic Product (GDP) are structurally driven by differential rates of growth between sectors and the operating ratios (cash and profit) which can be extracted from the various sectors. Krugman, the American economist, argues that the shift in structure at a macro level releases labour resources into new sectors where the prospects for value added generation and wages are higher (Krugman 1992).

Gross domestic product and national rates of growth

Before we turn to develop these issues we will start with a consideration of overall economic growth of a sample of countries. GDP is a national measure of value added. It measures total gross output of national firms minus what the economy purchases from other nations in order to generate that value added. Different economies experience different rates of overall GDP growth or growth trajectories and we can express changes in GDP using an index or per cent per year rate.

In Table 3.1 we illustrate the average percentage growth rates in GDP for a range of countries over the period 1970 to 1993. During this period the newly industrialized countries (NICs) experience the most rapid of growth rates. Taiwan, Korea and Malaysia are experiencing rates of growth in the range 6 to 14 per cent in these sub-periods. The economic environment for businesses operating in the mature industrial economies is, by way of contrast, less

Table **3.1:** Growth in real GDP (per cent per annum)

	1970–75	1975–80	1980–85	1985–90	1988–93
Malaysia	7.9	8.4	3.8	6.8	8.8
Korea	2.5	3.5	13.2	6.2	6.9
Taiwan	9.0	10.6	7.5	8.9	7.1
UK	2.4	2.2	3.0	3.2	0.1
USA	2.6	3.4	3.4	2.4	1.6
Germany	5.5	4.2	7.0	–1.4	–1.7
Japan	4.7	4.7	3.6	4.6	2.6

(Source: *Handbook of International Trade and Development Statistics,* UN Economic and Social Survey of Asia and Pacific 1995, UN)

attractive. Economic growth rates are in the range negative 2 to positive 5 per cent. In general terms, the more rapid the growth of GDP the more favourable will be the financial condition for business. When growth is sluggish and/or negative it is not possible to maintain employment and income increases at their pre-existing level because the fund of value added generated by the organization limits employment and wages. In a situation where output is cyclical, revenues and cash flow are also cyclical (see Chapter 2 for the relationship between market conditions and cash generation).

Apart from the output growth (GDP in real 1990 money values or constant money values) we can observe how rapid output trajectories translate into high levels of productivity by looking at Table 3.2 which shows the output per head in various countries. We observe in Table 3.2 that the NICs have substantially higher productivity growth per capita. In the last 25 years output per head of the population has been running in line with the differential in output growth namely at a rate which is three to four times higher than the advanced mature economies: USA, UK and Germany and even Japan.

The main impact of the rapid growth in output and productivity has been to raise the overall standard of living for the population of the NICs. Growth in GDP per capita within the population in turn fuels an increase in domestic

Table **3.2:** Growth in real GDP/capita

	1970–75	1975–80	1980–85	1985–90	1988–93
Malaysia	5.3	5.9	1.0	4.0	5.9
Korea	7.0	6.3	–1.7	8.9	5.9
Taiwan	6.9	8.5	5.9	7.9	5.7
UK	2.2	2.1	2.9	2.9	–0.1
USA	1.6	2.3	2.2	1.6	0.6
Germany	3.0	3.0	3.8	1.1	–1.2
Japan	3.3	3.8	2.9	4.1	2.2

(Source: *Handbook of International Trade and Development Statistics,* UN Economic and Social Survey of Asia and Pacific 1995, UN)

consumption. As national income and consumer expenditures increase so positive multiplier effects feed the rest of the economy and so further increase the demand for manufactured goods and services.

Apart from the fact that different countries exhibit different rates of productivity-led growth we also observe shifts in the composition of national output. Economic activity moves from basic primary raw materials processing and agriculture towards a more advanced economy composition of national output. That is, growth is driven by a shift of employment and resources into manufacturing activities and services.

Manufacturing share of GDP

In 1970 manufacturing accounted for just 14 per cent of national GDP in the low income regions of the world (UNIDO, 1998) but by 1994 manufacturing accounted for 32 per cent of national GDP by output composition in these regions. Growth in the manufacturing share of national GDP is a characteristic which is common to the newly industrializing countries but not so for the advanced economies.

Industrialization in the NICs is the motor of national economic development but for the advanced mature economies we observe a process of deindustrialization. In the mature advanced economies the share of manufacturing in total national GDP is generally falling as Table 3.3 demonstrates.

In Table 3.3 we can also observe that in all the advanced countries, even surprisingly in Japan, there has been a reduction in the contribution of manufacturing value added in GDP (national value added). In the UK and USA there has been a marked reduction in the contribution of manufacturing in total national output. In the UK and USA there has been a 6 to 8 percentage point drop in the share of manufacturing in GDP since 1970, with manufacturing now accounting for just 19 to 21 per cent of total national GDP. In Germany and Japan the share of manufacturing in GDP has also fallen by roughly 10–11 percentage points.

Table **3.3:** Manufacturing share of national GDP

	1970	1975	1980	1985	1995
Malaysia	14	21	27	20	33
Korea	21	26	30	29	30
Taiwan	29	29	36	38	30
UK	29	n/a	23	23	21
USA	25	23	22	21	19
Germany	38	n/a	33	n/a	27
Japan	36	30	28	28	26

(Source: UNIDO Industrial Statistics, 1998)

In the NICs, by way of contrast, manufacturing now accounts for over 30 per cent of national output and since 1970 Malaysia and Korea show a substantial shift in the composition of GDP towards manufacturing. In Malaysia the share of manufacturing in GDP has risen steadily from a 14 per cent share to a 30 per cent share in the early 1990s reaching a share of GDP which corresponds to that in Korea and Taiwan. Over the last 20 years investment in manufacturing has generally been a positive business opportunity because growth has underwritten a strong trajectory of cost recovery and cash generation.

Apart from the wide differences in growth rates internationally we should also pay attention to the fact that within national economies there are substantial adjustments in the composition of output (value added) between the major sectors of agriculture, manufacturing and services.

Internationally there are large differences in the structure and composition of national output of economies. Internationally, the share of manufacturing in GDP now stands at 22 per cent. However it is still the case that many countries within the African region have less than ten per cent of national output in manufacturing and their economies are essentially low-wage low-income agriculture or subsistence based economies (see Table 3.4).

In terms of the share of world manufacturing value added, it is still the case that a high share is taken by those economies that also have a high income per head. UNIDO (United Nations International Development Office) observe that in 1995 roughly 50 per cent of world manufacturing value added output is appropriated by the high-income regional economies, which in the same year accounted for just 17 per cent of world population (see Table 3.5).

However for those economies that have achieved the sectoral shift from agriculture to manufacturing, the result is one of rising national income and income per head of the population. In NICs like Taiwan and Korea rapid expansion of manufacturing output growth has created financial business opportunity because businesses that experience rapid output expansion are often cash generative.

Table **3.4:** Share of manufacturing in national GDP

	1980	**1995**
Industrialized Economies	**23.7**	**22.2**
Eastern Europe	31.6	30.6
European Union	26.2	23.4
North America	18.7	18.7
Developing Countries	**18.7**	**20.7**
Africa	10.0	11.5
Latin America	24.2	20.8
South and East Asia	18.5	23.6
West Asia and Europe	13.3	17.1
World Total	**22.9**	**22.0**

(Source: *UNIDO Industrial Statistics, 1998*)

Table **3.5:** Share of world manufacturing value added by low to high regions of the world

Country Group	Share of World Manufacturing Value Added		Population Share in %	
	1980	**1995**	**1980**	**1995**
Low Income	20.7	22.6	67.3	67.3
Middle Income	26.5	28.3	15.8	16.0
High Income	52.8	49.1	16.9	16.7

(Source: *UNIDO, Industrial Statistics, 1998*)

If we take the case of Korean motor vehicles and electrical engineering, Table 3.6 presents the basic data on labour's share in motor vehicles and electrical engineering. It shows that right through the period 1976–88 the Koreans invert the usual 70/30 ratio; where competitors are lucky to realize 30 cents in each dollar of value added as cash, the Koreans realize the best part of 70 cents as cash. This performance is similar to that of Japan when it was a new entrant; labour's share of value added was below 50 per cent in Japanese manufacturing as a whole in the 1950s and at or below 55 per cent throughout the 1960s. The explanation is relatively simple. The Japanese, as new entrants in the 1950s and 1960s, were, like the Koreans in the 1970s and 1980s, selling on their export markets at prices which reflected the cost recovery requirements of their high labour cost western competitors. However, because their labour costs per unit were dramatically lower, their cash recovery was strong (Williams *et al.* 1995).

Strong cash-generative businesses and industrial sectors enter into a virtuous circle of expansion funded by their surplus. As we have already noted during the 1980s, real manufacturing value added (MVA) or net industrial output has grown by around 10 per cent per annum in economies like Korea, Malaysia and Singapore; whereas the established Western economies have MVA growth rates of only 1.5 to 3.5 per cent. Rapid compound growth from a small base produces significant results fairly rapidly; the Korean vehicles industry currently produces two million vehicles

Table **3.6:** Labour's share of value added in the Korean motor vehicle manufacturing and electrical engineering sectors

	Motor Vehicles (384)		Electrical Engineering (383)	
	Labour's share	**Profit's share**	**Labour's share**	**Profit's share**
1976	36.0	64.0	33.9	66.1
1980	55.4	44.6	43.6	56.4
1985	30.0	70.0	28.3	71.7
1988	26.0	74.0	28.8	71.2
1995	26.0	74.0	20.0	80.0

(Source: *Industrial Statistics Yearbook*, United Nations; *Yearbook of Labour Statistics*, various years)

per annum and its electronics industry accounts for 40 per cent of televisions traded internationally. The factories of the new entrants are always fully loaded because in export markets they can sell entry-level products at very attractive prices. Cash generative businesses also have the capability to move across and up national markets; the cash from entry-level products allows them to price in a predatory way, undertake expensive investment in distribution and invest in an endless stream of new models and production facilities which take them up market.

The interesting question concerns the conditions under which a business moves on and then off the trajectory of high growth and ultra-high cash generation. Low wages are an important reason why Korean manufacturers were able to generate substantial cash from operations, but low wages alone are not a sufficient condition for sustaining performance. On the basis of Japanese experience (see case study at end of this chapter), a number of supplementary conditions are equally important: a growing domestic market which provides an unproblematic volume base for a business, a stable and predictable exchange rate; and a stable corporate financial structure.

Countries move off the trajectory of high growth as money and real wages rise through the combined effects of concessions to the workforce and currency appreciation; as a Renault executive observed 'wages don't stay low for long'. They do however stay low for long enough for multinational business to relocate capacity and/or create major new corporate players. In the first phase of Asian low-wage competition, between 1978 and 1991 US car production fell by 3.7 million and Japanese car production increased by more than 4 million. The beneficiaries of this expansion are firms like Nissan and Toyota. Korean manufacturing expansion will also leave a similar legacy of production capacity and new household names like Hyundai, Daewoo and Samsung. As wages rise, these firms will, like their Japanese predecessors, lose their low-labour cost advantage but that does not remove them from the global scene nor ease the low-wage pressure on Western producers if the Koreans are succeeded by another generation of new entrants. In any case, the labour market tightening effect only operates strongly in relatively small countries. Established Western producers may be grateful that the Korean workforce includes only 19 million workers and the Malaysian workforce just 7 million. However the Chinese workforce numbers 583 million and it will take some time for wages to drift upwards and hours worked to fall. Already China's share of total world manufacturing output has risen from a 2 per cent share in 1985 to a 4 per cent share in 1996.

From manufacturing into services

For the advanced economies such as the USA, Japan, Germany and the UK manufacturing has increasingly less weight in national economic output as these economies shift from manufacturing progressively into services. The added advantage of services is that they are, to all intents and purposes, sheltered from international competition and the exchange rate but this is not to say that internal competitive forces are driving costs out of the provision of services. In these economies the growth in services has outpaced the growth in manufacturing and in all of these countries services now account for two-thirds of all national output.

In Table 3.7 services are on a positive and strong growth trajectory. The manufacturing sector, by way of contrast, shows slow growth and in some cases this growth is punctuated with periods of cyclicality. The implications of this analysis for business strategy is rather compelling because it suggests that growth in value added and cash is more easily obtained where a business has a portfolio of service-related activities. The service sector(s) of these major industrialized economies do still generally have favourable cost recovery conditions which also combines with a relatively favourable operating architecture which generates more cash in value added.

In Table 3.8 we calculate the overall growth in the value of real national output and then account for this growth by broad sector: manufacturing, services, government and other. In an earlier period, 1950–1973, manufacturing makes a 25 to 40 per cent contribution to GDP growth with services accounting for 40–55 per cent of GDP growth. The general observation in the second later period, 1974 to 1993, is that manufacturing makes a progressively weaker contribution to the growth in national output. In Japan, an economy renowned for its industrial prowess, the contribution of manufacturing to the overall growth in national output was just 15 per cent in the period 1973–1995. In the USA and UK manufacturing barely makes a positive contribution to national value added growth. Services by way of contrast in all the advanced economies make an increasingly strong contribution to national output growth accounting for two-thirds to four-fifths of output growth (see Table 3.8).

The result is that, as far as the US, Japanese, German and UK economies are concerned, the service sector has increased its share in national output. In our four country case the service sector has increased its share of GDP from

Table **3.7:** Value added output growth for four main industrialized economies

	USA		Japan		Germany		UK	
	Manufacturing	**Services**	**Manufacturing**	**Services**	**Manufacturing**	**Services**	**Manufacturing**	**Services**
1970	100.0	100.0	100.0	100.0	100.0	100.0	100.0	100.0
1975	102.5	113.2	97.9	124.8	101.3	126.3	105.3	114.8
1980	110.7	128.4	115.0	149.1	112.9	155.8	103.5	125.3
1985	114.4	166.5	132.8	185.9	111.9	175.4	105.2	143.2
1990	120.8	196.4	158.9	241.4	133.9	226.8	114.4	193.2
1994	119.3	210.6	143.3	260.4	120.2	262.3	109.0	226.3
Growth 70–94%	19.3	110.6	43.3	160.4	20.2	162.3	9.0	126.3

Note: Services are wholesale and retailing, transportation and communication, financial services and community and personal services.
(Source: OECD)

Table **3.8:** Sectoral contribution to gross domestic product growth

		Contribution to Gross Domestic Product %			
		Manufacturing	**Services**	**Government**	**Other**
Germany	1950–93	25.9	54.9	12.0	7.2
	1950–73	37.9	38.3	12.3	11.5
	1974–93	10.8	76.3	12.0	0.9
UK	1950–93	11.9	60.2	15.9	12.0
	1950–73	24.9	40.9	17.1	17.1
	1974–93	–1.4	81.1	13.2	7.1
Japan	1950–93	24.5	54.0	7.8	13.7
	1950–73	33.9	45.4	7.2	13.5
	1974–93	15.0	61.8	8.5	14.7
US	1950–93	14.2	67.4	12.7	5.7
	1950–73	22.8	54.8	14.7	7.7
	1974–93	4.8	79.7	9.7	5.7

(Source: OECD, various years)

between 30 to 50 per cent in the 1970s to between 50 and 60 per cent in the 1990s (see Table 3.9).

We now ask the question 'From which service sectors has this growth in share of national output been derived?'

The analysis suggests that financial services account for between 20 and 40 per cent of total national output and in the UK and the USA Financial Services generate double the value added of manufacturing. Between 30 and 45 per cent of total national value added is generated from wholesale and retail activities. That is, from car dealing to hotels and accommodation, restaurants and catering to clothes shops and grocery stores. The two sectors – financial

Table **3.9:** Services share of gross domestic product and employment (%)

	1970		1993	
	GDP %	**Employment %**	**GDP %**	**Employment %**
Germany	34.3	29.7	51.1	42.0
UK	42.0	35.7	54.6	55.4
Japan	42.4	37.9	52.0	50.5
US	49.3	48.2	60.5	60.3

(Source: OECD, various years)

services and wholesale and retail – alone account for between 55 and 66 per cent of total national value added generated in a given year (see Table 3.10).

We even find similar patterns of development in the NICs. For example in Taiwan a shift has taken place in the composition of manufacturing and services in national output (see Table 3.11). Over the last ten years we find that even within Taiwan there has been a rapid shift in the composition of national output so that this country is now predominantly a service-based economy. Growth in manufacturing output acts to shift labour resources away from agriculture because it creates employment at higher wages – for example in Malaysia wages in manufacturing per hour are 2.5 times higher than agriculture. These more highly paid employees in turn spend a considerable proportion of their income on services from retailing to take-away meals, entertainment and leisure activities. This is turn creates an added boost to the development of the service sector of an economy.

The contribution to the growth in value added from manufacturing in Taiwan has fallen off in recent years. In an earlier period, 40 per cent of national output growth was derived from manufacturing and agriculture and these sectors exceeded the contribution from wholesale and retail and financial services by a factor of 2:1. In the period from 1990 to 1995 the ratio had adjusted such that the contribution from wholesale and retail and financial services now exceeds that of manufacturing and agriculture in the ratio 2:1.

Table **3.10** Service sector and service sub-sector contribution to gross domestic product growth 1970–93

	Contribution to Gross Domestic Product %			
	Total Services	**Financial Services**	**Retail, Community, Personal**	**Transport & Communications**
Germany	72.5	22.0	45.8	4.7
UK	74.0	37.1	28.9	8.0
Japan	60.6	20.7	34.1	5.8
US	75.8	38.6	31.8	5.4

(Source: OECD, various years)

Table **3.11:** Contribution to value added output growth in Taiwan

	1955–1975	**1975–1995**	**1990–95**
Agriculture	11.8	2.6	2.5
Manufacturing	31.7	27.8	19.5
Wholesale and retail	13.0	16.2	19.0
Financial services	10.5	20.0	23.1
Community and personal services	3.9	10.8	13.8

(Source: National Accounts 1951–1995, Taiwan)

Our value-added national accounting analysis can be used to observe changes in the degree to which particular sectors contribute towards national output growth. In our mature industrial economies the majority of national output growth is to be found in service-related sectors of their respective macro economies. The analysis can also be used to establish where strong sectoral growth trajectories are to be found. From this analysis we observe that two service sectors account for strong growth and structural shift in the four main economies.

Macro-economic shift and business opportunity

To take the analysis further we can use our value-added accounting framework to establish the extent to which these shifts present a strategic business opportunity. That is, in what sectors should a business be looking to consolidate activities and secure financial advantage. In the section on the value added framework we argued that some businesses are more cash generative and so it is with sectors within a national economy. Using the value added accounting framework we are able to calculate labour's share of value added (see Table 3.12) and cash generation (the gross operating surplus). Cash generation is found by deducting from value-added total labour costs including social charges.

Table **3.12:** Labour's share of value added 1970–93

		Manufacturing %	Services %
Germany	1970–93	65.9	40.5
	High	71.6	44.0
	Low	60.0	37.4
UK	1970–93	78.4	55.6
	High	81.8	56.8
	Low	69.8	49.6
Japan	1970–93	52.4	45.7
	High	58.7	48.9
	Low	39.6	37.2
US	1970–93	69.6	51.1
	High	78.3	52.8
	Low	65.6	49.7

(Source: OECD, various years)

In Table 3.12 we contrast labour's share of value added in manufacturing and services. We find that, in general, manufacturing has a higher labour cost share in value added than services. On average, manufacturing labour's share of value added in our four main countries is in the range of 40 to 80 per cent and services 40 to 55 per cent. That is for every yen, dollar or Deutsche Mark of value added generated from sales, services generally have the capacity to generate more cash out of value added generated from operations.

A business sector that has increased its weight and significance in national output in the developing and developed economies is that of financial services. This sector now accounts for a 20 per cent share of national value added in the major economies. Financial services have the capacity to generate a high value added per employee and this is also associated with a low labour's share in value added (see Table 3.13).

The observation is that business opportunity is limited in the manufacturing sector(s) of the advanced economies and that a cash surplus is difficult to sustain. Opportunity does however lie with the development and consolidation of service activities generally (and specifically business or financial services) within a portfolio of business activities. By far the most cash generative are those activities associated with the provision of financial and business services because these combine both a high value added per employee and a low labour's share in value added.

In each of our four countries covered, financial services generate a higher share of operating surplus than the sector's share of GDP (national value added). In the USA a 27 per cent share of national value added generates a 40 per cent share of national operating surplus. Likewise in Japan, Germany and the UK financial services share of operating surplus is much higher than the sector's share of national value added (see Table 3.14).

At a macro level our analysis allows us to observe a general shift in the composition in national output from agriculture to manufacturing and then increasingly into services. The first of these shifts released labour from agriculture. This labour was then employed within manufacturing. Manufacturing establishes the possibility of generating higher wages and profits but the trajectory of growth in output slows relative to the growth in services. The growth in services creates more employment in activities which generally deliver a lower labour's share in value added and a higher operating (cash)

Table **3.13:** Financial services sector value added and cash generation

	Value Added per Head in National Currencies	Labour's Share of Value Added	Cash Share of Value Added
USA ($ mill)	116,566	37%	63%
Japan (Yen mill)	29,715	21%	79%
Germany (DM mill)	425,907	20%	80%
UK (£ mill)	56,219	40%	60%

(Source: OECD)

Table **3.14:** Financial services share of total national operating surplus

	USA $ million	Japan Yen billion	Germany DM million	UK £ million
Total Economy Cash Generation	2,789,504	255,745	1,544,325	231,662
Financial Services Cash Generation	1,129,015	65,471	324,712	89,188
Financial Services Share of National Cash Generation	40.47	25.60	21.03	38.50
Financial Services Share of National Value Added	26.7	16.8	14.4	25.2

(Source: OECD)

surplus. To a greater or lesser extent the same shifts in the composition of national output can be observed in the NICs.

The problem facing manufacturers of durable and non-durable products is that labour costs do not stay at internationally low levels for long. Movements in the exchange rate combine with shorter hours worked and increased pay in national currencies to increase labour's share in value added unless growth in output compensates for the increase in labour costs. Intensified international competition works through to generate a crisis of cost recovery for manufacturers. The main manufacturing sectors of our four main industrialized economies now exhibit patterns of sluggish and/or cyclical growth. Services are less exposed to international competition and the distribution of value added favours cash generation.

For the business manager this macro/sectoral analysis can be used to shape long-term corporate decisions and answer a number of key strategic questions. For example 'what sectors and activities do we wish to migrate into in the next few years?' and 'what is/are the likely financial consequence(s) of such strategic manoeuvrings?'

Business analysis should inform the strategic calculations of management and enhance our understanding as to why firms consolidate some activities and uncouple others. Many organizations operate to financially consolidate a matrix of business segments covering a range of industrial and commercial sectors. The Ford Motor Corporation now generates more cash from its Financial Services Division than its does from its Automobile Division. The future strategic development of the Ford Motor Company is firmly located in the extension of its financial services division. In UK grocery and mixed retailer sector companies like Tesco, Sainsbury's and Marks and Spencer are consolidating financial services into their overall activity mix. Customers generate more cash for Sainsbury's or Tesco and profit when they use a store card or put their savings into a wider range of financial services such as pension funds and household insurance.

Using the value-added framework it is possible to identify a structural shift in activity towards services rather than manufacturing. This shift is the mix of national macro-economic activity and is to some extent determined by the fact that household expenditure patterns are increasingly shifting from durable goods consumption to the consumption of services. Intense competition in the manufacturing sectors of many national economies has put pressure on firms to reduce costs. Lower costs of food and consumer durable manufacture have been passed on to households. This frees up disposable income that can be spent on the purchase of services, for example: restaurant meals; take-away food; home cleaning; and household services and entertainment. Manufacturers in the advanced economies are caught between the rock of market maturity and the hard place of continuous cost reduction. Reduced volume sales combine with lower unit cost to undermine the ability of manufacturing organizations to sustain value added generation at previous levels so requiring a reduction in employment. This combination of trends puts a severe brake on the expansion of national manufacturing capacity and we illustrate these issues by looking at the case of manufacturing in Japan.

Case study: A brake on Japanese manufacturing?

The Japanese economy in the post-war period grew rapidly and businesses were generally highly cash generative as domestic consumer demand rose year on year without faltering. This domestic home market context was, however, to change in the 1980s with the onset of slower growth. Japanese management systems have been used to represent world-class business practice, where attention is constantly paid to market expansion through improved product differentiation and cost reduction through the application of Kaizen (steps towards improvement) systems.

If Japanese home-based manufacturers were masters of cost reduction and cost recovery, we would expect the real value added per employee to increase steadily as labour comes out and value goes in. The reality is completely different. Table 3.15 shows that real value added per employee shows no sustained upward trend; in 1995 it is no more than 12 per cent higher than in 1983. A closer examination shows also that labour productivity is not being actively managed; with total numbers employed in Japanese manufacturing more or less flat, the trend in real output determines productivity and this varies cyclically and passively. In years such as 1986 and 1992, when real sales drop, productivity falls sharply; conversely in the Hesei boom of the late 1980s a temporary increase in labour productivity of nearly 25 per cent more or less exactly matches the increase in output over the same period. This cyclically driven pattern of output growth is similar to that which we have observed in many manufacturing sectors internationally.

Not only have home market conditions deteriorated for Japanese manufacturers but Japanese hourly labour costs per employee, converted into dollars at the prevailing exchange rate, show that Japan in the early 1990s was a high-wage industrial country. Labour costs were in dollar terms roughly equal to those paid by American competitors and in 1994 the Japanese had become the second highest labour cost industrial country behind Germany (see Table 3.16).

Table **3.15:** Productivity and cash generation in Japanese manufacturing

Year	Nos. Employed	Real sales index	Nominal VA per employee index	Real VA per employee index	Labour share of VA	Labour + dep share of VA
1983	2,724	100.0	100.0	100.0	55.3	70.7
1984	2,738	105.6	110.1	101.7	52.7	67.7
1985	2,757	105.7	108.7	104.3	56.1	72.2
1986	2,719	97.32	102.2	97.5	60.1	78.0
1987	2,654	99.71	109.5	104.3	56.8	74.3
1988	2,659	108.9	124.0	117.4	53.2	69.2
1989	2,700	116.1	132.7	108.0	52.8	68.8
1990	2,771	123.4	137.7	123.7	53.8	70.3
1991	2,836	122.1	133.4	116.1	56.9	75.1
1992	2,858	116.0	124.9	106.9	60.4	80.4
1995	2,610	110.0	133.6	112.0	52.8	74.7

Notes: Calculations are averages based on a sample of 44 Japanese manufacturing firms which account for 22 per cent of total manufacturing output.
(Source: Japan Development Bank 1993)

Table **3.16:** Employer labour cost per employee hour for major industries 1980–94 (in US$)

Country	1980	1985	1990	1991	1994
Japan	7.40	11.15	18.03	20.52	28.60
USA	12.67	22.65	20.22	21.24	24.87
France	10.03	10.20	15.57	16.42	18.54
Germany	13.70	13.72	26.03	26.95	35.88
Italy	9.05	10.40	16.94	19.13	17.23
UK	7.63	8.70	15.48	16.15	16.80
Spain	6.95	6.76	16.31	17.91	16.86
Sweden	15.70	12.33	26.40	27.52	24.70

(Source: VDA, fax communication 1992; *Financial Times*)

Japanese manufacturing in the 1980s was structurally exposed and vulnerable on a number of fronts. The Japanese were unable to manage their physical inputs of labour and capital – continued profit depended on first, the maintenance of high output levels and second, a slowing of currency appreciation. Neither condition has been satisfied, especially after 1989 when the Japanese economy turned down cyclically for the first time since the first oil crisis.

These changed structural circumstances in the Japanese manufacturing sector are further examined in Table 3.17 which summarizes the operating performance of 44 large Japanese corporations involved in the manufacture of cars and car components, household electrical goods and electronic equipment. All these sectors are heavily oriented towards export and in all of them nominal and real sales have been falling

Table **3.17:** Value added per employee, cash flow to sales and break-even point of operations in Japanese automobiles, household electrical and computers/electrical equipment 1983–95[2]

	1983	**1988**	**1995**
Automobile Industry			
Cash flow as a % of Sales	8.6	7.9	4.1
Lab + Dep as % of value added	73.1	74.1	92.7
Real VA/Employee (mill yen)[3]	10.02	11.2	9.7
Household Electrical Industry			
Cash flow as % of Sales	9.1	8.3	3.8
Lab + Dep as % of value added[1]	53.0	65.5	85.0
Real VA/Employee in mill yen[3]	8.2	9.0	8.9
Computers and Electrical Equipment			
Cash flow as % of Sales	10.0	9.8	5.6
Lab + Dep as % of value added operations[1]	68.8	73.2	65.3
Real VA/Employee (mill yen)[3]	10.75	9.74	10.40

Notes:
(1) Labour costs plus depreciation as a per cent of the value added fund in each year also serves as a crude proxy for the break-even point.
(2) The 44 Japanese companies surveyed account for 22 per cent of total Japanese manufacturing output.
(3) The real value added per employee figure is for 1992 in household electricals and electrical equipment.
(Sources: Handbook of Industrial Financial Data, Japan Development Bank)

since 1991. In each of the three sectors we have calculated the average real value added per employee in million yen, cash flow as a percentage of sales and the labour plus depreciation share of value added.

The problems facing Japanese manufacturing as a whole can be understood if we consider the record of these three sectors since 1983. Japanese inability to reduce costs by taking physical labour out or cost recovery by moving the product up market emerges very clearly from the sectoral record on real value added per employee. Over the whole period 1983 to 1995, there is no sustained increase in any of the sectors.

In these three sectors, as in Japanese manufacturing as a whole, accumulating problems had been covered by output increases and high-capacity utilization in the later stages of the Hesei boom. However the classic upturn effect of a decline in labour's share as output increases cannot be observed. Instead, the share of labour plus depreciation in value added (the break-even point – see Figure 3.1) rose sharply in two of the three sectors between 1983 and 1988; in electronics, the combined share rises by more than 10 per cent. The downturn after 1991 and 1995 dramatizes the underlying deterioration in structural fundamentals. In all three sectors, cash flow as a percentage of sales is more or less halved and the

The break-even point is generally calculated as the point at which Total Revenue = Total Costs. Using the value added accounting framework we can approximate the break-even point as where value added just covers the labour cost and depreciation but no contribution to profit is made.

The degree to which a business in any given year is operating below or above break-even is expressed as:

(Labour costs + Depreciation)/Value Added

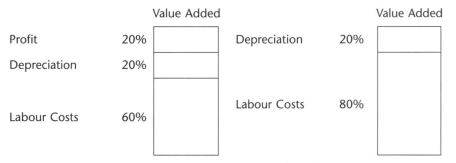

In the first case labour costs and depreciation = 80 per cent of value added so the company is breaking even at 80 per cent of operations in that year and in the second case the BEP is 100 per cent of operations.

Figure **3.1:** The break-even point

labour plus depreciation share rises alarmingly in cars and electrical/electronic products to squeeze residual operating profit. In both these sectors, a capacity utilization of around 95 per cent has now to be sustained before a positive contribution to net income is made after labour costs and depreciation have been covered.

These sectors operate in saturated and cyclical markets and this is a major problem because it means that firms are unable to sustain full capacity utilization and healthy profit contribution. Cyclical recovery would go some way to restoring cash generation but it could never restore the lost competitiveness of the pre-1985 period because structural conditions have changed irrevocably in a way which now makes Japanese manufacturers weak and vulnerable to every market downturn and exchange-rate movement.

In aggregate, Japanese corporate profits have been badly damaged by the conditions of market maturity and cyclicality with real profits still some 25 per cent down on the peak in 1990. During the last recession and after the Hesei boom which ended in 1990 corporate profits were down 40 to 50 per cent at their lowest which were equivalent to real corporate profitability of some 20 years earlier (see Figure 3.2).

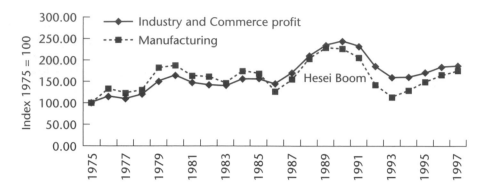

Figure **3.2:** Japanese industry real profit

Workshop questions/exercises

Q1 'In the advanced countries manufacturing is in decline but business opportunity is to be found from locating activities in the service sector.' To what extent do you agree with this statement?

Q2 Why does the service sector of an economy tend to operate with a higher level of cash generated per financial unit of value added?

Q3 What are the main lessons we can learn from an understanding of the changes in macro-economic structure?

Q4 What factors have undermined Japanese manufacturing performance in the 1990s?

Table **3.18:** French GDP by kind of activity in current prices

				Electricity Gas and Water		Wholesale and Retail Trades		Finance Insurance and Real Estate	Community and Social Services	Government Services
	Agriculture	Mining	Manufacturing		Construction		Transport			
France mill FF										
1970	50542	6652	224957	13603	58315	83540	42766	105033	46284	78681
1975	73247	12334	397391	26097	110558	161215	75722	214153	100577	162571
1980	112943	23003	722004	59215	182028	277420	154162	457451	213548	331015
1985	182310	40112	1033139	116869	243898	575507	289050	861137	231374	795561
1990	221865	29754	1394503	138739	335812	811345	378473	1390152	363473	1015534
1994	177196	31271	1415399	176232	335104	888522	427520	1704649	446240	1270319

Q5 Using the information provided in Table 3.18, comment on how the structure of GDP (value added output) by industrial and commercial sector has changed in the last 25 years in France.

Q6 Referring back to this chapter are the changes in the composition of national GDP similar to or different from those in Germany, Japan, UK and USA?

References

Krugman, P.R. (1992) *Age of Diminished Expectations: US Economic policy in the 1990s*, Boston: MIT Press.

Magaziner, J.C. and Reich, R.B. (1982) *Minding America's Business: the Decline and Rise of the American Economy*, New York: Harcourt Brace.

Williams, K. *et al.* (1995) *The Crisis of Cost Recovery and the Waste of the Industrialised Nations, Competition and Change*, Vol. 1, pp. 67–93.

Useful statistical references

International Monetary Fund (IMF) *International Financial Statistics Yearbook, New York*.

Organisation for Economic Cooperation and Development (OECD), *Comptes Nationaux, Volume II*, Paris, various years.

United Nations (UN) *National Accounts Statistics, Main Aggregates and Detailed Tables*, New York, various years.

CHAPTER 4

Competitive business: Industry and sector matrix analysis

In economics the production function describes the relationship between inputs of land, labour, capital and materials to produce a particular output for the firm. At the industry level or sector level firms are competing within a particular industry producing similar products as defined by their shared technology e.g. steel production or glass manufacture.

This understanding of the firm as a linear supply chain and industry as a collection of firms producing similar output sharing a common technology is the specification used by Porter to construct the concept of the value chain.

Within the value chain firms are constantly struggling to enhance cost recovery and reduce costs of manufacture. They may, in the end, pursue these objectives globally by expanding markets or accessing lower labour costs. Analysis is constrained within a linear supply chain and industry-centred view of the world of business and so strategic choice(s) are also limited by the value chain model constructed by Porter.

To add to and complement this analysis we add here the concept and framework to undertake a sector matrix business analysis. We accept that the struggle is still to enhance cost recovery and reduce costs to maintain a return on capital. But rather than see the firm as operating within an industry defined by common technology the firm in a sector matrix is viewed as one that consolidates income from a range of activities running across sectors. Rather than restrict the demand side to the consumption of output by individuals e.g. the individual car purchaser, we see the household as the unit of consumption and that household expenditure on motoring or food and clothing, etc. acting to define the economic space within which firms will consolidate their income and profits.

Introduction

In a market economy, management is often judged primarily against financial standards of productive efficiency and profitability. In economic terminology the task of management is to adjust inputs of labour and capital and materials to produce the largest output and realize a surplus for capital. In a positive sense this requires that management expand output by satisfying the consumer with products and services provided at lower cost. In economics the production function describes the relationship between output and factor inputs.

Porter's (1985) value chain analysis describes a chain definition of an industry in which the linkages (supply chain) between firms within a particular industry are described. In its most abbreviated form this concept of an industry and supply chain is found in most introductory micro-economic texts. Production here means the combination of inputs to produce output in the form of a finished product or service. In the more elaborate, rather more realistic, schemas of business policy production takes place in space and time so that production has a double meaning.

KEY CONCEPT 4.1
The production function

In economics the production function is a mathematical statement of the relationship between output of the business or firm and the factor inputs required to produce that output. Where

$$*Q = f (K, L, Lab, M)$$

The production function is used to describe various physical combinations of capital, labour, materials and land required to produce different products. If we attach costs to the resources employed in production it is possible to define not only technical relations of production but also the economic relations that determine cost and price.

The firm is therefore represented as a black box in which inputs are transformed into a saleable product.

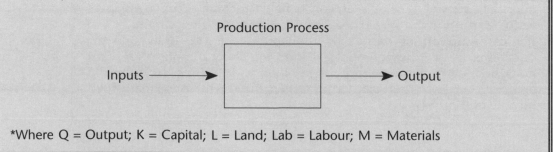

Production Process

Inputs ⟶ [ ] ⟶ Output

*Where Q = Output; K = Capital; L = Land; Lab = Labour; M = Materials

---

The production function

The production function is generally presented linearly in economic input/output analysis and within the business policy literature as a series of linear functions or stages in the transformation process of raw materials to finished product. These stages include: design/development; purchase; assembly and manufacture; marketing and distribution. Production is therefore a chain of activities/exchanges where money moves back down the chain as the physical product or service is transformed up the chain. This concept of production also carries with it a concept of an industry defined as a group of firms producing similar products/services using a common or shared technology whose output appears on the demand side as competing products.

For example, a steel producer manufactures steel and the process is one of converting raw materials (coke, limestone and iron ore) into steel through a series of process stages – blast furnace, rolling, strip, bar and billet, etc. The manufacturer of steel is identified as belonging to the steel industry because the business shares a common technology and shared products.

To illustrate how this works we can combine two fundamental elements of Porter's work on competitive advantage: the value chain (see Figure 4.1) and industry structure analysis.

The value chain describes production as a series of functions in a supply chain. Suppliers provide raw materials and services which have costs added to them before they reach an organization's factory gates. Inside the factory, further production takes place with the addition of costs of production. Once the internal conversion process is completed products leave the organization and enter into a distribution system and then to the final consumer.

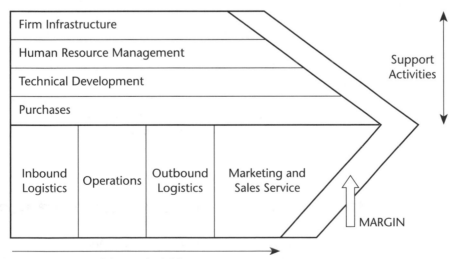

Figure **4.1:** The value chain

The supply chain concept of business operations is located within the concept of a value chain and the question as to how a business manages its supply chain relations depends upon the strategic analysis of the industry in which the organization operates. The industry is defined as a group of competing firms operating a similar technology producing similar products. The car industry, for example, contains a number of organizations that utilize relatively common assembly technologies (although the organization of work within this technology may be hybridized). Each organization competes against others by producing relatively similar products. Corporate strategy can then be represented as a series of responses that attempt to position your business relative to competitors so that it secures competitive advantage relative to the industry.

The strategic imperative of an organization is to enhance cost recovery (volume multiplied by price per unit) and reduce costs. Within the industry a particular organization will strategically try to ensure that it maintains home market share and exploits the variability of price structures in a portfolio of markets. An organization in a particular industry will also work towards ensuring that costs of production of a product or service are kept to a minimum unless particular market conditions permit the recovery of high unit costs.

Output growth trajectory

The analysis we have presented establishes the point that we can identify national economies and industry sectors that have favourable growth trajectories. With new products or services the first players in the market experience a rapid trajectory of output growth as new demand creates the financial conditions for further investment and expansion.

The video recorder is used here as an example to illustrate how sales volumes follow an arc-like trajectory. During the growth phase of the product market trajectory cost recovery is strong and a sustained expansion of cash flow is generated and this facilitates further expansion of productive capacity and distribution networks. After a relatively short period of exceptional growth, the rate of physical output increase year on year tends to fall away. In our video recorder example it takes just 12 years before the European market demand for video recorders reaches a point of market maturity where replacement demand becomes the norm at around 8.5 to 9 million units (see Table 4.1 and Figure 4.2).

Market maturity and replacement demand

A general problem faced by organisations is that the national home-market demand for particular products or services reaches a point of saturation and maturity (see Key Concept 4.2). When this takes place demand for the output of an organization is very much determined by replacement rates. The

Table **4.1:** Volume sales of video recorders in the four major EC markets France, Italy, Germany and the UK

Year	Colour TVs sold (million)	Video recorders sold (million)
1976	5.482	0.046
1977	6.900	0.069
1978	7.675	0.148
1979	7.909	0.688
1980	8.461	0.983
1981	9.288	4.160
1982	10.115	4.217
1983	9.450	4.274
1984	10.044	3.692
1985	10.720	4.111
1986	12.090	5.247
1987	12.500	6.380
1988	14.150	7.380
1989	15.200	8.040
1990	15.651	9.530
1991	15.866	8.733
1992	14.715	9.105
1993	15.600	8.500
1994	16.100	8.600
1995	16.300	8.800
1996	16.600	8.900

(Source: Consumer Europe)

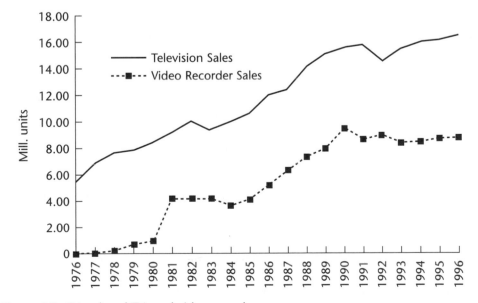

Figure **4.2:** EU: sales of TVs and video recorders

KEY CONCEPT 4.2
Replacement demand cycle/Cyclical markets

A product market reaches maturity when demand for the product is determined by replacement. Some products such as washing machines have a relatively long replacement cycle, maybe up to ten years before a consumer needs to replace the product in their kitchen. Other products have a relatively short replacement cycle, because they deteriorate more rapidly through frequent use and are a relatively small expenditure for the household.

A cyclical market is generally a mature market in which volume fluctuates at or around a steady pattern of demand. A fall in retail sales may be the result of consumers deciding to postpone their replacement purchase for a period of time. The effect of this postponement is to create a cyclical trend in sales.

Car markets are generally mature and cyclical. On the one hand most households in the industrial economies now own a car and so demand each year is replacement demand. When consumers decide to postpone their replacement because of uncertainty relating to economic recession they will postpone their purchases. This causes the market to turn cyclical.

In a mature market competition intensifies and replacement demand exacerbates cyclicality in the market. An organization's revenue and value added from sales also becomes cyclical and cash generation alternates from surplus to deficit.

---

replacement rate may also decline because the product itself has been made more durable. In an earlier period, 10 per cent of the population might replace each year, but now 8 per cent or less of the population replace the product because durability and reliability are enhanced.

When market and cost recovery conditions deteriorate management calculation turns towards a more cost-effective utilization of resources. Cost recovery conditions generally deteriorate because volume growth slows and this combines with aggressive price competition.

The objectives of corporate strategy will change as industries move along the life cycle of growth maturity and cyclicality. It is well known that US car assemblers have been operating in a mature market since 1973 when sales on the US market peaked at roughly 11 million units. The European and Japanese home car markets were still expanding at this stage and so corporate strategy across the various nationally-based car assemblers would therefore be variable. In Europe and Japan a fragmented industry structure survived with relatively small players generating sufficient sales revenue to maintain product and process renewal. In the US corporate strategy emphasized downsizing and a slower rate of model replacement accompanied by economy in the use of financial resources.

When both the European and Japanese car markets reached maturity and cyclicality in the 1990s the corporate strategies of the major car assemblers changed and like their American and European competitors, Japanese producers discovered economy in resource use and corporate downsizing and turned it into a virtuous strategic necessity.

Up until the mid-1970s, car registrations in the US were expanding but in 1973 the market peaked at roughly 11 million units sold. In contrast Japanese producers and West European producers were taking advantage from being located in buoyant domestic markets in which unit sales were expanding. In the mid-1970s the West European and Japanese domestic car markets were at 50 per cent of their peak level of demand. It is not until the late 1980s that these two markets also mature and become cyclical (see Table 4.2). In the late 1980s and early 1990s it was the turn of Korean producers to experience a period of rapid domestic market growth. The point that emerges from market analysis is that organizations are located on different points along a trajectory because country-specific market conditions are variable. If an organization is located at a favourable point along a growth trajectory this is likely to underwrite strategic freedom because cash generation is strong year on year. An organization which is located on a cyclical and mature point on a product market trajectory is more likely to have variable and uncertain cash flows and the degree of strategic freedom much more constrained.

As market conditions deteriorate so increasing effort is directed towards cost reduction as the means by which competitiveness can be sustained. The importance of cost reduction is that it can, to some extent, offset the loss of cash that arises from adverse cost recovery conditions. How and which costs an organization reduces depends on where the costs are located and which

Table **4.2:** Passenger car registrations in main advanced country markets

	W. Europe		Japan		USA	
Year	Units 000s	Index Peak Year = 100	Units 000s	Index Peak Year = 100	Units 000s	Peak Year = 100
1961	3,346	24.79	229	4.49	5,855	51.58
1965	5,368	39.76	586	11.48	9,314	82.05
1970	7,049	52.21	2,379	46.62	8,388	73.90
1973	8,503	62.99	2,934	57.50	11,351	100.00
1975	7,668	56.80	2,738	53.65	8,262	72.79
1980	8,888	65.84	2,854	55.93	8,761	77.18
1985	10,618	78.65	3,104	60.83	10,889	95.93
1990	13,233	98.02	5,103	100.00	9,295	81.89
1991	13,500	100.00	4,868	95.39	8,176	72.03
1992	13,497	99.98	4,454	87.28	8,211	72.34
1993	11,451	84.82	4,199	82.28	8,518	75.04
1994	11,904	88.18	4,210	82.50	8,992	79.22
1995	12,303	91.13	4,450	87.20	9,650	85.01
1996	12,903	95.58	4,700	92.10	10,250	90.30
1997	12,844	95.14	4,850	95.04	10,850	95.59
1998	12,642	93.64	4,650	91.12	n/a	n/a
1999	12,530	92.81	4,600	90.14	n/a	n/a
2000	12,558	93.02	4,500	88.18	n/a	n/a

Notes: Figures for 1995 to 2000 are estimates from Economist Intelligence Unit
(Source: Society of Motor Manufacturers and Traders)

categories of cost are of importance to the particular organization. The value-added accounting framework can be used to discriminate between internal and external costs and also draw management attention to the structure of costs.

Cost structure: Internal and external costs

Looking at Table 4.3, in the case of Company A, the calculation of value added establishes that most of the costs are outside the supply chain as purchases of materials or services from external suppliers. If cost reduction is a priority attention should then be directed towards ensuring a reduction in the purchase costs per unit from suppliers and/or the costs of out-sourced services. In the Japanese economy firms are generally highly vertically disintegrated. This means that most of the cost of the final output is located in the supply chain and management of supplier relations is therefore of critical importance. Cost reduction within the supply chain can be achieved through aggressive purchase ordering and tendering which places responsibility for cost reduction with suppliers. This policy may work more effectively where suppliers are in an adverse power relation to the final purchaser. Where suppliers are dominant, purchase cost reduction may be much more difficult.

Company B, in contrast, has a low purchase to sales ratio and a high value added to sales ratio. This means that most of the cost of this product or service is located within the organization and most of this cost will generally be labour cost. Strategic management action(s) should therefore be directed at reducing internal value added conversion cost and especially labour cost embodied in the product or service.

It is important to remember that an individual organization may operate within a value chain that may be fully located within a national economy or is a global value chain (Gereffi *et al.* 1994, 1996) where various segments of the chain are located across national boundaries. In Table 4.4 company D operates at the end of a supply chain where three other companies (two overseas and one on the home market) are its main suppliers.

In the schematic example in Table 4.4 the three suppliers account for 76 per cent of the total value added in the chain and 90 per cent of the cash generated within the supply chain. Company B needs to pay attention to reducing its labour costs because they account for 88 per cent of total value added and set the limit on internal cash generation. However, strategically,

Table **4.3:** Variation in vertical integration

	Company A	Company B
Sales Revenue	1,000	1,000
Purchases	800	200
Value Added	200	800
Labour Costs	140	600
Cash from Operations	60	200

Table **4.4:** Schematic example of a value added supply chain

$	Supplier Company A Overseas	Supplier Company B Overseas	Supplier Company C Home	Company D Home	Total
Sales	500	1000	1600	2000	5100
Purchases	300	500	1000	1600	3400
Value Added	200	500	600	400	1700
Labour Costs	100	250	450	350	1150
Cash from operations	100	250	150	50	550

company D needs to reappraise its relations with the supply chain companies A, B and C. Most of the cost is outside of the control of company D but it is clear that the suppliers overseas have a much lower labour share in value added. This could be explained as the result of producing in a low-labour cost economy but selling onwards into economies with a more favourable price structure. The result, in any case, is that suppliers are generating by far the greater share of the cash within the value chain and company D might therefore be concerned to negotiate price so adjusting margins and cash shares taken within the value chain.

Company D needs to reduce costs in the supply chain in addition to adjusting its internal labour cost structure if it is to strategically enhance cash generated from operations. Accessing cost in the supply chain to reduce conversion costs requires that labour costs embodied in the output be reduced because labour costs account for 68 per cent of total value added within the supply chain. There are a number of ways in which labour cost could be productively reduced within the industry supply chain. These policies generally take time to execute and the benefits are often limited because cost savings might be passed on to the consumer or lost because gains at one level in the organization are lost at another. The three levers of cost reduction explored briefly below are: design and development; flow improvement; and quality control.

Design, development and cost reduction

Design and development requires a large commitment of physical and financial resources. In this pre-production stage, or in advance of a service being provided, there is an opportunity to anticipate and build into the organization's processes cost reduction at a time when systems are being reorganized.

The design and development process itself requires especially large financial expenditure, in particular the labour time spent on the design and development activity. It is estimated for example that the design and development costs of a car can amount to $2 to $5 billion. Attention paid to reducing the design lead-time from the concept to execution could result in a more cost competitive provision.

According to Marco Iansiti, systems-focused companies form a core multi-function team of scientists, managers and engineers at an early stage in the design and development process. The result is that 'System-focused companies achieve the best product improvements in the shortest time and at the lowest costs' (Iansiti, 1993).

It is possible for the design and development process to function on a basis where each department or function separately undertakes input into the design and development process and that a stages approach to each phase of the development cycle taken. After each stage of the development cycle is finished then the next phase can start. We can represent this linear approach to design and development below. A simultaneous or concurrent approach to design and development can shorten the concept to market lead-time (see Key Concept 4.3).

KEY CONCEPT 4.3
Linear and simultaneous design processes

Linear
In which the stages of the design and development process are completed as discrete operations before the next stage of the product's development starts.

| Concept stage | Prototype | Re-design | Tooling up |

Development to market lead-time

Simultaneous
Here the stages of the design and development cycle of the product overlap. Where multi-function teams are put together on a development project it is possible to start the next stage before the previous stage has been fully completed.

Development to market lead-time

It must be noted that shorter development to production lead-times would require an increased intensity of resource commitment at any moment in time and so financial savings may be more elusive than time saving.

Improvements to the design of a system of manufacture or the provision of a service can anticipate cost reduction. Japanese managers, it is argued, also appreciate the importance of design and its contribution to cutting the costs of manufacture. According to the executives at Sony electrical some 80 per cent of 'Kaizen' (cost improvement) takes place in the design and development stage (company interview, 1990). The objective in this case is to pass design improvements to suppliers so as to reduce labour cost embodied in the supply chain. An example of the contribution made to cost reduction from better design is illustrated in the case below using the Computer Workstation Mouse as an example.

According to Nicols, (1992) the results shown in Table 4.5 were achieved from design for manufacturability for a computer mouse.

Improved flow and cost reduction

In most business activity, materials or information flow through the organization and at various points labour time (wages and salaries) is required to transform materials and/or process information.

It is normally a difficult task to manage improvements in flow because it requires constant attention to detail. A general principle of flow is to bring the work past the employee at a fixed position in a linear fashion. Improvements can be made to this system by multi-tasking so that one person does the work of two or bringing the placement of tasks closer together so that indirect labour required to manage materials or information flow is reduced. Moving labour with the flow of information and material could also reduce the costs of production still further (as illustrated in Key Concept 4.4). In this case it is accepted that the cycle time to do the work is longer but that an individual employee undertakes more tasks within the longer cycle time.

Quality control

In the 1940s the American government and associated companies such as Western Electric and General Dynamics developed a statistical quality control

Table **4.5:** Production cost savings resulting from redesigning a computer mouse

	Production Cost Saving
Part count reduction (%)	50
Assembly time reduction (%)	65
Reduced assembly operations (%)	33
Part cost savings (%)	40

(Source K. Nichols (1992) p. 224)

KEY CONCEPT 4.4
Conditions of flow

The concept of linear flow can be represented in the diagram below in which the work or tasks flow past employees. All tasks take 3 minutes and are undertaken by 5 employees.

Linear Flow – Employee Static at each Task

```
      Time elapsed to finish 3 minutes
Flow ───────────────────────────────▶  Linear

       *     *     *     *     *
      /*\   /*\   /*\   /*\   /*\
      / \   / \   / \   / \   / \

Task   1     2     3     4     5
```

In the above case 5 workers are producing and completing 1 unit every 3 minutes. So in 1 hour 20 units are completed by 5 employees at a rate of 4 per employee.

Flow Configuration Variable – Employee Dynamic and Multi-tasked

Assuming a longer cycle time of 6 minutes, 10 units can be completed by 1 employee. 20 units of output would therefore need 2 employees and physical output per employee would be 20/2 or 10 units which is 2.5 times more than the linear flow configuration.

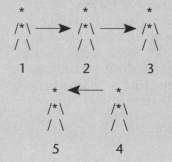

In the above case the worker starts off from position one and moves through all the tasks to complete 1 unit in 6 minutes or 10 units per hour. To maintain the volume of 20 complete tasks a further employee is needed and additional equipment.

Whilst this configuration is more capital intensive, the cost of capital is generally much lower than the cost of labour in Value Added.

(SQC) system. Statistical quality control systems were developed and promoted in the 1940s and 1950s by Juran (1993) and Demming (1981). Improvements to quality ensure that labour resources within the value chain are not wasted on producing an output that does not function or deliver a quality service. Statistical quality control takes a sample of throughput to test for failure in terms of size or function. It is still possible in complex multi-stage operations for faults to pass through and affect the consumer of the product or service.

Yashiro Monden suggests a system of total quality control to ensure that all the output is saleable and consumer satisfaction maximized. To ensure that total quality control is maintained he presents the following rules to be followed:

(i) Ensure small batches of supplies are received so that checks establish that everything supplied is of the standard required.
(ii) Ensure that problems revealed at one stage are not passed on to the next.
(iii) Do not continue until the problem is resolved.

The objective of any quality control system is to reduce the percentage of output not functioning properly and therefore not meeting customer requirements. Quality control therefore works to reduce wasted labour costs associated with the production of output that cannot be sold. In addition enhanced quality control reduces re-work required which also unnecessarily adds to costs of production.

Improved design and development, flow and quality control are all capable of accessing and reducing labour costs embodied in the product or service and they often require a medium- to long-term managerial commitment. All of these systems of cost reduction can also improve cost recovery because better design and quality/reliability can often improve an organization's reputation.

In recent years it has become fashionable to combine the above cost reduction policies within one overall strategic concept that of the 'Lean Enterprise' or 'Lean Management'. In order to remain competitive an organization should work in partnership with other firms in the supply chain to ensure that it and its partners all make a positive contribution towards increasing efficiency (reducing costs) within the industry supply chain.

In this respect Porter's concept of the industry and value chain make an important contribution to competitive business analysis. Porter's value chain analysis focusses on the activities performed in designing, producing, marketing and distributing product (Porter, 1985). Porter presents the value chain as: 'the basic tool for diagnosing competitive advantage and finding ways of enhancing it'.

In the work of Porter in the 1980s, and Womack *et al.* and Andersen Consultants in the 1990s on lean enterprise, there is a common shared understanding. All observe that competitiveness of the firm in its industry sector can be restored, sustained or enhanced by taking cost out of the supply chain. Arthur Andersen Consultants observe that:

> The common factor across all the world class plants is process discipline and control. This was not limited to internal processes, but extended along the whole supply chain and encompassed quality, inventories, planning horizons and schedules.
>
> *(Arthur Andersen Consultants, 1994)*

Porter's industry-structure analysis and the concept of the linear value chain appears within the analytical framework of the Andersen Lean Enterprise benchmarking studies of the 1990s. The underlying framework of analysis is one that locates an organization within an industry chain. On the supply side the analysis locates the organization within an industrial sector generally defined by a common or shared technology that has its correlate on the demand side as competition between firms producing similar products.

In *Foundations of Corporate Success* (1993) John Kay proposes the concept of a business located within a network of contractual relations between stakeholders rather than a Porterian value chain. Competitive advantage is obtained by applying the firm's 'distinctive capabilities' of innovation, reputation or architecture in relevant markets.

But Kay still defines an industry as 'a group of products associated by common technology or supply or distribution channels' (Kay, 1993).

The business policy literature on globalization and the multinational business extends the concept of the value chain to accommodate the fact that value added is determined by international industry characteristics that straddle national boundaries. The global supply chain provides a basis for business analysis of the international cars business (Williams *et al.*, 1994, and Womack *et al.*, 1990). Womack *et al.*'s *The Machine that Changed the World* describes Japanese style 'lean production' and prescribed it as the one best way for struggling Western mass producers. This text was organized into sections that take the reader through a linear value-chain analysis of the industry from suppliers to the final assemblers, research and development and distribution.

Industry value-chain analysis, as it is constructed, restricts the field of business analysis because it limits the definition of the business on the supply side. On the supply side we confine the analysis and definition of a business so as to locate it in a particular industry sector. On the demand side the analysis of international business focusses on selling, distributing and marketing similar new products or services to individual consumers. In order to take the analysis one stage further we will shift from an industry value chain to a matrix form of business analysis.

Supply chain to sector matrix analysis

Case study: A sector matrix analysis of motoring

In order to take up the task of moving from an industry-chain approach to a matrix alternative we will use the case of motoring as an illustrative case. This case is used as an example because motoring represents a large component of consumer and household expenditure in all the major advanced economies (Froud *et al.* 1999).

Industry linear supply-chain analysis can be used to assess the strategic possibilities and limitations facing firms which operate in simple, durable, throw-away products, like sports trainers. These products require distribution before they can be sold but do not require a complicated infrastructure and complementary services before they can be used. The case for a sector-matrix approach to business analysis applies with most force for products that require a complex support infrastructure and complementary services such as pharmaceuticals and motoring. It could also be argued that many simple commodities are now bundled with services so that potentially a sector-matrix value-chain analysis has a broad application, for example in retailing.

The limits of an industry-chain analysis are set on the demand side by competition between finished products and on the supply side by the common technology applied to manufacture (see Figure 4.3).

Industry value-chain analysis places a great deal of emphasis on the supply side because it is centred on the vertical linkages between suppliers and final producers/distributors. This analysis informs strategic decision making by suggesting how a series of interventions or re-organization of the value chain can deliver advantage. On the demand side, weak horizontal linkages suggest that competition is defined by the decisions of those organizations in the final stage of the production process. That is, competition on the demand side is between the major car assemblers that produce similar products. The assumption of this model of analysis is that it captures the relevant information for informing strategic business policy. Strategy in the cars business is therefore centred on which value chain is best suited to generate competitive advantage – Ford mass production, the Toyota model, German (Volkswagen) or some other hybrid model of the organization of production.

In order to break from the industry-value chain approach to business analysis we make two rather more broad assumptions to construct a matrix framework of analysis:

1 On the demand side rather than limit this to expenditure on the new product by an individual consumer, broaden the definition to include all household expenditure on motoring.
2 On the supply side rather than limit the definition of a business as operating in an industry defined by a common technology and similar finished product, broaden the definition so that a business is defined as the financial consolidation of a range of activities which cut across industry sectors.

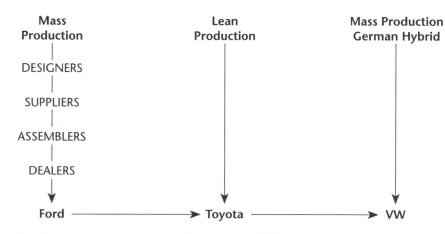

Figure **4.3:** New car supply chains (see Froud *et al*, 1999)

At a regional block level or a national level the space defined in the motoring matrix (see Figure 4.4) is governed by the demand for motoring from households and firms which sustains cost recovery for a range of supply side activities. On the supply side this cost recovery will sustain corporate surpluses which will often be reapplied to consolidate activities within and across industry sectors.

This understanding of a business as a consolidation of a range of activities was fully recognized by Alfred Sloan in his President's address given in September 1928. In this address he outlines the 'principles and policies behind General Motors'. And observes:

> General Motors' profits, like its businesses, have increased rapidly during the past two or three years. . . Now, this aggregation of profits is the largest that any corporation has ever made in times of peace and, as a matter of fact, has ever made in the whole history of industry with the exception of a single instance in times of war. Unfortunately, this has led to a false impression due to a lack of understanding of the facts that General Motors must be making a very large profit per car. This is absolutely not true. General Motors profit per car is less today than it has been at any time except the one year in which we made no profit, or as a matter of fact, made a loss.

> The statement that I made as to the increase in our profit account and the statement I have just made as to the reduction in profit per car, may appear to you to be somewhat contradictory. I think, therefore, that I should perhaps explain the statement a little more in detail. It is not realised that General Motors profits come from many different sources. As a matter of fact, not more than half General Motors profits come from the manufacture of motor cars in the sense that other manufacturers manufacture motor cars . . . money has been invested in the expansion of our motor car operations direct in increasing capacity of existing lines and in the establishment of the Pontiac and Lasalle, but very large sums have gone in entirely different directions,

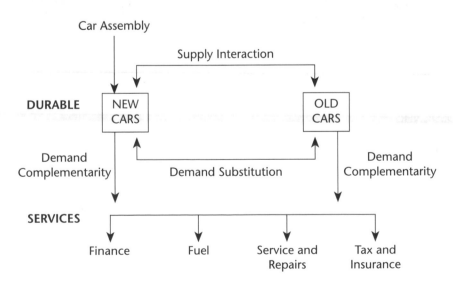

Figure **4.4:** A motor sector matrix (see Froud *et al*, 1999)

viz., in expanding and establishing new activities entirely independent of the motor car operations and some even out-side the automotive industry.

(Alfred Sloan, September 28 1927, GM Archives)

The objective of a matrix form of business analysis is to understand how a more complex web of demand and supply side relations interact and shape business policy responses. On the demand side we are interested in household demand for finished products and all complementary and substitutable products and services which are part of the buyer's consumption. The result of this form of analysis is not an industry chain analysis but a matrix of horizontal and vertical relations.

Close substitutes

Most households never buy a new car but instead purchase a second-hand car because this is a good close substitute. A second-hand car costs less to purchase and the buyer does not incur the high initial depreciation costs of owning the product. Demand substitution is possible as households move from purchasing a new to a used car and then back to a new car as their financial circumstances permit. The second-hand car market in the UK accounted for 7 million car unit sales in 1996 compared to 2 million new cars and in France 4.5 million used to 2 million new cars were sold. It is likely that in all the major advanced economies the stock of cars is such that second-hand and third-hand car dealing is a significant market in its own right.

Supply interaction is also made possible and visible in our matrix analysis because car manufacturers have to interact with the second-hand car market through their dealerships and are often now to be found offering nearly new cars with manufacturers' warranties still valid.

Complementary services

New and used cars are purchased but the expense of running the vehicle does not end at the point of purchase. Consumer credit needs to be paid off during the life of the loan or credit purchase agreement. The car requires continuous purchases of fuel, servicing and repairs, insurance and tax. This bundle of services is often expensive and accounts for a large proportion of household expenditure on motoring.

On the supply side the employment in services, pumping gas, fixing and repairing and selling cars often exceeds those manufacturing the car by a factor of 2:1 in the UK and over 3:1 in the USA. The supply side of the matrix therefore includes a population of organizations that consolidate the surpluses from manufacturing in addition to the provision of services associated with the consumption of the new and used car. The technologies of these organizations are diverse and the financial performance of these organizations variable. These organizations may operate predominantly inside or outside the matrix. Financial services such as loans and insurance would generally be provided by organizations that have their main business interest outside the motoring sector matrix.

A matrix, rather than industry chain analysis, establishes a much more complex series of possibilities and outcomes involving production, market and financial interaction within and between sectors as major actors struggle within the matrix to capture a financial surplus from inside and outside their sectors. From this alternative sector-matrix perspective, an industry value-chain analysis limits the field of view and analysis in a way that makes it more difficult to understand what is going on and why. A sector-matrix framework opens up the field of analysis and can better inform corporate actors as to the possibilities and limitations of particular courses of strategic action.

We can start in the upper left hand-side of the motoring matrix. It has been generally argued that within the conventional industry-chain analysis of the cars business that the right organization of production and appropriate product can be a source of competitive advantage. Williams *et al.* (1994) note that the benefits of these cost-reduction policies have been eroded in a world where build hours to make a complete car have converged. This limit to cost reduction has also combined with market maturity to undermine the financial performance of many large players such as Toyota, Nissan, Ford and GM. Niche marketing and moving the product up market exploits new and more lucrative segments but here too there is limited market space. The benefits of locating in new growing markets are soon lost as close competitors enter the market or it becomes volatile, mature and cyclical.

Where the conventional strategic moves within the value chain are unrewarding matrix fusion that combines car manufacture with other related services is interestingly different and can be strategically rewarding. In the macro and sectoral analysis of this text we observe that the major growth opportunity in the advanced and even newly industrializing economies is that to be derived from the service sector. Within the broad definition of private-sector services the trajectory of growth and opportunity to generate cash from operations has been noted. Ford like GM combines car manufacture with customer and dealer finance, credit cards, private customer loans and finance deals such as Ford Options. In effect whilst Ford's main business up to 1985 was selling people cars it has now increasingly become selling people the finance to buy the car and after sales repair and maintenance services, with the acquisition of Kwik Fit in the UK.

Ford provides credit to finance the sale of its own cars to the customer and in 1996 financed 38 per cent of its total US sales, 29 per cent of Ford cars sold in Europe and 23 per cent of cars sold in Asia-Pacific. In 1996 the Automotive Division generated 80 per cent of sales revenue for the company but contributed just 34 per cent of the consolidated cash from operations. Financial services, on the other hand, generated just 15 to 20 per cent of total sales revenue but generated a 45 to 60 per cent share of the organization's cash generated from operations depending on the nature of the automotive market in these years (see Table 4.6).

Senior Ford executives are keenly aware of the benefits to the company of its involvement in the provision of financial services.

> Financial Services gives Ford and our customers a competitive advantage. It supports our automotive business with vehicle financing and by generating cash to keep exciting new products coming.

> Customers who finance with Ford Credit are the most loyal to our dealers. Fifty-seven per cent of US customers financed by Ford Credit buy another Ford product and about 80 per cent who lease for two years remain loyal to the company.

> *(Ford Annual Report and Accounts, 1996, pp. 17 and 19)*

Table **4.6:** Ford sales and cash shares by division

	1998	**1995**	**1993**	**1991**
Automotive share of Sales	84.5	81.0	84.0	85.0
Automotive share of Cash	53.4	41.0	49.0	55.0
Financial Services Share of Total Revenue	15.3	19.0	16.0	16.0
Financial Services Share of Total Cash	46.5	59.0	51.0	45.0

(Source: Ford Consolidated Accounts)

The lesson of matrix fusion is one that many organizations can strategically try and replicate. Marks and Spencer, the UK mixed retailer, ten years ago launched its Financial Services business and has the fastest growing UK store or loyalty card and is amongst the top ten in Europe. The company is offering personal loans and finance, opportunities to save via unit trusts and is preparing to move into Life and Pension Funds. In 1995 the company generated 1 per cent of sales revenue and 5 per cent of operating profit from Financial Services.

At a financial level the generation of cash flow from other activities like finance reduces the impact of cyclicality and market maturity which affects the core business. Matrix fusion into financial services is an option for some but not all. Fiat and Toyota have been unable to fully develop their financial services divisions. In 1995 Fiat generated just 8 per cent of cash from operations from its Financial Services activities and has since sold the business, and in 1996 Toyota generated 17 per cent of its total cash flow from financial services. The problem facing many of the European players is that selling for credit is limited by conservative private customers who buy for cash or make their own credit arrangements.

The most important strategic development in the car business is not changes in the product or technology but in the selling of cars using new forms of finance. Ford's Personal Contract Purchase (PCP) introduced through its Options scheme was subsequently imitated by other car companies. The strategy here was to convert motorists from owners of cars to renters of cars so as to increase car sales and generate extra cash for the financial services division.

From this matrix perspective it is finance, rather than manufacturing the product, which ensures strong financial returns. The problem facing many of the major car assemblers is that this is an opportunity which is likely to be exploited by other strong players who are situated on the outside of the matrix such as finance houses, banks and other financial institutions. These strong finance providers are likely to migrate into the matrix and appropriate the financial surplus that can be extracted from the provision of finance. In Europe, bank and finance company finance support up one-third of all car purchases made on credit.

On the supply side, sector-matrix analysis broadens the field of the visible because we observe that firms can migrate into other more lucrative activities. A matrix financial analysis treats the business as a consolidation of various business segments and broadens our understanding of the supply side of a business.

Connecting the way in which firms migrate into other activities the social and institutional context in which they operate allows us to understand why migration is possible in some sectors and not others and in some economies and not others. From a supply side perspective the more narrow value-chain or supply-chain analysis establishes the point that the problem facing car producers is the mature new car market. A demand-side sector matrix analysis adds a broader insight because it is concerned to understand the pattern and distribution of household expenditure within and across national boundaries.

It is the household that consolidates income from those who are economically active in the labour market. We find that within national economies household income is unequally distributed and that this inequality of income impacts on the corporate sector in terms of the patterns and composition of household demand. In the UK, as with the USA, the top to bottom range of household income distribution is roughly the same at 6:1 (see Table 4.7). Comparing the two country household populations also establishes that between countries there are also large differences in income per head. This income difference goes a long way towards explaining why households in the US run roughly two cars per household compared to one on average in the UK.

The pattern of income distribution impacts on the pattern of household expenditure. In the UK as with the USA the stock of cars on the road increases every year. In the UK it stands at 25 million and in the US 170 million. Households with low income tend not to buy an expensive new car but settle on a nearly new or not so new second-hand car.

From this household distribution of income perspective we can ask the question 'why can't manufacturers sell more cars to the private buyer?' To understand the limits to demand for new cars we must understand how an unequal distribution of household income combines with the fact that running an old car is just as expensive as running a new car. For the household on low income the purchase of a new car is not an option because of the depreciation costs involved. But owning a car places a severe expenditure constraint on households with low income because they spend up to 20 per cent of their weekly income on maintenance and services. On the demand side the problem for car manufacturers is that the distribution of household income puts a social break on consumption and business opportunity. In the period 1984 to 1995 US middle income households have a reduced propensity to buy new cars (see Table 4.8).

The shift from a value-chain analysis to a sector-matrix analysis opens up a more complex web of demand and supply-side relations. Household expenditure

Table **4.7:** Household income in the USA and UK

	Q1	Q2	Q3	Q4	Q5
USA Income in each Quintile $	17,940	31,300	47,000	69,998	120,043
UK Income in each Quintile $	8,824	12,180	16,475	29,112	51,668

UK incomes converted into $ at £1 = $1.60 dollars
A Quintile splits the household population into five equal segments.

Table **4.8:** US household propensity to buy new cars

Household disposable income 000 $	1984 % of households prepared to buy a new car	1995 % of households prepared to buy a new car
$40–60	90	32
$25–39	58	30
$15–24	45	28
<$15	32	15

determines the cost-recovery opportunities for the corporate sector of any economy. Within and across national boundaries there are large differences in household income and the patterns of expenditure. Within the economic and financial space created by this household expenditure actors from within the matrix or outside the matrix compete to appropriate the cash that can be extracted from expenditure within the matrix. The corporate relations that exist and consolidate financial results within this sector-matrix space are relatively unstable because they are so competitive. This instability is a product of the patterns and growth in household expenditure and the intensive nature of competition within the matrix to appropriate the surplus.

Within this unstable space the operating architecture of a business cannot always withstand the intensity of competitor interaction from actors within and outside the matrix. Competition to appropriate the surplus from within the financial space created by household expenditure establishes the precondition for a supply-side consolidation or rationalization of business activities where the bundling and unbundling of assets becomes commonplace.

Sector-matrix analysis can be extended to other areas of household expenditure and the sectors/businesses this expenditure sustains on the supply side. These sectors are not distinct, water-tight compartments on the supply side because surplus can be and is consolidated through a process of competition in which the various corporate actors come from many different business sectors. The diversified and global firm's success and its continued viability is being increasingly determined by the ability to identify and exploit financial opportunity inside and across different sectors and countries where surplus can be consolidated into your report and accounts. This is exemplified by UK food retailers' move into motor services via petrol retailing and then into financial services, or by French water utilities' movement into what are now British contracted-out public services. Global business is no respecter of a linear national value chain. Within the context of a restless pursuit of surplus these chains are being fractured and broken as previously segregated demand and supply relations increasingly interfere with each other. Corporate actors from inside and outside a sector matrix recombine activities to compete for operating surpluses and the capitalization of activities that buttress cost recovery and cash generation.

Workshop questions/exercises

Q1 Using the data given in Table 4.9a and b discuss how the age of the stock of cars in use in the USA is ageing over time.

Table **4.9a:** US cars in use by age 1965 to 1994

Year	Under 5 years	6–8 years	9–11 years	12+ years	Totals mill units
1960	32.5	12.4	9.2	2.8	56.90
1965	39.6	13.6	9.8	5.9	68.90
1970	49.3	18.4	7.7	4.9	80.30
1975	52.7	22.0	13.8	6.6	95.10
1980	52.3	25.2	14.6	12.5	104.60
1985	48.7	27.8	17.2	21.0	114.70
1990	56.5	22.6	19.1	25.1	123.30
1994	45.4	27.7	25.1	31.4	129.60

(Source: Statistical Abstract of the US (1996), US Department of Commerce, Washington DC Tables 1002 from 1996 edition, Table 1073 from 1977 edition and Table 959 from 1975 edition)

Table **4.9b:** US cars in use by age 1965 to 1994 percentage breakdown

Year	% under 5 years	% 6–8 years	% 9–11 years	% 12 + years	Totals
1960	57.12	21.79	16.17	4.92	100.0
1965	57.47	19.74	14.22	8.56	110.0
1970	61.39	22.91	9.59	6.10	100.0
1975	55.42	23.13	14.51	6.94	100.0
1980	50.00	24.09	13.96	11.95	100.0
1985	42.46	24.24	15.00	18.31	100.0
1990	45.82	18.33	15.49	20.36	100.0
1994	35.03	21.37	19.37	24.23	100.0

(Source: Statistical Abstract of the US (1996), US Department of Commerce, Washington DC Tables 1002 from 1996 edition, Table 1073 from 1977 edition and Table 959 from 1975 edition)

Q2 It is often argued that services are replacing manufacturing as the main driver of employment and output growth in the mature industrial economies. Use the information provided in Table 4.10 and 4.11 to answer and discuss the following question. To what extent are US motor sector services becoming more important than the manufacture of cars?

Table **4.10:** US employment in motor manufacture and motor services 1967 to 1993

Services Employment 000's	1967	1972	1977	1982	1987	1993[2]
Auto Dealers[1]	906.6	1,073.0	1,115.0	1,051.0	1,373.0	1,993.0
Service Stations[1]	575.2	747.7	673.0	604.0	702.0	In above
Auto Equipment[1]	341.1	391.8	423.0	433.0	483.0	489.0
Services and Repairs[1]	316.2	392.5	483.0	553.2	785.0	904.0
Total Services Employment	2,139	2,605	2,694	2,641	3,343	3,386
Total Manufacturing[1]	939	806.6	876	616	748	703
Ratio of motor service to car manufacturing jobs in the US	2.28	3.23	3.08	4.29	4.47	4.82

Notes[1]: Auto Dealers SIC 55 excluding 554
　　　　　Service Stations SIC 554
　　　　　Auto Equipment SIC 501
　　　　　Services and Repairs SIC 75
　　　　　Manufacturing SIC 371
Note[2]: After 1990 Service Stations and Auto Dealers are combined into one in SIC 55
(Source: Statistical Abstract of the US (1996), US Department of Commerce, Washington DC)

Exercise: Complete the information given in Table 4.11 by calculating the pay per employee in dollars.

Q3 To what extent has the growth in US motoring services created well paid jobs relative to those in the car manufacturing sector of the US economy?

Table **4.11:** Payroll per employee in US motor services and motor manufacture 1967, 1982 and 1993

	1967			1982			1993		
	Employ 000	Payroll $ bill	Pay per employee $	Employ 000	Payroll $ bill	Pay per employee $	Employ 000	Payroll $ bill	Pay per employee $
Auto Dealers[1]	906.6	5.2		1051	16.9		1993	43.5	
Service Stations[2]	575.2	1.9		604	4.8				
Auto Equipment	341.1	2.1		433	7.5		489	12.0	
Services and Repairs	316.2	1.5		553.2	7.1		904	17.0	
Services Average									
Car Manufacturing	939.0	5.9		616	15.3		703	26.2	
Service pay per employee as % of manufacturing									

Notes[1]: Auto Dealers SIC 55 excluding 554
　　　　　Service Stations SIC 554
　　　　　Auto Equipment SIC 501
　　　　　Services and Repairs SIC 75
　　　　　Manufacturing SIC 371
Note[2]: After 1990 Service Stations and Auto Dealers are combined into one in SIC 55
(Source: Statistical Abstract of the US (1996), US Department of Commerce, Washington DC)

Exercise: Using the information in Table 4.12 calculate employment in an average US car dealership.

Also calculate separately the average new and used cars sold per dealership and collectively used and new car sales per dealership.

Q4 To what extent is the growth in cars sold by an average dealer the result of selling new or used cars?

Table **4.12:** US franchised new car dealerships: summary of operations 1970 to 1995

Year	Dealerships 000's	New Cars mill	Used Cars mill	Employment 000	Employees/ Dealership	New Cars/ Dealership	Used Cars/ Dealership	New and Used Cars per Dealership
1970	30.8	8.4	11.3	703				
1980	28.25	9.0	9.7	754				
1985	24.7	11.0	13.0	861				
1990	24.8	9.3	14.2	916				
1995	22.8	8.6	18.5	1010				
Change 1970–1995	−26%	+2.4%	+64%	+43.7%				

(Source: Statistical Abstract of the US (1996), US Department of Commerce, Washington DC: Table 1262: Franchised New Car Dealerships – 1970–1995. Source derived from National Automobile Dealers Association, Mclean, UA, NADA Data, Annual)

Using the information from Table 4.12 and also from Table 4.13 discuss why car dealing is relatively unprofitable (see profit before tax as a percentage of sales in Table 4.13 below).

Table **4.13:** US franchised new car dealerships: profit to sales and stock turn 1970 to 1995

Year	Profit before Tax as % of Sales	Total Car Sales (New and Used)	Total Stocks (Domestic and Imported Cars)	Physical Stock Turn[1]	No of weeks Stock held on average[2]
1970	2.0	19.7	1.9	10.37	5.01
1980	0.61	18.7	2.0	9.35	5.56
1981	1.16	18.7	1.9	9.84	5.28
1982	1.30	17.9	1.7	10.53	4.94
1983	2.14	20.0	1.46	13.70	3.80
1984	2.18	22.7	1.616	14.05	3.70
1985	2.20	24.0	1.771	13.55	3.84
1986	2.16	24.7	2.092	11.81	4.40
1987	1.88	23.5	2.251	10.44	4.98
1988	1.71	24.9	2.126	11.71	4.44
1989	1.0	24.4	2.35	10.38	5.01
1990	1.0	23.5	2.033	11.56	4.50
1995	1.4	27.1	2.022	13.40	3.88

Notes: 1. Physical stock turn based on dividing total inventory (domestic and imported cars) in
millions of units into physical new and used car sales.
2. Number of weeks of physical stock held calculated by dividing the physical per annum
stock turn into 52 weeks.
(Source: Statistical Abstract of the US (1996), US Department of Commerce, Washington DC: Table
1262: Franchised New Car Dealerships – 1970–1995. Source derived from (National Automobile
Dealers Association, Mclean, UA, NADA Data, Annual))

The information contained in Table 4.14 shows US household expenditure
data on motoring by income quintiles.

We start with total household expenditure by quintile and then total spend
on motoring. This latter figure is split into three major sub-headings: vehicle
purchases; gasoline and motor oil; and other vehicle expenses.

Q5 To what extent do the poorer quintile households (quintiles 1 and 2) in
the US spend more or less on motoring than quintiles 4 and 5, the richest
households? (Remember to take into account the number of vehicles
owned in each quintile and the change over the period 1986 to 1997.)

If you are in the business of selling motor vehicle services generally in the US,
which are the more attractive households as far as spend on motoring is
concerned?

Table **4.14:** United States total expenditure and motoring expenditure in 1984 split by
quintile groups. Motoring expenditure as a % of total expenditure. All money totals in US$
in 1995 prices

	QUINTILE GROUP					All Households
	1	2	3	4	5	
Total Expenditure (in $US)	15,974	21,023	28,548	38,327	61,329	32,223
Total Spend on Motoring (in $US) *of which (split in %)*	2,661	3,900	5,381	7,310	11,025	5,937
Vehicle purchases (net outlay) *sub-category split*	40.5	41.9	41.1	44.5	48.1	44.8
Cars and trucks, new	22.6	20.3	19.2	22.0	32.9	25.4
Cars and trucks, used	17.2	20.9	21.1	21.8	14.6	18.7
Other vehicles	0.7	0.7	0.9	0.7	0.6	0.7
Gasoline and motor oil	30.8	30.0	28.8	26.1	21.9	26.1
Other vehicle expenses *sub-category split*	28.7	28.2	30.1	29.4	30.0	29.1
Vehicle finance charges	3.2	4.2	4.6	5.6	6.4	5.3
Maintenance and repairs	14.9	12.1	13.5	12.0	11.0	11.9
Vehicle insurance	7.6	8.9	9.2	8.8	8.4	8.6
Veh. rent., leas., licen., oth. chges	3.0	3.0	2.8	3.0	4.1	3.3
Vehicle Ownership (no. of vehicles)	1.0	1.4	1.9	2.4	2.8	1.8

(Source: US Consumer Expenditure Survey, US Bureau of Labor, 1986)

Table **4.14:** (continued) United States total expenditure and motoring expenditure in 1995 split by quintile groups. Motoring expenditure as a % of total expenditure. All money totals in US$ in 1995 prices

	QUINTILE GROUP					All Households
	1	2	3	4	5	
Total Expenditure (in $US)	14,607	22,126	29,125	39,395	62,639	32,264
Total Spend on Motoring (in $US)	1,876	3,811	5,511	7,279	10,276	5,659
of which (split in %)						
Vehicle purchases (net outlay)	34.9	46.6	49.0	46.7	47.1	46.6
sub-category split						
Cars and trucks, new	11.5	22.6	15.2	19.6	25.5	21.2
Cars and trucks, used	22.9	23.6	33.5	26.1	21.1	24.8
Other vehicles	0.4	0.3	0.3	1.0	0.5	0.6
Gasoline and motor oil	25.1	18.8	17.9	17.5	15.8	17.8
Other vehicle expenses	40.1	34.6	33.1	35.8	37.1	35.6
sub-category split						
Vehicle finance charges	3.2	3.3	4.9	5.4	4.7	4.6
Maintenance and repairs	16.1	12.3	11.3	11.7	11.0	11.5
Vehicle insurance	14.2	13.8	12.2	12.3	12.3	12.6
Veh. rent., leas., licen., oth. chges	6.6	5.2	4.7	6.4	9.1	6.9
Vehicle Ownership (no. of vehicles)	1.0	1.5	2.0	2.5	2.9	1.9

(Source: US Consumer Expenditure Survey, US Bureau of Labor, 1997)

Q6 What do you understand by constant or real money values (that is adjusting for changes in inflation)?
To what extent has US household motoring expenditure increased in real terms over the period 1986 to 1997?
Q7 Describe Porter's value chain? How can the concept of the value chain be used to understand the factors that sustain competitive advantage?
Q8 What do you understand by the concept 'sector matrix'? How can this concept broaden our understanding of the factors that influence competitive advantage?

References

Arthur Andersen Consultants (1992, 1994) *Lean Enterprise Benchmark Survey(s)*, London.

Deming, W.E. (1981) 'Improvement of Quality and Productivity Through Action by Management', *National Productivity Reviews*, Vol. 1, pp. 12–22.

Froud, J., Haslam, C., Johal, S. and Williams, K. (1999) 'Breaking the Chains: A Sector Matrix Analysis of Motoring', *Global Competition and Change*, Vol. 2.

Gereffi, G., Korzeniewicz, M., Korzeniewicz, R. (1994) 'Introduction: Global Commodity Chains', in Gereffi, G. and Korzeniewicz, M. (eds) *Commodity Chains and Global Capitalism*, Westport, CT: Praeger.

Gereffi, G. (1996) 'Global Commodity Chains: New Forms of Coordination and Control Among Nations and Firms in International Industries', *Competition and Change* Vol. 4, pp. 427–439.

Iansiti, M. (1993) 'Real World R&D: Jumping the product generation gap', *Harvard Business Review*, May/June, pp. 138–149.

Juran, J.M. (1993) *Quality Planning and Analysis: From Product Development Through Use*, New York, McGraw-Hill.

Kay, J. (1993) *Foundations of Corporate Success*, Oxford: OUP.

Monden, Y. (1994) *The Toyota Production System*. Peoria, GA: Industrial Engineering and Management Press.

Nichols, K. (1992) 'Better, Cheaper, Faster Products by Design', *Journal of Engineering Design*, Vol. 3, no. 3.

Porter, M. (1985) *Competitive Advantage*, New York: Free Press.

Williams, K. *et al.* (1994) *Cars: Analysis, History, Cases*, Oxford: Berghahn Books.

Womack, J., Jones, D. and Roos, D. (1990) *The Machine that Changed the World*, New York: Rawson Associates.

Sloan, A. (1927) *The Principles and Policies behind General Motors*, Sept – GM Archives, Flint Michigan – Sloan, A.P. Jnr C.2 83-12.16.

CHAPTER 5

Restructuring, financialization and competitive advantage

In this chapter we turn to consider the process of restructuring and the increasing pressure that is put on firms to achieve the market rate of return on capital. In the mature advanced economies mature product market conditions combine with limits to cost reduction to drive restructuring. Restructuring is reinforced by a process of financialization whereby shares are increasingly managed by fund management businesses and the pressure to maintain a return on capital intensified.

In the UK and the USA where fund management and the equity market are more fully developed, the expenditure on mergers and acquisitions is equivalent to 50 per cent of total capital expenditure on plant and equipment.

We discuss how Economic Value Added (EVA^{TM}) and other consultancy-firm metrics require that firms return more on the capital they employ in their balance sheets. Value-based strategies are prioritized by managers because they are paid on the basis of particular financial yardsticks tied into shareholder value. EVA^{TM} is distinguished from value added as used in this text.

Mergers and acquisitions are a risky business because they often fail to deliver all that they promised. We use in our case study the merger between Glaxo and Wellcome to illustrate how product market pressures established limits to value added and cash generation in these two companies. The merger allows the two companies to rationalize capacity and so release shareholder value. We also show that this process of restructuring promises a once off improvement in finances when difficult product market conditions remain. Extracting more shareholder value sets up the precondition for further merger and takeovers in the pharmaceuticals business.

General Motors employed capital during the last three years has increased roughly $400,000,000. This investment carries with it an obligation as to a return.

(Alfred Sloan, 1927)

Introduction

We have already observed that business operations often require the complex financial consolidation of various business segments spanning a variety of industrial and commercial sectors. Within a meso-economic space an organization will consolidate new activities and abandon old in the struggle to obtain a higher return on capital. This struggle to appropriate a higher surplus on capital is best understood using a sector matrix analysis that displaces the traditional economic concepts of industry and supply chain. The issue with the traditional economic model is that it constructs a framework where organizations are assumed to operate in a particular industry (defined as utilizing a common technology) producing similar products. The problem for business analysis is that organizations operate a complex mix of business segments that straddle sectors and product markets.

Factors determining favourable
cost recovery

The generation of a surplus from the provision of products and services is generally best achieved when market conditions (cost recovery) and productive (resource management/cost reduction) are favourably disposed to generate the required financial outcomes. However such interventions reach natural limits defined by the size of a national market, the exchange rate, income levels and technical limits to cost reduction. The practical point is that a high return on capital employed is often the result of rather exceptional circumstances that are difficult to imitate. The reputation of a brand may help cost recovery by a few leading firms, like Coca-Cola, which can franchise the name to bottlers or BMW which can sell its output without discounting as the mass manufacturers do. These premium positions cannot be occupied simultaneously by all cola or car manufacturers. In pharmaceuticals or computer software the numerator in the return on capital employed ratio (profit surplus) is flattered because advantage comes from being able to sell at fancy prices due to the protection of intellectual property rights (see Table 5.1). The case of Microsoft and Intel are here used as examples of the special case. Both organizations are able to exploit the advantage of monopolistic type property rights that lock the consumer into the initial purchase and further subsequent upgrades at favourable prices to the

Table **5.1:** Microsoft revenue mix and unit cost of software

	1995	1998	2000E
Revenue Mix			
Windows 3X	99%	5%	2%
Windows 95/98	0%	80%	63%
Windows NT	1%	7%	35%
Unit Mix			
Windows 3X	97%	9%	1%
Windows 95/98	0%	79%	51%
Windows NT	3%	12%	48%
Average $/unit	**$33**	**$53**	**$62**

(Source: SG Cowen, market analysts)

producer. The wildcard for Microsoft in the late 1990s is the anti-trust suit that might result in a loss of monopolistic conditions and for Intel the technical superiority of its new micro-processor and the period of time prices per unit are held at a favourable level.

Microsoft provides the software loaded in our personal computers and the volume of PC shipments world-wide is still expected to grow rapidly from 47 million units to 150 million units by 2002. For PC manufacturers revenues are likely to soften because the price per PC unit is expected to fall from $2,100 per unit sold in the early 1990s to $1,600 by the year 2002. However unlike the hardware manufacture Microsoft's strategy of software product upgrade continues to pay dividends as Table 5.2 outlines.

The switch from Windows 3X to Windows 95 and 98 generation of software very quickly adjusted the composition of product revenue mix such that by 1998 80 per cent of volumes and revenue are from the latest software. In the next phase of development Windows NT (it is expected) will also

Table **5.2:** Return on assets and equity: Microsoft and Intel Corporation 1988 to 1996

Year	Microsoft Corporation		Intel Corporation	
	Return on Assets	**Return on Equity**	**Return on Assets**	**Return on Equity**
1988	31.5	40.0	14.3	26.0
1989	27.9	36.1	10.3	16.7
1990	30.1	37.1	13.4	20.5
1991	33.4	40.4	13.9	20.2
1992	32.5	39.3	14.7	35.5
1993	29.1	34.6	23.6	35.5
1994	25.0	29.8	18.3	27.4
1995	23.1	29.7	22.8	33.3
1996	25.4	35.9	25.0	35.6

(Source: Standard and Poor's Stock Reports)

favourably adjust the volume and revenue mix. Microsoft has managed to lift the revenue per unit received from each new generation of software package retailed or installed in the PC by the original equipment manufacturer. By the time Windows NT is up and running we will be paying twice the unit cost compared to that paid five years earlier for the Windows 3X generation of software. The difference between Microsoft and the hardware manufacturer is that whereas international competition drives down the cost of making the box and electrical componentry Microsoft's licensing arrangement protects the ex-factory price of the product.

The return on capital

In business services like recruitment agencies or security services the denominator (capital employed) is often small or negligible (see, for example, media agencies). These activities also tend to generate healthy returns on their capital base.

Management strategy is not just about the generation of surplus from productive and market intervention, it is also concerned with the extraction of surplus value from the manipulation of the capital base of the business. A matrix analysis of business brings out the importance of the struggle to consolidate activities that have a high return on capital employed. Car manufacturers like Ford and GM have profitable positions in finance that gives them a competitive advantage over those firms that do not have these strategic positions. We have already seen in the previous chapter that Ford generated on average 50 per cent of its profit from the 15 per cent of its turnover from its financial services division. Bolting on financial services is yet another way of finding a more favourable cash generation from assets and counteracting the effects of the business cycle on the manufacturing side of the business.

> The US automakers' finance subsidiaries have acted like a shock absorber providing a steady stream of profits that have partially absorbed staggering automotive losses during sustained down-turns.
>
> *(Bernstein Research, Oct. 1997)*

In a more low key way the struggle within sectors takes the form of passing on assets which are generating a low return on capital to another organization that finds that this return on capital is acceptable. In the UK *The Times* newspaper prints a league table of firm performance using shareholder value indicators.

The table of *The Times* rankings serves practically to demonstrate that organizations generate variable returns on capital employed. In the case of the top companies like Shell and Glaxo-Wellcome the return on capital employed is greater than the cost of capital and so the organizations are generating a profit which exceeds the return on shareholder funds and debt in the form of long- and short-term loans.

An organization's return on capital represents the average return on a portfolio of operations where some business segments will be returning more or less than this average. In order to increase the average, an organization might offer for sale low return segments and/or purchase new activities that increase the organization's overall return on capital employed. From Table 5.3 we can observe why SmithKline Beecham would be a financially attractive acquisition for Glaxo-Wellcome. The similarity of return on capital goes a long way towards explaining why merger talks had taken place between the two parties. For the dominant partner (Glaxo-Wellcome) the deal offered to bolt on new assets with a return on capital which was slightly higher than its own operations. A merger or take-over involving SmithKline Beecham would not reduce Glaxo-Wellcome's overall ratios and just like the Wellcome merger, the deal would also offer the possibility of rationalizing duplicate activities thus reducing the overall cost base of the combined business and releasing cash.

A great deal of corporate effort is directed towards financial calculations relating to the bundling and unbundling of financial assets through a process of financial engineering. Rappaport's list of moves includes rationalizing, merger, selective divestment and new business formulae. These moves are all generally presented in a positive way and fitted into an upbeat framework. In general the arguments that are used to support these financial calculations are often partial and in the interests of one particular stakeholder, the

Table **5.3**: Top and bottom UK listed companies: return on capital employed

	Capital 1997 £ mill	Return on Capital %	Cost of Capital %
Top (Selection)			
Glaxo-Wellcome	11,669	18.5	11.1
Shell	54,745	13.4	12.1
British Telecom	16,600	15.3	11.3
SmithKline Beecham	6,087	19.9	10.7
Reuters	1,001	55.6	13.9
Cable and Wireless	16,600	15.3	11.3
Zeneca	4,396	16.2	12.2
Vodafone	2,088	21.6	15.1
Bottom (Selection)			
Redland	2,857	5.6	12.1
Inchcape	2,206	3.2	12.2
GEC	7,612	8.5	11.5
Rolls-Royce	2,948	4.3	11.8
ICI	6,954	6.2	10.2
Hanson	12,253	7.3	9.4
British Aerospace	3,980	3.3	10.5
British Steel	5,117	5.1	12.4
Grand Met	10,541	5.0	11.9

(Source: *The Sunday Times*, Sept 1997)

KEY CONCEPT 5.1
The cost of capital

The cost of capital is normally made up of two components **the cost of debt** and the **cost of equity**.

The cost of debt is simply the weighted average of interest costs on loans. For example a company has two loans X and Y.

Loan X = 20% of total debt at 10% rate of interest
Loan Y = 80% of total debt at 20% rate of interest
Cost of debt = $(10 \times 0.20) + (20 \times 0.80)$
Cost of debt = 18%

The cost of equity **where there is no widespread share ownership structure** is estimated using a risk-free bond rate as the financial benchmark. In addition an additional percentage is added which represents the risk of this equity where returns are not guaranteed.

Cost of Equity $E(R) = Ri + Rr$

Where Ri = Risk free bond rate and Rr = particular added risk of this equity.

The cost of equity **where there is a widespread stock market and trading structure** is estimated as the risk free rate on equity plus the average cost of equity in the market multiplied by a beta factor (β) which is an index of this particular share's volatility.

Cost of Equity $E(R) = Ri + \beta(Rm - Ri)$

For example we assume that the risk free rate of return Ri = 10%. The return on all shares is 15% and the market volatility of the company's shares has a β of 1.5 (i.e. fluctuating 1.5 times the market average). The cost of equity would then be:

$10 + 1.5(15 - 10) = 17.5\%$

Note: β factors can be obtained for a company from various sources e.g. for US companies these factors are disclosed in Standards and Poor's 500 Guide, 1998.
See also Lynch, 1997, pp. 320–325.

---

shareholder. In addition these strategic moves might only deliver short-term results. Witness the case of direct insurance operations that at first attracted healthy margins but the new business formula was easily copied and the result of intensified competition is that margins are once again squeezed. The strategic objective is to ensure that the return on capital exceeds the cost of capital and many organizations achieve this objective but just as many organizations keep going even when the return on capital is less than the cost of capital.

Generating a surplus over and above the cost of capital

In circumstances where existing market conditions and organization structure make it difficult to increase the spread between the return on capital and costs of capital (increase shareholder value and generate a positive Economic Value Added (EVA^{TM})). Management strategy will increasingly prioritize the bundling and unbundling of assets so as to generate extra shareholder value. It is argued by some that the pursuit of the single objective of shareholder value is congruent with sustaining competitive advantage and satisfying the conflicting interests of all the various stakeholders. The introduction of new shareholder value models such as EVA^{TM}, it is argued, will change strategic management for the better, particularly when the metrics are internalized into the organization's corporate governance procedures.

> Chase managers quickly pulled out of low-return activities that may have increased net income but did not add SVA (Shareholder Value Added). The capital, thus liberated, can now be reallocated more profitably or handed back. Even the bank's senior management has been surprised by the speed with which its executives, now paid at least according to SVA, have reacted.
>
> (The Financial Times, *12 June 1998*)

In a recent battle to acquire the UK-based car manufacturer Rolls-Royce, Volkswagen (the German car assembler) paid an extra £90 million to shareholders and they accepted the deal. Rolls-Royce had spent the last ten years building up a strategic alliance with BMW for the supply of much-needed engines and equipment. BMW supplies all the engines for the Rolls Royce and Bentley car range. Productive logic might have determined that BMW would have been the better partner but shareholder value won the day.

It is not at all certain that corporate restructuring delivers sustained financial improvement when the fundamental productive and market dynamics of the business have not been transformed. Often merger, take-over and rationalization are justified financially but are defensive in nature because the productive and market fundamentals of the business have deteriorated in some way. As Kay (1993) observes:

> No consistent pattern of either improved or deteriorated profitability can therefore be claimed across the seven countries. Mergers would appear to result in a slight improvement here, a worsening there.

We do know that within the UK there has been a substantial history of merger and take-over activity and rationalization of capacity over the last decade. In terms of the spread of EVA^{TM} we observe in Figure 5.1 that most of the top 100 and 200 UK companies (by market capitalization that is, the market value of their share capital) are clustered around a range of +/− £100 million of EVA^{TM}.

In highly competitive mature advanced economies it is increasingly difficult to sustain excess profit return on capital over and above the cost of

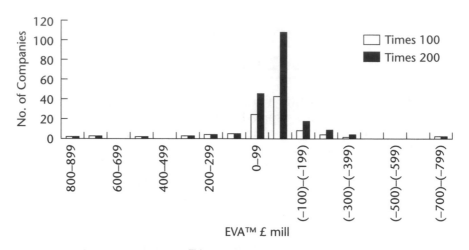

Figure **5.1:** Times 100 and 200 EVA™s

capital even when asset churning is so extensive. Intensified competition coupled with market maturity sets limits on revenue growth and this often combines with various factors limiting cost reduction. Even where these conditions are favourable they too can be offset by the requirement for a high level of capital employed in the balance sheet.

Restructuring to release shareholder value

In aggregate, the returns to restructuring may be uncertain but for city finance operations mergers and acquisitions (M&A) are big business. At a national and international level rationalization and the sale and re-purchase of business assets has become major international business in itself. By the end of 1998 it is expected that $2,000 billion (1997 $1,600 billion) will have been spent by international business on mergers and acquisitions. To put this into some sort of macro-economic context, this spend is a factor of two to three times larger than total UK national gross domestic output in 1997.

These deals often involve a combination of domestic rationalization where a fragmented domestic base consolidates into larger operating units and/or cross border mergers and acquisitions which involve consolidation of international markets. The possible take-over of Chrysler by Mercedes-Benz is one example of a cross-border deal that will cost £39 billion. The Daimler-Chrysler deal was notable because of the complementary nature of the activities and the suggestion that rationalization will be less significant as in a deal where overlap and duplications exist within or across a national boundary. Whilst cross border deals have expanded significantly in recent years they account for approximately 20 per cent of the total international spend on mergers and acquisitions.

Table 5.4 illustrates the sheer scale of the bids pending in 1998, the majority of which are between US companies. The impression is that most

Table **5.4:** 1998 top ten mergers and acquisitions world-wide

Target	Acquirer	Status	Value $ bill
Citicorp (US)	Traveller (US)	Pending	72.6
Ameritech (US)	SBC Comm (US)	Pending	62.6
BankAmerica (US)	NationsBank (US)	Pending	61.6
Chrysler (US)	Daimler-Benz (Ger)	Pending	39.5
Monsanto (US)	American Home Products (US)	Pending	35.6
Wells Fargo (US)	Norwest Corp (US)	Pending	34.3
First Chicago NBD (US)	Banc One (US)	Pending	29.6
Mellon Bank (US)	Bank of New York (US)	Withdrawn	24.2
Toronto-Dominion (Can)	Canadian Imperial Bank of Commerce	Pending	15.4
Waste management (US)	USA waste services	Pending	13.3

(Source: *The Financial Times*, 26 June 1998)

mergers and take-overs are between organizations within a particular national economy and that a fragmented industrial and commercial base is consolidating into fewer larger organizations.

Many of these strategic mergers and acquisitions which consolidate assets and return on capital employed are risky and as Meeks (1977) and Kay (1993) observe are often disappointing marriages. Rationalization of duplicate operations and divestment of poorly performing business segments deliver one-off gains but often do not transform underlying financial performance.

In a world where internationally-based fund managers manage shares and also often hold a majority ownership stake in a business, the strategic ambitions of an organization will be affected by shareholders who require year-on-year increases in shareholder value. Business strategy texts have emphasized the competitive advantage to be gained from productive and market calculations that privilege organic growth and innovation. Grocery retailers should choose the right site, airlines pick the right landing slots and hub airports, and car manufacturers invest in new technologies and lean production systems. If the organization achieves a productive and market advantage this could stabilize sales and may even reverse the fortunes of the business. The message of shareholder value is that management should think more carefully about strategies that tie up capital that does not deliver strong margins and return on capital.

Business policy texts and management journals are now promoting shareholder value metrics such as Economic Value Added (EVA^{TM}) and Market Value Added (MVA). These calculations are designed to establish whether a business is adding to or destroying shareholder value. Andrew Higginson, finance director of Burton's, a clothing retailer, is currently designing an EVA^{TM} bonus system. He observes that:

> ... the company used to pay store managers bonuses based on sales. That encourages them to order stocks in the hope that they might shift them and safe in the knowledge that could always get rid of the stuff in a sale. It was good for sales figures, and hence bonuses, but

lousy for profits. It (EVA^{TM}) fits with the way we are trying to run our businesses. It gives the store manager an incentive to focus on the cost of capital.

(The Sunday Times, 10th December 1995)

All things being equal, the increase in shareholder value requires higher earnings and profit margins from revenue generated by the organization. In many sectors of international business, market maturity and intensified competition puts pressure on margins. At this point the composition of costs becomes a problem and management needs to then identify and reduce the large controllable costs which are likely to be labour costs. UK utilities such as gas, water and electricity operate in mature markets where price competition has intensified due to deregulation. Profit margins and shareholder value have been extracted at the expense of the employees and the reduction in the share of value added paid to employees has been redistributed to shareholders in the form of dividends, but this also reaches practical limits.

Financial calculations that result in a loss of employment can purchase a one-off gain in shareholder value but they cannot transform the productive and market operating context within which the organization operates. Merger and take-over rationalizes ownership structures and strips out duplicate activities releasing more cash and improved margins. This form of financial engineering is well known and is demonstrated well in the case of Hanson Trust UK–USA conglomerate.

Hanson Trust has been dedicated to the creation of shareholder value. In 1997 Hanson was ranked second-worst performer amongst *The Times* Top 100 firms ranked by shareholder value. The problem(s) facing Hanson Trust related to the fact that the organization's investment portfolio exposed the business to market maturity and cyclicality in the USA and UK. The fundamental problem was that the underlying productive and market characteristics of the business generally were not sound. Strong financial performance results from a positive and virtuous relation between the market and productive dimensions of the business.

This point is accepted in the latest UK survey on shareholder value. The noteworthy feature is that the companies which come top of the rankings are those which have managed to generate strong rates of organic growth.

> Companies such as Glaxo-Wellcome, SmithKline Beecham, Reuters, BskyB, Marks and Spencer and Vodafone are all businesses that have managed to build huge volumes of sales largely without acquisitions ... organic growth and expansion, appear to be the best way to generate the best returns.

(The Sunday Times, 27th September 1997)

On the one hand it is argued that long-term shareholder value is best maximized through organic growth but this all depends on market conditions and growth trajectories within particular national economies and sectors. We have already explored the pattern of these trajectories and argued that the general tendency is for slow down and cyclicality in the advanced markets. Organic growth across a large number of sectors in the advanced economies and NICs is much more problematic than it was 20 or so years ago. Adverse changes in market conditions combine with the operating architecture of a business to undermine and frustrate financial performance.

Sears Roebuck and Co, a US general retailer, has recently streamlined operations and its capacity and asset base. Sears experienced market difficulties during the period 1987 to 1993. In the early part of this period real sales were stagnant and in the last two years of this period sales revenue fell in real terms by roughly 20 per cent. Sears was no longer an expanding business and this obviously had implications for the financial operating ratios after 1993 (see Table 5.5).

In the period when real sales revenue was flat, net income fluctuated up or down by as much as 50 per cent but dividends were being maintained at $2.00 per share. The net result is that the payout ratio (dividends as a per cent of earnings) fluctuates between 50 to 80 per cent. The crisis year of 1992, when dividends were paid out of a net loss, provoked the company into a process of restructuring. Sears exited a number of its non-retailing activities: Dean Witter, Discover and Co in 1993; Coldwell Banker Residential Services and Sears Mortgage and Banking Group were sold in 1993; Sears spun off its 80 per cent stake in Allstate Corp to shareholders in 1996; and its stake in Advantis data services in 1997.

Sears Roebuck suffered the misfortune of operating in a mixed retail market that had matured such that company sales growth had stagnated and turned seriously down after 1992. In these circumstances restructuring and divestment become inevitable as a way of preserving the operating ratios and protecting shareholder value. By 1996 the financial operating ratios (earnings per share and P/E ratio) had been normalized but the business was no longer what it once was. The common equity base of the business had been halved by 1996 to $5 billion as against $10 billion in 1993 and the total asset base of the business is one-third of what it was in 1993 (see Table 5.6).

As organizations move through their particular trajectory it becomes progressively more difficult to sustain growth in output and this again

Table **5.5:** Sears Roebuck and Co. real sales index

Year	Sales $ billion	US Consumer Price Index	Real Sales $ billion	Real Sales Index
1996	38.2	1.2	31.83	100.00
1995	34.9	1.16	30.09	94.53
1994	54.5	1.13	48.23	151.52
1993	50.8	1.11	45.77	143.80
1992	52.3	1.07	48.88	153.57
1991	57.2	1.04	55.00	172.79
1990	56.0	1.00	56.00	175.93
1989	53.8	0.95	56.63	177.91
1988	50.2	0.91	55.16	173.30
1987	48.4	0.87	55.63	174.77

(Source: Company Annual Report and Accounts)

Table **5.6:** Sears Roebuck and Co. assets, equity and payout ratio and net income

Year	Total Assets $ Bill	Total Common Equity $ Bill	Payout Ratio	Net Income
1996	36.2	4.9	29	1.2
1995	33.1	4.0	50	1.0
1994	91.9	9.2	51	1.2
1993	90.8	10.1	26	2.4
1992	83.5	9.2	100+	−2.6
1991	106.4	13.8	54	1.3
1990	96.2	12.8	77	0.9
1989	86.9	13.6	47	1.4
1988	78.0	14.0	72	1.0
1987	75.0	13.6	46	1.6

increases the internal operating architecture and associated structure of costs. Eventually the organization is forced into making a series of tactical and strategic financial moves which off-load or consolidate new activities with the objective of appropriating surplus.

In order to explore these issues further we will turn to the case of pharmaceuticals. On the one hand the pharmaceutical business is represented as being R&D led, delivering organic growth and strong financial returns. But by way of contrast the *Investors Chronicle* (Sector Focus on Pharmaceuticals 19 June 1998) observes:

> mergers are likely to dominate the sector for some time yet. . . .
> . . . there is little doubt there will be more. Merger activity has characterised the industry for several years already; accountants Price Waterhouse estimate that the 30 biggest deals in the period 1989–97 were worth about £125 billion. The trend is likely to continue until two or three players each have more than 10 per cent of the market.

Case study: Pharmaceuticals

Pharmaceuticals are widely represented as one of the most successful international businesses. Glaxo-Wellcome, is most successful European pharmaceuticals company. The imagery suggests that pharmaceutical manufacture is the practical realization of all the possibilities of prosperity in a dynamic case that realizes the potential of knowledge-intensive, high-value added activity. This observation is made without ever checking to see whether the underlying market conditions and operating architecture support the case. John Kay identifies Glaxo, as 'Europe's most successful company' (Kay 1993, p. 30), whilst Davis *et al.* represent Glaxo as the most successful company in the world (Davis *et al.*, 1991).

In general terms the pharmaceuticals business is characterized as an R&D-led business and that this underlying productive/market strategy has established strong organic growth and robust world-class players.

Internationally the world pharmaceutical market is dominated by US firms followed by the Japanese and European producers (see Table 5.7).

In terms of global output share, the UK sector is no larger than the German, French or Italian pharmaceutical industries. The explanation for this apparent paradox is that internationally the industry is fragmented and nationally based. All the main European countries have a domestically based pharmaceuticals industry consisting of indigenous firms and foreign owned affiliates. These play a major role in satisfying domestic demand just as in the UK where more than three-quarters of domestic demand for pharmaceuticals is met by domestically-based firms.

Pharmaceuticals: A fragmented business

From a European perspective, the most striking feature of the world pharmaceutical industry is its fragmentation and the absence of the concentration we find in most other capitalist manufacturing activities such as car manufacture where the top ten firms produce 80 per cent of world output. The world's three leading drug companies (Glaxo-Wellcome, Merck and Hoechst Marion Roussel) have world market shares of just 3.5–4.7 per cent and the average top 20 drug company has a 2.5 per cent share. Halfway through the recent merger boom, the top twenty companies together accounted for no more than 50 per cent of the global market (*Financial Times*, 30 September 1994) and there are no fewer than 50 drug companies with annual sales of more than $1 billion (*Financial Times*, 22 August 1995). In 1996 it was estimated that the top ten companies together accounted for 36 per cent of the world market for 3.6 per cent each on average.

After the 1995 merger of Wellcome with Glaxo, Glaxo-Wellcome is now the world's largest drug company by share of industry turnover. Glaxo-Wellcome has also recently been in merger talks with SmithKline Beecham. If Glaxo-Wellcome were to merge or take over SmithKline Beecham then its share of the world market would consolidate out at eight per cent until the next mega-merger. The fact is that large-scale take-overs are possible because the industry is still internationally highly fragmented.

Table **5.7:** Estimated percentage share of world pharmaceuticals output, 1994

USA	30
Japan	22
Germany	7
France	7
UK	6
Italy	6
Rest of world	22

(Source: Trade Estimates (Key Note, 1995, p. 11))

Patents and intellectual property rights

The global fragmentation of the business was made possible by the existence of intellectual property rights in a period of biochemical advance: this condition allowed ethical drug companies to capture the benefits of market growth in the form of monopolistic rents. In the period from the early 1940s to the mid-1970s, a series of relatively simple biochemical advances produced antibiotics, tranquillizers, respiratory drugs, anti-ulcerants, etc. which created new possibilities of therapeutic treatment and management. Ordinarily, the rents or profits of innovators would be competed away by new entrants (see Chapter 1 on Perfect Competition). In pharmaceuticals those companies which patent new chemical entities effectively obtain the right to block new entrants and charge a higher price. The pharmaceutical industry generally argues that these property rights are necessary if firms are to undertake research and development. It is equally true that, in a period of fundamental biochemical advance, patents were effectively a licence to print money for any company which had an ethical product that sold in volume. Ethical pharmaceutical companies typically sell their products at prices that are much higher than generic manufacturers charge for similar preparations. Generic drug manufacture is possible when drugs go out of patent and because such firms do not need high R&D budgets they can sell at a much lower cost than that required by the original ethical drug manufacturer.

The result is that the ethical companies operate in a different business where, thanks to intellectual property rights, cost structures look very different from those of companies in generics. The hypothetical example in Table 5.8 shows that the main difference is not in the commitment to R&D in the two types of business. The main distinguishing features of ethical pharmaceuticals are much lower (manufacturing) cost of sales and much higher costs of marketing in pursuit of margins which are twice as high as in generic manufacture.

Pharmaceuticals: An R&D-led business?

At this point, we can return to the stereotype of pharmaceuticals as a 'knowledge intensive' industry driven by the input of R&D and the creative activity of people in

Table **5.8:** Typical cost structures of an international pharmaceuticals company and a generic drugs company

	Generic	International
Cost of sales manufacturing	70%	25%
Selling and general admin	15%	35–40%
Research and development	3%	13–15%
Profit margin	12%	20–27%

(Source: BZW, 1991, pp. 162–3)

white coats. As so often with imagery, this is both a true and misleadingly partial view of what the industry is about because it obscures understanding of the activity and the conditions of its success. In pharmaceuticals, aggressive marketing is the main lever of success.

'R&D' is something of a misnomer because the routine development component of this activity is much more important than creative research. The research has never been highly creative because most of the industry's products have always been imitative 'me too' variants on existing products which vary the formulation so as to allow another patent to be created.

According to the leading consultants Pharma, development accounts for 92 per cent of R&D costs with research (including discovery and pre-clinical trials) accounting for just 8 per cent (EIU, 1994, p. 45). New product development is a slow business in pharmaceuticals with a mean time of 12 years from synthesis to first launch largely because clinical tests of safety, dosage, efficacy and side effects typically take 6 years (EIU, 1994, p. 45). The management task is therefore much more routine than the R&D stereotype suggests.

According to industry analysts, leading pharmaceutical companies' average spend on R&D has increased from 10.4 per cent on sales revenue in 1990 to 11.4 per cent in 1996 with some firms spending as much as 20 per cent. The net result is that the productivity of R&D spend is falling for the top 20 companies.

In any case it is wrong to present pharmaceuticals as a business which is led by R&D; while traditionally organized companies need the labs which generate (imitative) new products, aggressive marketing of products is the major object of expense and probably the major lever of advantage. According to Lehmen Brothers, world-wide drugs companies spend $60 billion (£34.2 billion) on sales and marketing that absorbs around one quarter of sales revenue whilst the Economist Intelligence Unit estimate the spend slightly higher at 26–30 per cent of sales with half that sum spent on the sales force. Observers agree that the industry spends twice as much on marketing as it does on R&D. This sets up pharmaceuticals very much in the mould of a business which is distinguished more for its marketing than manufacturing and technical capability.

When drug companies depend on the careful selection and aggressive promotion of 'me too' products, their competitive struggles are much more like Procter & Gamble versus Unilever. If this similarity is not immediately obvious it is because the marketing effort and distribution expense is hidden from the consumer because pharmaceutical companies concentrate on influencing the doctor. Where the stereotype represents pharmaceuticals as technicians in white coats; it would be more accurate to represent the business as sales representatives driving around in saloon cars.

The conclusion therefore is that pharmaceutical manufacture is an activity in which the overemphasis on R&D is significant because it misrepresents the activity as one where input leads to reward and output. The industry is more like a lottery. Success goes to the company which comes up with the right 'me too' product, patents it effectively and markets it aggressively. Glaxo shows that a patent protected drug, coupled with aggressive marketing can turn an industry also-ran into the 'most successful company in the world'. *Zantac* was a cynical copy of SmithKline's *Tagamet*, the first effective anti-ulcerant in the marketplace; by clinical standards Zantac was also a better drug which generally commanded a higher price. Zantac was effectively patented so that the first effective competition came 15 years later, with the next generation anti-ulcerants. While the going was good, Glaxo applied intelligent and aggressive marketing to boost sales. An shrewd early move was that of using Hoffman La Roche to get into the American market and an effective later move was to step up sales effort. Research indicates a strong correlation between number of calls made by a sales representative and the sales volume and Glaxo increased the number of representatives serving doctors.

Conditions of restructuring

Only weak companies merge.

(Sir Paul Girolami, Glaxo chief exec 1981–5, chairman 1981–November 1994, when Glaxo made no acquisitions)

This industry is consolidating and we had to lead that consolidation, not be carried along with it.

(Sir Richard Sykes, Glaxo chief exec 1993 to date, when Glaxo acquired Wellcome in 1995)

The most obvious first adverse structural change facing pharmaceutical companies is the decline in rates of market growth. The world pharmaceuticals market grew by 6–8 per cent in 1994 (Key Note, 1995, p. 10) and current projections are of future growth at 4–5 per cent per annum; the industry had previously expected 10 per cent plus rates of growth. It must be said that market trends internationally are not even. The Clinton health reforms in the USA will actually increase demand for medicines by extending drug benefits for those already on Medicare and those otherwise uninsured. US pricing formulae are not onerous (Key Note, 1995). But most of the other advanced countries have introduced various forms of controls that aim to curb expenditure on drugs. The Italian reforms of January 1994 aimed to cut the drugs bill by 30 per cent and by the end of the year had reduced the bill (Key Note 1995). The socialized agencies that pay the bill for drugs are finally exerting themselves against the pharmaceutical companies. As SmithKline Beecham's (SKB's) chief executive observed, 'We used to market to pharmacists, physicians and hospitals . . . now it will be governments and companies' (*Financial Times*, 24 March 1995). The *Investors Chronicle* observes that one of the main threats to the pharmaceutical companies will be 'Governments and health management organisations squeezing profit margins' (*Investors Chronicle*, June 1998).

The second structural feature is declining effective patent protection in an era when the industry is apparently unable to produce major biochemical advances. All this may seem paradoxical when all the Western countries have rapidly ageing populations whose chronic ailments require medication; while conditions like HIV/Aids and infertility open up new possibilities for drugs which treat long-term chronic disorders. Drug companies have responded to this challenge by increasing their expenditure on R&D.

If the industry's R&D and marketing are increasingly irrelevant, its lobbying is as effective as ever. The European industry has obtained an extension of patent protection through the 1994 EU Supplementary Protection Certificates Scheme that responds to industry concerns about the way in which lengthening development has shortened effective patent protection. The new regulation offers patent protection for 15 years from launch after the 10-year allowance for development.

A third structural feature is that, globally and nationally, the industry is spending more to get less as clinical testing takes longer and becomes more expensive. Clinical development that took an average of three years in the 1960s took seven years in the 1980s. Current estimates from HSBC put the cost of developing a new product at roughly $800 million on average for the top 20 manufacturers. While the cost of developing each new drug increases, fundamental advances are elusive probably because the industry has solved the easy problems that are amenable to biochemical treatment. The industry of the 1990s has been unable to produce the number of blockbuster drugs that create new treatment possibilities. An Economist Intelligence Unit (EIU, 1994) report observed:

> most of the development pipelines are stuffed full of chemical class variations which will provide low grade improvements in safety or efficacy and have limited potential to create meaningful differentiation over existing brands or lower-cost generic or therapeutic substitutes

The pharmaceuticals industry was never entirely different and is becoming much more like industries that experience an excess supply. In this situation the production of new drugs of which all perform perfectly adequately tends to undermine cost recovery.

The industry's difficulty in producing new must-have blockbuster drugs coupled with patent protection running out, establishes the possibility of generic product further undermining the industry. The main impact of generic products is that they destabilize price structures of the world pharmaceuticals industry. Given the universal attempt by western governments to reduce healthcare costs, the trend towards generics is set to continue; with European sales of generics estimated to double to £12 billion by the year 2000 (*Economist*, 30 September 1995). The impact of this growth can already be seen in the USA. While generics only account for 12 per cent of dollar market share they account for fully 40 per cent of total prescription units.

Against this background of a more difficult market, diminished effective patent protection and the rise of generics, the pharmaceutical industry faces the return of its old problem of revenue volatility. Before the blockbusters of the late 1970s and early 1980s, 'substitute competition' was intense and company fortunes were tied to the often short-lived success of one or two major products. The Hinchcliffe Committee in the UK observed in 1959, 'there must be very few industries in which a market can be lost as quickly as in the pharmaceutical industry'.

Unlike car manufacture, pharmaceuticals represents a different and more volatile case because cheap generics very quickly steal the volume and spoil price structures as patents on blockbuster drugs begin to expire.

> on losing patent protection, branded ethical drugs annually lose up to 50 per cent of sales within two years to cheaper generic competition that could cost as little as a quarter of the branded drug.
>
> *(Jordans, 1993)*

Glaxo's vulnerability to patent expiry was common knowledge and the point is registered in Kay's (1993) *Foundations of Corporate Success*. Kay recognizes that Glaxo's position is 'knife edged' but 'the company must hope that Zantac's reputation is sufficiently powerful to maintain its position against generic equivalents'. That hope was hardly realistic if we consider that in the space of 12 months, after losing patent protection on Zantac and Zovirax in the US, sales of the two products fell 21 per cent representing roughly 10 per cent of Glaxo-Wellcome combined sales revenue for 1997.

> The year saw the expiry of US patents on two of our largest selling products, Zantac and Zovirax. Global sales of these two products declined by over 21 per cent with a resulting loss of sales of £583 million.
>
> *(Sir Richard Sykes, Chairman's Statement,*
> *Glaxo-Wellcome 1997 Annual Report and Accounts)*

The industry has responded to these external changes by initiating a wave of internal reorganization. In the two years 1994–5, the industry spent four times as much on buying other pharmaceuticals companies as it did on researching and developing new drugs. According to analysts there is little doubt that there will be more merger activity, and accountants Price Waterhouse estimate that the biggest pharmaceutical sector deals in the period 1989–97 were worth approximately $200 billion. The global restructuring of the pharmaceuticals industry takes two forms: first, defensive horizontal merger between ethical companies; and second, acquisition and joint venture which takes companies (further) out of ethical pharmaceutical products into related health care businesses. The defensive merger phase began in 1988–90 with the merger of Bristol Myers Squibb and Rhone Poulenc Rorer as well as the SmithKline acquisition of Beecham. In the current wave of defensive mergers, larger companies are buying smaller ones. The Hoechst acquisition of Marion Merrell Dow for $7.1 billion in May 1995 is in this respect like the Roche purchase of Syntex or the Glaxo purchase of Wellcome. More recently we observe negotiations between increasingly large players, for example Glaxo-Wellcome and SmithKline Beecham which were terminated by SmithKline Beecham in February 1998 but the merger between Astra and Zeneca goes ahead to form Astra-Zeneca.

It is necessary to explain this behaviour at company level, we can see that the pharmaceutical companies are prisoners of their own earlier success. The problem of the industry, as structural conditions deteriorate, is that it is highly cash generative but it has accommodated high cash generation by making high dividend disbursements, R&D and marketing expenditure. These expenditures will still have to be met if firms are to sustain their momentum in the product market and to retain their status in the capital market. To illustrate our points we present financial data on three companies that illustrate aspects of this dilemma: we will focus the argument on Glaxo-Wellcome using SmithKline and Zeneca as comparators.

Glaxo's operations (here examined prior to its merger with Wellcome up to 1995) are hugely cash generative because it is 100 per cent ethical and thanks to Zantac this yields the best ratios in the business. Glaxo with a purchase to sales ratio around 40 per cent and a labour share of value added under 40 per cent (see Table 5.9) generates nearly 40 per cent of cash out of its sales revenue. The other two companies

Table **5.9:** Value added to sales and labour's share of value added for three pharmaceutical companies

	Glaxo		SmithKline Beecham		Zeneca	
	Value added to sales (%)	Labour's share of VA	Value added to sales (%)	Labour's share of VA	Value added to sales (%)	Labour's share of VA
1997	52	36	49	48	48	48
1996	65	35	46	49	46	53
1995	63	46	45	54	42	60
1994	61	38	41	63	44	58
1993	63	39	49	54	44	55
1992	63	37	51	51	44	57
1991	66	36	52	50	n/a	n/a
1990	67	34	48	51	n/a	n/a
1989	64	33	44	59	n/a	n/a

(Source: Company Annual Report and Accounts)

combine pharmaceuticals with other activities and find it difficult to generate much more than 20 per cent of cash out of sales revenue (see Table 5.10).

Glaxo-Wellcome has increased its good fortune: its spend on R&D is merely average at approximately 25 per cent of value added but its distribution of a further 25 per cent of value added as dividends is well above the average for the sector. If we add on an estimate for marketing expense, then Glaxo-Wellcome's position starts to look less than comfortable. The 1997 Glaxo-Wellcome accounts disclose that the company then employed 26,000 in sales and admin, roughly three times as many as the 8,800 in R&D so the claim of marketing on value added is around 45 per cent. Strictly, we should be cautious about adding these expenses as claims on value added because some of the company's development is contracted out and appears as external purchases rather than internal staff cost. Roche estimates that 15–25 per cent of the

Table **5.10:** Cash per pound of sales revenue for three pharmaceuticals companies

	Glaxo	SmithKline Beecham	Zeneca
1997	40	25	25
1996	42	24	22
1995	28	21	17
1994	38	15	19
1993	39	22	20
1992	40	25	19
1991	42	26	18
1990	44	24	20
1989	43	18	n/a
Average			

(Source: Company Annual Report and Accounts)

industry's R&D is contracted out (*Financial Times*, 17 June 1994) and that the percentage is increasing. But a calculation based on sales revenue avoids these difficulties; in Glaxo, dividends and R&D separately account for 15 per cent each of sales revenue whilst marketing probably accounts for another 45 per cent making 75 per cent of sales revenue mortgaged (see also Table 5.11 and 5.12).

It is relatively easy to understand the motives behind defensive horizontal merger because in this case two companies into one will go. Rationalization of activities will leave better ratios, some improvement in cash generation and useful gain in the profit margin. The precondition is that there must be some scope for rationalizing two overlapping R&D operations and two marketing networks and the latter condition is obviously fairly easily met.

Table **5.11:** Dividends as a percentage of sales and value added for three pharmaceutical companies

	Glaxo		SmithKline Beecham		Zeneca	
	Dividends as a % of sales	Dividends as a % of VA	Dividends as a % of sales	Dividends as a % of VA	Dividends as a % of sales	Dividends as a % of VA
1997	16	25	7	14	7.0	14
1996	14	22	7	15	6.0	12
1995	15	28	6	13	6.0	14
1994	15	24	6	15	6.0	14
1993	14	22	5	10	4	10
1992	13	20	5	10	n/a	n/a
1991	14	19	6	11	n/a	n/a
1990	12	17	4	9	n/a	n/a
1989	10	16	3	7	n/a	n/a

(Source: Company Annual Report and Accounts)

Table **5.12:** Research and development as a percentage of value added for three pharmaceutical companies

	Glaxo	SmithKline Beecham	Zeneca
1997	23	22	26
1996	21	21	24
1995	28	21	27
1994	25	24	26
1993	24	19	27
1992	23	18	30
1991	21	18	n/a
1990	22	17	n/a
1989	20	18	n/a

(Source: Company Annual Report and Accounts)

This logic of better ratios through rationalization was quite explicit in City comment on the previous Glaxo-Wellcome merger. The acquisition of Wellcome manifestly did not solve Glaxo's major strategic problem about patent expiry because Zovirax, Wellcome's best selling herpes treatment, was (just like Zantac) close to patent expiry. As the FT then observed 'the only logic behind Glaxo's bid, therefore, is the potential for cost savings through "slash and burn"' (*Financial Times*, 27 January 1995). At this point, NatWest Securities estimated that the 'cost base' of the two companies could be reduced by £1 billion to £4.7 billion.

The on-off $16 billion merger negotiations between Glaxo-Wellcome and SmithKline Beecham offered a similar prospect of rationalization of the cost base. Glaxo-Wellcome and SmithKline Beecham operate with a similar return on capital employed, of between 17 to 18 per cent. Strategically mergers and take-overs in the pharmaceuticals sector offer the prospect of rationalizing costs so as to improve margins, cash generation and dividends paid. Restructuring of the international pharmaceuticals business takes place within a market and productive context that undermines the prospects for strong organic growth based on blockbuster drugs. Firms whose revenue is highly exposed to patent expiry will seek inorganic growth to reconcile the demand of the earnings growth and a higher dividend yield.

Much of the restructuring of international business involves deals between companies which are quoted on the European, Asian and American stock exchanges. Mergers and acquisitions (M&As) are always attractive when there are willing buyers and sellers. Deals that offer generous bid premiums over yesterday's closing price for the ordinary shares can be put together. A bid premium of 50 per cent was enough to persuade the Wellcome Trust to sell its 30 per cent plus stake in Wellcome to Glaxo and thus effectively guarantee the success of the bid. Buyers are willing to pay these kinds of premiums in cash because the alchemy of the stock exchange is such that it can continue to generate substantial increases in shareholder value from a relatively modest reduction in employment. Where securities markets are volatile, as they have been in 1998, it becomes increasingly difficult to put together deals based on share exchanges where the closing price today could be 4 or 5 per cent down on the day before.

International stock markets have been particularly volatile over the last few years with falls ranging from 10 to over 30 per cent at times when the market does turn down. This increases the uncertainty regarding the cost of take-over deals especially when the take over bidder is offering its own shares in exchange at a price which in three months could have dropped by over 20 per cent. In these circumstances deals are often increasingly cash deals and in the case of large mega deals the loss of liquidity for the purchaser is sufficient to cancel or postpone merger and acquisition strategies (see Table 5.13).

At a micro level we have argued that market conditions facing the organization become progressively constrained as the trajectory of cost recovery deteriorates because volume growth slows and price competition intensifies. Actions at the level of the organization are necessary, but often not sufficient, to sustain advantage. We argued that the concept of an organization operating in an industry oversimplifies the situation because on the supply side organizations often consolidate a range of activities which cut across sectoral boundaries. Most businesses consolidate a number of activities, some of which are more cash generative and profitable than others.

Table **5.13:** Major stock market fluctuations: August to October 1998

Major Stock market	Close 12/10/98	Percentage change over day	Percentage change previous week	Percentage change previous 3 months
FTA All Share	2,226.4	+2.2	+0.8	−20.6
FT-SE 100 Share	4,823.4	+2.7	+1.5	−19.2
Dow Jones Industrials	7,899.5	+2.2	+1.5	−13.1
S&P Composite	984.4	+2.6	+1.8	−15.0
Nikkei-Dow Jones	1,355.5	+5.2	+4.7	−15.8
Tokyo SE Ordinary	1,023.3	+4.2	+2.7	−17.6
Amsterdam CBS General	581.0	+3.4	+5.6	−28.3
Australia All Ordinaries	2,501.6	+0.4	+0.6	−9.0
SFB 120 Index	2,103.4	+3.8	+1.3	−27.9
Deutsche Aktien (DAX)	3,983.6	+2.2	+0.5	−33.6
Hong Kong Hang Seng	8,990.3	+5.7	+18.8	−9.6
Jo-Burg SE Industrial	5,548.4	+1.7	+0.2	−34.1
Madrid Stock Exchange	656.8	+2.1	+1.9	−29.1
Milan Banca Com. Ital	1,063.5	−0.4	−3.1	−31.6
Singapore Straits Times	885.3	−2.8	−5.1	
Swiss Market Index	5,419.0	2.4	+3.1	−34.0
Toronto SE Composite	5,481.8	1.5	−0.6	−26.1

Within this framework of analysis the business imperative becomes one of bundling and unbundling assets in a restless struggle to appropriate a surplus on capital employed from sales revenues. But this is a game of winners and losers because one organization's gain is another's loss when there are only a few seats at the top of the return on capital employed league table, growth in cash flow, return on capital and dividends paid per share.

Workshop questions/exercises

Q1 The strategic success of pharmaceutical companies results from its knowledge-intensive, R&D-driven activities. Discuss.

Q2 'This industry is consolidating and we had to lead that consolidation, not be carried along with it.' Sir Richard Sykes, Glaxo chief executive, discussing the 1995 Glaxo take-over of Wellcome.
What factors have made restructuring inevitable?

Q3 'Mergers and acquisitions have become an increasingly important corporate initiative for increasing shareholder value.' To what extent would you agree with this statement?

Q4 Why do Microsoft and Intel have such strong cash generation and return on capital employed/assets?

References

Bernstein Research (1997) *Auto finance: Industry Shock Absorber Losing Some Bounce*, Oct, Washington, USA.

BZW (1991) *Industry and Perspectives: The World's 50 Best Selling Drugs, 1965–1989*, London: BZW.

Davis, E. Flanders, S and Star, J. (1991) 'Assessing Corporate Performance', *Business Strategy Review*, Vol. 2 (2).

Economist Intelligence Unit (EIU) (1994) *The Pharmaceuticals Industry in 2000: Reinventing the Pharmaceutical Company*, London: EIU.

Jordans (1993) *The British Pharmaceuticals Industry*, Bristol: Jordan and Sons.

Kay, J. (1993) *Foundations of Corporate Success*, Oxford: OUP.

Key Note Marker Review (1995) *UK Pharmaceutical Industry Key Note*, London.

Lynch, R. (1997) *Corporate Strategy*, London: Pitman Publishing.

Meeks, (1977) *Disappointing Marriage: A case study of the gains from merger*, Cambridge: Cambridge University Press.

Sloan, A. (1927) *The Principles and Policies behind General Motors*, GM Archives, Flint Michigan, Sloan, A.P. Jnr C.2 83-12.16.

CHAPTER 6

The financial environment

The separation of ownership and control ensures that shareholders retain control through their share ownership and managers take over day-to-day and strategic responsibility for the business. The influence of the shareholder on business behaviour and corporate strategy operates indirectly through the relationship between the shareholder (for which read fund management firm) and the firm.

Internally management decision making will be influenced by the requirement to make the necessary return on capital for the shareholder. This usually takes the form of a hurdle rate (or discount rate) when the organization is assessing future investment plans using Discounted Cash Flow calculations. It can also take the form of a price earnings (P/E) ratio or dividend yield calculation against current earnings. In this way the capital market impacts upon management action(s).

In general we find that firms use their internal funds for investment in new plant and equipment and rarely use external funds for long-term capital projects.

The growth in fund management has institutionalized share ownership and fund management firms are increasingly turning the stock of equity in order to drive up share prices. On average shares were held for a period of 4 to 5 years in the early 1970s but now shares are held for an average of just 18 months. In the UK and USA the P/E ratio now stands at 30 times current earnings and the disconnection between share prices and national, sector and corporate value added is dramatic.

It is structurally difficult for firms to maintain the return on capital as established by rises in share prices. The combination of market conditions, internal operating ratios and capitalization in the balance sheet all need to be favourable. If one of these is unfavourably disposed then the firm will find it difficult to sustain a surplus EVA^{TM} or return on capital (after tax) greater than 12 per cent.

Our case study on fund management companies explores these issues and illustrates that even for the fund management firms shareholder value and abnormally high return on capital employed is difficult to sustain in a competitive market.

Introduction

The separation of ownership and control

The financial calculations of business take place within a specific context where there has been a separation of ownership and control. Ownership of a company generally resides with shareholders where the business has listed issued capital unless the business is a partnership or a sole proprietorship. Shareholders elect the Board of Directors and typically delegate operational control to professional managers who, although they may have substantial shareholdings, in no sense own the firms that employ them. The financial calculations employed by management for both operational and strategic decision making reflect the interests of the shareholders because they are designed to either control costs or plan for profit.

Apart from the shareholder claim against profit there are also other providers of finance looking to secure a return on capital, for example banks and all those who provide a business with loans overdrafts and debt finance and working capital funds.

Management must account for the use of funds to the various stakeholders in the business and the annual report and accounts provide information on current profitability and the ability of the business to generate a level of cash from operations which covers finance charges. Apart from the need to account for the use of funds and the return on those funds, management

---

KEY CONCEPT 6.1
Separation of ownership and control

Most shares in large corporations are owned not by individuals but by financial institutions such as insurance and pension funds that manage shares on behalf of the personal sector or households. These institutions employ fund managers whose objective is to obtain a return on managing this capital in the form of dividends from the corporate sector or capital gains from dealing in second-hand shares.

These institutional investors are able to intervene and influence the way managers organize and operate the businesses under their charge. For example fund managers can adjust their expectations as to what constitutes a fair return on shareholder funds. They can sell shares onto another pension fund or another firm such as a take-over bidder and so exchange ownership rights. In Chapter 5 we noted the rapid expansion in merger and take-over activity nationally and internationally.

In an earlier period shares, and hence share ownership, were dispersed and in the hands of many individuals. The power of a dispersed set of owners limits the impact that ownership has on firm behaviour (Berle and Means, 1932). The concentration of ownership is such that over 50 per cent of shares in the UK are owned by pension funds and insurance companies and in some cases over 80 per cent of a firm's shares are institutionally owned and managed.

calculations will be influenced by the need to deliver an adequate return on capital. So where capital funds are to be appropriated to a particular investment project, the financial returns from the investment will be subjected to a hurdle rate or cost of capital test. Financial calculations such as Discounted Cash Flow (DCF) and NPV (Net Present Value) are employed to predict whether or not a project will cover its cost of capital. It is important to note that these calculations do not guarantee that the return on capital will be met but they do influence the way in which management allocates capital funds.

Consider the example in Table 6.1 for illustration. In relation to this investment, project management expect a future net cash flow (inflow minus outflows) shown in column 2. It is also established that the cost of capital is 10 per cent (that is, the weighted average cost of debt and equity finance for this project is 10 per cent). The cost of capital is used to establish the discount rate or factor that is applied to calculate the present value of future cash flows.

To calculate the present value of discounted future cash flows we use the following formula:

$$PVo = \frac{FVn}{(1 + i)^n}$$

Where PVo = The present value of future cash flows
FVn = The future value of net cash flows in each future year n
$(1 + i)^n$ = The compound discount factor based on the year in which net cash flow is obtained (n) and the market rate of interest or cost of capital (i)

To establish the Net Present Value (NPV) we deduct the initial investment outlay from the present sum of values.

$$NPV = \Sigma\ PVo - Io$$
$$NPV = 10,463 - 8,000 = 2,463$$

In this example the project returns a positive NPV. This means that the investment project delivers a return on investment that covers the cost of capital and provides a surplus of profit. In this way business accounting calculations DCF and NPV internalize a hurdle rate or cost of capital discount rate that represents the external interests of the providers and source of finance.

Table **6.1:** Illustrative NPV calculation

End of Year Col.1	Net Cash Flow £ Col. 2	Discount Factor Col.3	Present Value £ Col.4
Year 1	2,000	0.9091	1,818.2
Year 2	3,000	0.8264	2,479.2
Year 3	3,000	0.7513	2,253.9
Year 4	3,000	0.6830	2,049.0
Year 5	3,000	0.6209	1,862.7
Total present value of Discounted Cash Flows in £			10,463.0

It has been argued that capital allocation calculations like NPV and DFC strategically undermine the competitive position of the business. In 1980 and 1982 Hayes and Abernathy and Hayes and Garvin argues that American business set hurdle rates at a level that actively discouraged strategic long-term investment. Hayes notes that the calculation of DCF is like a reversed telescope in that near-term cash flows are assigned greater weight than medium and long-term cash flows because the discount factor progressively reduces the value of future net cash flows. Hayes argues a case for keeping the DCF calculation but managers must also take into account other variables that affect strategic outcomes and performance.

The problem is that many firms employ the calculation of DCF because it provides a means to allocate scarce capital resources. Klammer observes that application of the technique alone cannot guarantee the return on capital and that just a 10 per cent variation in the parameters of the calculation can undermine a particular choice of investment project.

On the one hand management employs a range of financial calculations like DCF and NPV to ensure that capital funds are allocated to those projects that secure a return that satisfies the external providers of funds. Paradoxically external finance is not the only source of funds to a business. The average business in the USA, Germany, France and the UK tends to employ its own profit or net cash flows for capital investment and only rarely goes to the capital market (shareholder) for more funds.

Internal versus external finance

UK, and more generally international, businesses traditionally rely upon internally generated funds from operations as a means to finance expansion. It has been generally argued that the motivation for using internal funds is that it allows managers to avoid the increased dependence on external finance giving them a greater sense of freedom. The obvious result of this is that UK and international businesses are therefore highly dependent upon the fortunes of the business and current profit performance. If a company hits bad times and turnover and profits are cyclically depressed for a period of time this will affect the level of investment that can be sustained by the business. This in turn will restrict expenditure on product and process renewal and possibly weaken the competitiveness of the business.

International comparisons of investment finance are difficult to make because of differences in accounting conventions and tax legislation. The research undertaken by Mayer (1988) suggests that in the UK and USA most, if not all, financing of private physical investment by enterprises comes from internally generated funds. This also accords with the fact that internal funding in German enterprise has accounted for over 100 per cent of gross asset funding in recent years. In 1995 and 1996 internal funds represented 117.2 and 120 per cent of gross asset formation of German enterprises (Deutsche Bundesbank Report, November 1997).

Mayer (1988) concludes that most UK Industrial and Commercial Companies (ICCs) invest in fixed capital out of retained earnings. In Table 6.2 the cumulative value of ICC fixed assets investment accounted for 85 per cent of their retained earnings. It has been a tradition with British business to invest in capital formation out of retained earnings and to borrow to cover the cost of working capital.

In Table 6.3 we calculate the ratio of investment as a per cent of cash flow after all other charges are deducted for tax, dividends, working capital adjustments and interest charges. The average reveals the high level of self-financing of fixed asset replacement in many sectors of UK business. However there are significant differences between sectors with diversified industrial companies investing roughly 60 per cent of cash on fixed asset replacement in 1997 and water utilities and food retail going above their cash fund. In the case of water utilities, environmental investment initiatives are forcing firms

Table **6.2:** ICC fixed assets investment and retained earnings

	Total ICC Fixed Assets Investment 1974–1995 £ mill	All ICC Retained Earnings 1974–1995 £ mill	Excess of Retained Earnings over Fixed Assets Investment %
1974–1995	624.43	715.2	15

(Source: UK National Accounts, 'The Blue Book', various years, ONS)

Table **6.3:** Investment as a percentage of internal cash flow for a range of UK industry sectors

Sector	Year	Cash flow pre-investment £ mill	Net payment for fixed assets £ mill	Net payments for fixed assets as a per cent of internal cash flow
Chemicals	1996	1,151	1,418	123.20
Diversified Industrial	1997	304	174	57.24
Electrical Equipment	1996	488	424	86.89
Electricity	1997	2,127	1,474	69.30
Engineering	1995	1,635	1,781	108.93
Food producers	1997	3,238	2,404	74.24
Food retail	1996	1,893	2,159	114.05
Pharmaceuticals	1997	1,763	1,330	75.44
Telecommunications	1997	5,291	4,772	90.19
Water Utilities	1996	1,556	1,726	110.93
Total		19,446	17,662	90.83

Cash flow after working capital, net interest, dividends and tax paid.
Cash flow excludes finance from external sources.
Investment in fixed assets is net fixed asset payments.
(Source: Datastream ICV)

to invest up to and slightly beyond internally generated cash limits. Grocery retailers like Tesco and Sainsbury continue to expand supermarket sites and often borrow externally to cover the cost of expansion and recover the cost of finance from future expansion in grocery and allied retail sales.

There are a number of important implications for firms that have a heavy reliance on internal funding for capital expenditure and these relate to the indirect pressure that is exerted on free cash for investment.

On the one hand neo-classical economics assumes that a firm's share value or market capitalization reflects confidence in future profit and a fall in share value will undermine investment. The fact that investment behaviour is independent of share value is not surprising (see Bond and Devereux, 1988). Movements in share values are often the result of the speculative activities of pension funds and insurance companies and prices are independent of corporate profits. Neo-classical theory also suggests that there is an inverse relationship between business investment and interest rates. We would not disagree with the view that higher interest rates discourage investment though the empirical evidence on this suggests that interest rate does not have a significant impact on investment (Savage, 1978).

We would argue that the relationship between the financial environment and the business is rather more indirect and operates via the profit and loss and source and applications of funds account. External finance in the form of debt or equity exerts variable pressure upon the distribution of profit in a business. The cost of capital charge made against profits will be less uncomfortable when market conditions of the business are strong. The competitive condition of a business can be adversely affected because structural or macro-economic conditions are deteriorating. If profit and cash generated from operations decline because of adverse market conditions the cost of debt and equity can undermine retained earnings and re-investment. In this situation a business will find it difficult to maintain capital expenditure and the competitive reproduction of business through product and process renewal.

In addition aggressive fund managers in pension funds and insurance companies dealing in the share capital of a business inflate the market value of its share capital so increasing the pressure to pay higher dividends because the firm is locked into a dividend yield and price earnings expectation.

Stock market growth versus

corporate earnings

In Figure 6.1 it can be seen that in the USA and the UK growth in the stock market (that is the market price of shares) has outstripped the growth in real earnings to such an extent that the P/E ratio in the USA and UK has touched 25–30. That is, the market has discounted earnings to the point where it would take 25 to 30 years for the current earnings to recover the current market price of the share. When stock prices inflate this puts pressure on

KEY CONCEPT 6.2
Price-earnings ratio (or earnings yield)

P/E ratio   =   Market Price of a Share/EBIT (as a factor)

Earnings Yield   =   EBIT/Market Price of a Share (as a %)

The price-earnings ratio reflects the relationship between the earnings per share of a particular business (normally earnings before interest and tax minus EBIT) and the price of the share as quoted on the stock exchange. An increasing P/E ratio suggests that the stock market is discounting future revenue growth and has positive expectations about a firm's earnings performance and growth. The inverse of the price-earnings ratio is the earnings yield or EBIT as a percentage of the market price of the share.

Dividend yield
The dividend yield measures the dividend paid to the market price of a share and is calculated as:

Dividend Yield   =   Dividend Paid/Market Price of a Share (as a %)

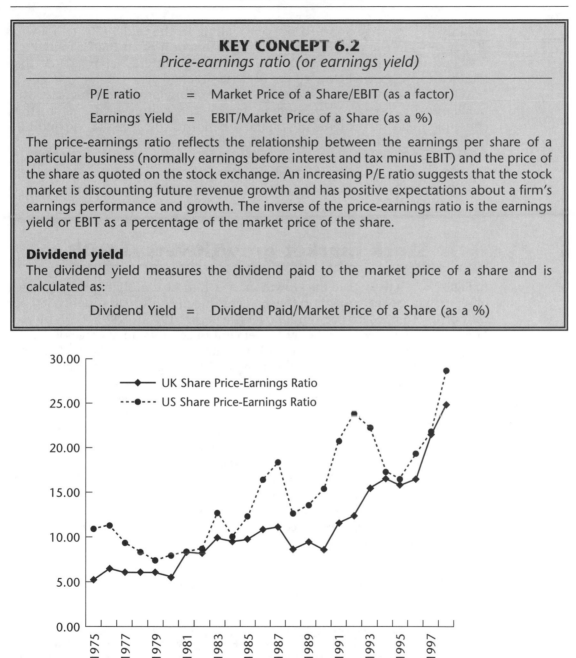

Figure **6.1:** UK and USA stock market price-earnings ratios

firms to maintain the dividend yield and so dividends distributed out of earnings tend also to increase.

In the early 1960s to the mid and late 1980s the share of dividends and interest charges and tax taken out of profit including depreciation stood roughly in the range 50 to 55 per cent, falling in the mid-1970s to a low of 40 per cent. In the period since 1985 the deduction of an increasingly high dividend charge combines with a relatively high interest charge such that retained earnings are below 40 per cent (see Table 6.4).

Where dividends as a percentage of operating profits do increase this mechanically operates to squeeze retained earnings and has further consequential effect of reducing capital expenditure. Real capital expenditure by the ICCs has dropped by 20 per cent on its peak of 1990.

The expectation in a bull market is that share prices will continue to rise at a rate which outstrips the growth of real output of the economy generally and more specifically the earnings growth of Industrial and Commercial Companies.

Stock market growth versus GDP

In Figure 6.2, if we deflate the growth in the UK industrial share price index we observe that the real growth in the market value of equity was roughly 350 per cent or 15–16 per cent per annum over the period 1975 to 1997. GDP, by way of contrast increases by just over 50 per cent or roughly an average of 2.3 per cent per annum. The growth in market capitalization of the UK stock market represents the capital gains from dealing and the degree to which firms issue new shares that are subsequently traded. In addition the privatization of once public corporations has added to the circulation of equities especially in the area of utilities and services. Since 1979 the share of GDP accounted for by public sector companies has fallen from 11 per cent in 1981 to 4.8 per cent in 1997 and what is left operates with low or negligible profitability.

To understand how the source of external capital funds exerts a significant and indirect burden on business finances we need to consider the place of business within the capital fund circuit and the relation between households, institutional investors and profit generating business. To illustrate these relations we use the UK as a specific case but make reference to international similarities and differences.

Table **6.4:** UK ICC dividends, interest charges, taxes and retained earnings as a percentage of gross trading profit 1963 to 1996

	Dividends	Interest Charges	UK Taxes	Retained Earnings	Total
1963	26.0	10.9	13.1	50.0	100
1970	18.0	17.1	16.2	48.7	100
1975	8.6	21.7	10.7	59.0	100
1980	8.2	32.7	13.8	45.3	100
1985	10.7	24.0	19.3	46.0	100
1990	19.4	31.5	15.6	33.5	100
1996	27.7	20.6	12.3	39.4	100

(Source: UK Economic Trends 1996/7 and UK National Accounts 'Blue Book', ONS, 1997)

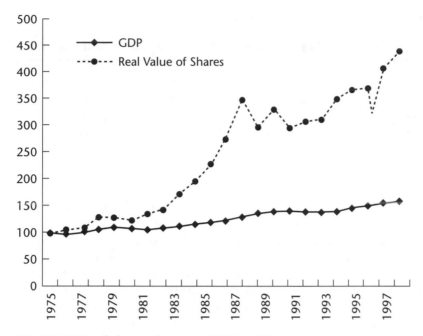

Figure **6.2:** UK GDP and share value index 1975 = 100

Stock market impact on business

The UK is recognized for its expertise in terms of equity investment and the emphasis placed on managing equity based assets structures. In Europe the UK accounts for one-third of funds under management. Reflecting the importance of its equity based assets structure we observe in Table 6.5 that in 1997 household equity holdings expressed as a percentage of disposable income has risen from 84 per cent of household disposable income in 1960 to a factor of 2.9 times household disposable income.

In the UK it is the equity market rather than bond market which dominates, and we further demonstrate this point by expressing bond market values versus equity market values as a percentage of GDP (see Table 6.6).

Table **6.5:** UK household equity holdings as a factor of household income

Year	Equity holdings expressed as a factor of total household income
1960	0.58
1971	1.79
1986	2.00
1997	2.86

(Source: Social Trends)

Table **6.6:** Bond and share market capitalization as a percentage of GDP

	Bond Market % of GDP	Equity Market % of GDP
UK	35	155
Germany	81	39
France	42	42
Japan	90	48
US	117	129

(Source: Deutsche Bundesbank, Monthly Report, April 1998, Frankfurt)

Expressed as a percentage of GDP we observe that in France, Germany and Japan the bond market dominates as a form of financial instrument and in the USA bonds and equity as a share of GDP are roughly equally split in 1997. The UK by way of contrast is much more biased towards equity funding with equity to GDP ratio of 155 per cent compared to 35 per cent for bonds.

Funded investment by UK households in life assurance is not new but has been greatly expanded in the past 30 years so that life assurance and pension funds now account for around two-thirds of household savings. Savings from the household come from two sources: savings made on behalf of the employer and employee which are deducted from gross wages and discretionary savings made out of household disposable income. At present 35 per cent of the UK population (top 40 per cent of UK households by income) account for 81 per cent of all current long-term savings provisions in the form of life assurance and pension funds. These households also accumulate discretionary savings through tax efficient/exempt schemes such as PEPs and TESSAs (and next ISAs). Voluntary participation by lower income households in private pensions is limited because they cannot easily afford to defer wages and make substantial contributions. Table 6.7 demonstrates how the distribution of household income reduces the capacity of low-income households to make discretionary savings. Low-income households and particularly quintiles 1 to 3 also have a relatively small claim on pension funds and other investments and managed on their behalf.

Table **6.7:** Investment expenditure and savings by UK non-retired households 1995

£ week and total per year	Lowest 25% by Income Quintile 1	Quintile 2	Quintile 3	Quintile 4	Quintile 5
Life Assurance and Private Pension	1.40	3.40	8.70	16.60	39.70
Savings and Investments	0.21	0.50	2.90	6.70	18.70
Total per Year	84	203	603	1,212	3,037

(Source: UK General Household Expenditure Survey 1995)

Given the pattern and distribution of income from employment the ultimate beneficiaries of investment and pension investment income are the top 40 per cent of UK retired households. Their income and employment profile while in work determines their claim on the assets managed by pension, insurance and mutual fund managers. The distribution of income from funds managed is highly skewed to the benefit of the top 40 per cent of retired UK households and Table 6.8 shows that 83 per cent of occupational pension income goes to the top two quintiles and 62 per cent to the top quintile.

Recent announcements by the Government envisage an extension of compulsory private pensions for the lower income groups and it is possible to envisage an increase in private fund savings as the switch from a state provision to private insurance funding takes place. Any adjustment that shifts more household savings into financial assets will further strengthen the trend towards holding household assets in the form of financial rather than tangible assets. Since 1975 the real value of residential buildings owned by the household sector has doubled, while equity in insurance and pension funds has risen six-fold. As a result by the mid-1990s household equity of nearly £1,000 billion in insurance and pension funds is almost equal in value to residential buildings.

UK pension funds and insurance companies have always invested their incomes in financial assets but in the last thirty years they have switched from holding government stocks and corporate debentures to UK ordinary shares. These now (as Table 6.9 shows) account for 50 per cent of pension fund holdings and 40 per cent of insurance companies long-term funds with government securities accounting for 10–15 per cent of pension funds and 15–20 per cent of insurance company funds. The institutions in the circuit effect a transformation whereby household savings become portfolios of issued British shares bought in a secondary market that is increasingly dominated by the funds.

If we add on investments in overseas securities then the pension fund asset base comprises 67 per cent and the insurance company asset base includes 52 per cent of equity investment. In so far as they buy issued (second-hand) shares, the pension funds and insurance companies are establishing claims by households on the income stream of the corporate sector and these claims

Table **6.8:** UK retired households' source of income

£ week and total per year	Lowest 25% by Income Quintile 1	Quintile 2	Quintile 3	Quintile 4	Quintile 5
Occupational Pension	385	928	1,388	3,340	9,647
Investment Income	304	328	408	1,015	4,311
Other	47	135	184	292	1,181
Total Before State Pension	736	1,391	1,980	4,647	15,139

(Source: UK General Household Expenditure Survey 1995)

Table **6.9:** Assets held in UK pension and insurance funds (%)

Pension Funds	UK Securities	Overseas Securities	Government Securities	Other
1988	53.6	13.3	12.6	20.5
1996	50.7	16.4	10.6	22.3
Insurance Companies				
1988	33.9	8.3	17.5	40.3
1996	40.6	11.3	16.6	31.5

(Source: UK National Accounts 'Blue Book', various years)

increasingly consist of professionally managed portfolios. Much of the investment in equity is speculative and the job of the fund/capital asset manager is to outguess the market and pursue shareholder value.

The behaviour of institutional investors:
Pension funds and insurance companies

Pension funds, insurance companies and fund management operations expanded because households have effectively delegated the management of their portfolios to professional fund managers who buy and sell shares on their behalf. The private individual typically has a very limited grip on saving, investment and personal finance. The point is proven by surveys where 60 per cent of respondents did not realize the return on an endowment policy was linked to stock market performance. In addition 28 per cent of unit trust investors believe that their investment is guaranteed to outperform deposit savings accounts (*Financial Times*, 27 June 1998). In the previous generation, the ignorant purchasers of what the industry calls 'savings products' were passive, sentimental shareholders whose motivations and calculations were very different from the fund manager. Witness the shareholder debate over the sale of Rolls-Royce by Vickers. Private shareholders criticized Vickers management for selling off a national treasure and said they didn't want their cash back. Fund managers voted for the sale of Rolls-Royce because the fund manager's job is to exchange shares to realize capital. This is because the personality of the investor has changed – the individual investor has become a fund management organization whose business is the calculation about how savings are invested and the implications this has for a corporate return on investment.

The impact of this change in personality is complex and profound. The most obvious effect over the past 20 years is a greatly increased velocity of dealing as fund managers engage collectively in attempts to outguess the market. Active rather than passive tracker funds are managed actively precisely because the expectation is that the manager will deliver more than the index and more than their colleagues at the next desk. It is hardly surprising that the velocity of share dealing has increased and the average holding period has fallen.

In the case of UK pension funds for example the average turnover rate for UK shares was roughly 5 years in the late-1960s, it was down to 3 years by the mid-1980s and is now just 18 months and holding relatively steady in the mid-1990s (see Figure 6.3). The financial results of speculation are bound to be disappointing when managers can't outguess themselves. Tracker funds have become increasingly popular in recent years. The W.M. Company estimates that tracker funds or index based funds account for 15–20 per cent of pension fund domestic equities and 25–50 per cent of overseas equity holdings that they manage.

> The move into index funds has been relatively recent with the proportion being relatively negligible only ten years ago. The main growth phase has been in the 1990s in the UK. In the US they are much further advanced in their use of trackers but the proportion has plateaued at around 30–35 per cent.
>
> *(The W.M. Company, 1997)*

Tracker funds have become popular, attracting lower management fees because they are essentially automatic programs based on a particular spread or portfolio mix. Many tracker funds do well because they simply consist of a portfolio of large blue chip stocks.

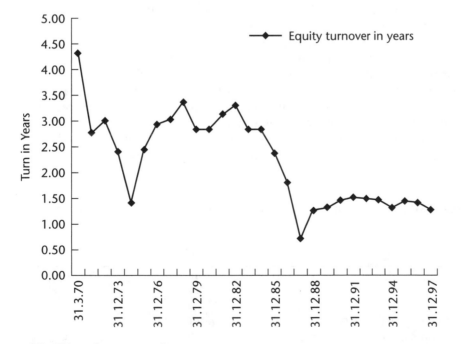

Figure **6.3:** UK equity turnover in years
(Source: UK Stock Exchange)

In the UK, for example the largest ten stocks returned more than 40 per cent against an overall index return of 23.6 per cent ... This out-performance appears to have created a surge of interest in indexation.

(Dyson, 1988, pp. 7–8)

Over the ten-year period to December 1996, active managers achieved a 13.9 per cent return on UK equities compared with a 14.2 per cent by index-tracking portfolios (*Financial Times*, 1998).

This return on equity is internalized by firms as a hurdle rate by which capital investment projects are judged. The cost of capital increasingly reflects the return on equity because at a national level the stock of quoted ordinary shares is four to five times the value of unquoted shares or bonds and preference shares and more than twice the value of bonds and unquoted shares (see Table 6.10).

UK households have increasingly ceded management of their investment portfolios to the fund management institutions. These funds are predominantly held as equities because the return on equity is relatively high compared to other types of finance instrument. The growth in the value of the UK and US stock market(s) out-run the growth in real output (value added) and earnings of the corporate sector such that the price-earnings ratio is generally increasing steadily.

The growth in the market value of equity and capital gains are determined by the dealing activities of asset managers but inflated equity values exert a claim on current GDP in the form of dividends out of corporate profits. In the UK ICCs (Industrial and Commercial Companies) account for 80 per cent of total equity and account for most of the profit generating part of the economy (see Tables 6.11 and 6.12).

ICC gross trading profits have increased by a factor of 18 since 1970 and dividends paid have increased by a factor of 30 with interest payments out of profits by 16, roughly in line with the growth in profits. A rise in the share of gross trading profits accounted for by dividends and interest charges reduces the share of profit that is retained as undistributed income or cash available for capital expenditure. From the late 1960s the share of profits distributed as dividends fell steadily to a low of 8 per cent which, when added to interest charges, left undistributed profit in the range 55–65 per cent of gross trading profit.

Table **6.10:** Ratio of UK quoted shares to unquoted and bonds and preference share capital 1993–97

£ bill	1993	1997
Quoted Ordinary Shares	536	1110
Unquoted Ordinary Shares	137	283
Bonds and Preference Shares	88	205
Ratio of Quoted Ordinary Shares to Bonds	6.1:1	5.4:1
Ratio of Quoted to Unquoted Ordinary Shares	3.9:1	3.9:1

(Source: UK Financial Statistics, ONS)

Table **6.11:** UK total gross profit share by sector

Year	ICCs	Public Companies	Central Govt.	Local Authorities	Total
1973	32.9	32.4	0.2	2.2	19.1
1980	31.7	28.9	0.9	1.1	17.7
1985	33.3	32.5	1.1	1.4	17.0
1990	31.8	20.4	1.6	1.4	14.5
1995	33.3	13.6	0.7	1.0	16.0
1996	33.9	12.8	1.2	0.7	16.5
Average 1973–1996	32.7	26.1	0.6	1.1	17.0

(Source: UK National Accounts, 'The Blue Book', 1997, ONS)

Table **6.12:** UK quoted company securities share by sector

	% share of UK Quoted Ordinary Shares		
	Banks	**Other Financial**	**ICCs**
1990	3.3	12.3	84.4
1993	3.9	15.2	80.9
1996	3.4	16.8	79.8

(Source: UK National Accounts 'The Blue Book', 1997, ONS)

Stock market expectations versus corporate performance

The demand for a high return on equity places a strain on the ICCs' appropriation account because they must adjust their disbursement of dividends in line with inflated equity values that often exceed profit growth. This in turn reduces their capacity to invest in capital expenditure. Expectations could also be further fuelled by the more recent concern to extract more shareholder value or economic value added. The extent to which an organization returns a positive EVA^{TM} depends on whether the ROE (Return On Equity) exceeds the average cost of equity.

If we assume that the Weighted Average Cost of Capital (WACC) of 12 per cent (which is not unreasonable) we find that most UK sectors have a negative EVA^{TM} (see Table 6.13). At the peak of a cycle, in 1997 UK businesses are finding it difficult to sustain a Return On Capital Employed (ROCE) or profit before tax that covers a cost of equity of 12 per cent. We observe that there are a number of exceptional cases, for example pharmaceuticals, or media, that can generate above 12 per cent WACC. These businesses have a number of distinct but rather exceptional

Table **6.13:** UK industry sector return on capital and EVA^{TM}

	ROCE	Year	Capital Employed	ROCE-WACC 12%	EVA^{TM}
Broadcasting	33.8	97	1,379	21.8	300.622
Pharmaceuticals	23.3	97	17,573	11.3	1985.749
Media	16.5	97	14,810	4.5	666.450
Food manufacturers	15.9	97	25,389	3.9	990.171
Telecoms	14.2	97	26,208	2.2	576.576
Retailer General	13.2	97	19,192	1.2	230.304
Diversified Ind	12.5	97	4,077	0.5	20.385
Retailers Grocery	12.2	97	16,011	0.2	32.022
Electricity	11.9	97	20,919	−0.1	−20.919
Speciality Chemicals	11.2	97	4,322	−0.8	−34.576
Distributors	10.7	97	4,351	−1.3	−56.563
Engineering	10.5	97	34,862	−1.5	−522.930
Water	10.2	97	19,654	−1.8	−353.772
Chemicals	10.1	97	15,841	−1.9	−300.979
Engineering Motors	10.1	97	4,010	−1.9	−76.190
Leisure	10.0	97	4,586	−2.0	−91.720
Construction	9.8	97	5,566	−2.2	−122.452
Building materials	9.4	97	25,307	−2.6	−657.982
Aerospace/defence	9.3	97	7,172	−2.7	−193.644
Pubs and Restaurants	9.2	97	16,898	−2.8	−473.144
Elect Equipment	8.9	97	1,957	−3.1	−60.667
Brewers	7.6	97	15,423	−4.4	−678.612
Hotels and Caterers	7.6	97	5,684	−4.4	−250.096
Tobacco	7.0	97	41,152	−5.0	−2057.600
Totals			352,343		−1450.189

Note EVA^{TM} = cost of capital at 12% deducted from earnings.
(Source: Datastream/ICV)

characteristics. Pharmaceuticals, media, and food processing have market place advantages where cost recovery is strong arising from intellectual property rights and brands. Media operates with little capital and so the return on capital is generally high. Losers who have a relatively low return on capital are correspondingly disadvantaged by their market position and degree of balance sheet capitalization. British Steel operates in a highly cyclical market where price competition is intensive, so limiting the margins per tonne of steel sold. The balance sheet of British Steel is highly capitalized because the business requires heavy long-term capital investment to generate the earnings.

The problem facing many firms is that market conditions combine with the internal operating architecture of the business and balance sheet capitalization to generate average or below average return on capital and negative EVA^{TM}. Pressure from the stock market, and especially fund managers of pension funds for higher returns, establishes the precondition for a distribution conflict between the various stakeholders in a business.

In the case of pharmaceutical companies, favourable market conditions and patent protection have ensured that UK companies have experienced sustained steady growth since the mid-1970s. In terms of operating architecture purchases take 49 pence out of every £ of sales to leave 51 pence in every £ as value added. Labour costs in value added are 47 per cent, leaving a favourable cash to sales revenue of 27 per cent. Compare this performance with that for grocery retailers like Tesco and Sainsbury: out of sales revenue 82 per cent is deducted to cover the cost of bought-in purchases, leaving just 18 pence in a £ of sales revenue as value added. Labour costs take a further 57 per cent of value added leaving just 7–8 pence in the £ of sales revenue as cash earnings.

These operating ratios (purchase to sales and labour's share of value added) are often stable over long periods of time. The stability of the ratios suggests that it is difficult for management to shift the ratios in favour of more cash earnings per £ of sales revenue (see Table 6.14).

The Return On Capital Employed (ROCE) is like all ratios, the combination of the numerator (earnings before interest and tax) and denominator (balance sheet capitalization namely shareholder funds plus long-term loans). In the case of pharmaceuticals, profit generated per £ of sales is twice that of our manufacturing company sample but the balance sheet capital employed per £ of sales is roughly the same as pharmaceuticals. The net result is that the ROCE for pharmaceutical firms is roughly double that of manufacturing. Water utilities are also highly cash and profit generative per £ of sales revenue with a profit to sales ratio of 23 per cent. The problem is that this income ratio combines with a highly capitalized balance sheet and so the return on capital is below average at 11 per cent.

The point is that various factors combine to determine a firm or sector return on capital. Market conditions and the cost recovery characteristics of the business or sector combine with the internal and variable operating

Table **6.14:** Activity ratios for a selection of UK industrial and commercial companies

Sector Activity Ratios: Five Year Averages, 1994–1998							
Sector	Purchases to Sales (P/S) %	Labour's share of value added	Cash Generated per £ of Sales in pence	Profit Generated per £ of Sales in pence	Balance Sheet value of Capital Employed per £ of Sales in £	Return on Capital Employed – Conventional ROCE %	ROCE Range
Pharmaceuticals	48.7	46.8	27.3	15.6	0.73	34.4	30–35
Manufacturing	62.1	64.7	13.3	8.9	0.66	20.9	17.8–24.0
Grocery Retail	82.3	56.9	7.6	3.83	0.35	16.0	8–22
Water Utilities	38.4	33.2	41.1	22.8	3.05	11.0	10–12

Sector Companies   Pharmaceuticals: SmithKline Beecham, Zeneca, Glaxo-Wellcome
Electricity: Viridian, British Energy, National Grid, National Power, Power Gen, Scottish and Southern Electricity, Scottish Power.
Grocery Retail: Tesco, Asda, Morrison, Iceland, Safeway, Sainsbury, Somerfield.
Water PLCs: Severn Trent, Anglian, Hyder, South Staff, Yorkshire.

(Source: Datastream/ICV)

architecture of the business to determine income ratios. These in turn variably combine with balance capitalization to determine the return on capital employed. In this respect we can understand that the return on capital is the result of a complex set of interactions between the product market, internal operating conditions and balance sheet capitalization. Many of these variables are outside management's control and difficult to influence.

Financialization of capital markets is running ahead of the globalization of product markets and product market competition. Deregulation of stock markets will provide opportunities for American and UK based fund management businesses. In recent years foreign ownership of the French equity on the CAC 40 index has increased to 40 per cent. American and UK fund management businesses set high return on capital targets and fuel the demand for higher EVA^{TM} on behalf of their clients – the pension, insurance and mutual funds. Pressure from the capital market (fund managers) for an increased return on capital as required by higher EVA^{TM} will intensify distributional conflict and the general restructuring of business. It can already be observed that the market value capitalization of UK business is increasingly concentrated in fewer firms.

At the end of 1997, 120 companies accounted for 76 per cent of the total market value of UK quoted share capital which was up from 65 per cent just five years earlier (see Table 6.15). At the end of 1998 the top 50 US corporations accounted for 50 per cent of the market value of NYSE stocks.

We have argued that firms generally avoid using external funding for the purpose of long-term fixed capital investment but may use loans and overdrafts to maintain working capital. Internally generated funds are the main source of capital and are used to invest in product and process renewal and strengthening the balance sheet.

Finance markets and especially the stock market, indirectly impact on corporate behaviour through the institutions that manage pension, insurance and mutual funds. We have observed how the growth in equity markets has been fuelled by expectations that increase the price-earnings ratio to levels that are two to three times the level of 20 years previous in the UK and the US. The spread of deregulation of stock markets and the privatization of pensions

---

KEY CONCEPT 6.3
Market capitalization

The market capitalization of a firm or sector is calculated as the volume of shares in issue multiplied by the market price of those shares on the stock market. In general, if there is a bull market where the price of shares is growing year on year then the market capitalization of a business will increase. In a situation where the share price of a business falls then the market capitalization of the firm will decline.

Market capitalization is an important component in the calculation of MVA – Market Value Added. This calculation measures the difference between total market value (what investors can take out of the company) and the total capital invested.

Table **6.15:** Distribution of UK quoted company market capitalization, December 1997

Equity Market Value Range £ mill	No. of Companies	Share of Companies %	Equity Market Value £ bill	Share of Equity Market Value %
2,000+	120	6.07	958.9	76.628
1,000–2,000	54	2.73	76.5	6.113
500–1,000	112	5.66	76.6	6.121
100–500	444	22.45	100.0	7.991
50–100	296	14.96	21.2	1.694
10–50	626	31.65	16.7	1.335
5–10	155	7.84	1.1	0.088
2–5	92	4.65	0.33	0.026
0–2	29	1.47	0.04	0.004
Unvalued securities	28	1.42		
Suspended	22	1.10		
	1978	100.00	1251.37	100.000

(Source: UK Stock Exchange 'Fact File')

provides an opportunity for the expansion of equity driven finance markets more generally at an international level.

The institutions that manage funds on behalf of households are themselves quoted companies and demand higher returns to cover their own costs before remitting the capital gains on to their clients. In addition fund management companies are able to influence the corporate governance of organizations through the new shareholder value metrics like EVA™ and MVA.

We have argued that the combination of market conditions, operating architecture and capitalization of balanced sheets often work to limit the generation of increased shareholder value as measured by EVA™. This will not stop managers from adjusting their strategies in a way which will increasingly privilege restructuring in an attempt to maintain or improve the rate of return on capital and the lump of surplus available for distribution to shareholders. The restructuring of business concentrates the market value of capital in fewer larger organizations in an attempt to sustain the return on capital hurdle rates demanded by institutional investors. In order to explore these issues further we will use as our case example the fund management business in the UK and the US.

Case study: Restructuring and the fund management business

In this case study we start by looking at the fund management business in terms of the cost recovery characteristics of the activity. It is important to understand that fund management organizations obtain income in the form of fees on the funds they manage, the Funds Under Management (FUM). These fees sustain their activity in terms of paying employees and covering the normal expenses of running, what are more often than not, quoted companies in their own right (see Table 6.16).

Competitor interaction and fee incomes

Let us consider the pressure on fees in the fund management business. These originate from the client base because they demand that fee structures become more competitive, that is, they (the pension funds, insurance companies and mutual funds) get more of their funds managed for the same or less fees. Fund management companies do not beneficially own the funds managed but they do charge a fee for managing a client's funds.

Trimming fee structures is also not just demanded by clients but competitor's interaction and the pressure to follow the market leader puts further pressure on fee structures. Overseas competitors, especially from the US, are able to use volume as the basis for offering lower fee structures in Europe. They may even loss lead on the basis that the European fund market will expand and they are in for a long-term battle.

In terms of the management fees on FUM the average sector firm obtains the largest fee margin on retail funds then investment trusts followed closely by private clients and institutional funds. In the case of retail funds the fee income is 4.3 times higher than institutional funds but the costs of managing such funds is also 4.3 times higher and so the margin on income from both products is roughly 30 per cent. By far the greatest profit margin is to be obtained from managing investment trusts (see Table 6.17).

Whilst the fee return on FUM matters we should also note that the scale of funds also matters because the scale of the funds managed determines the amount of profit.

We can therefore say that four key factors influence the level of profit generated per employee and the firm and these are:

1   The fee rates charged as a per cent of fund under management.
2   The composition of funds under management.
3   The level/scale of funds managed per employee.
4   The internal cost structure of the firm.

Table **6.16:** UK fund management sector revenue and margin characteristics 1997 (average % earned on funds under management – FUM)

	Institutional Funds	Retail Funds	Investment Trusts	Private Clients
1. Management fees	0.196	0.801	0.623	0.267
2. Other	0.013	0.099	0.023	0.081
3. Fees, etc. % return on FUM	0.209	0.900	0.646	0.348
4. Costs as % of FUM	0.145	0.631	0.341	0.268
5. Margin as % of FUM	0.064	0.269	0.305	0.080
6. Profit margin on Revenue (5 as % of 3)	30.7	29.9	47.2	22.9

(Source: PricewaterhouseCoopers, 1998)

Table **6.17:** Margin and funds under management per staff

	Institutional Funds	Retail Funds	Investment Trusts	Private Clients
Profit margin on revenue	30.7	29.9	47.2	22.9
FUM per member of staff £ million	120	24	51	36
Fees etc. % return on FUM	0.209	0.900	0.646	0.348
Income per staff member £	250,080	216,000	329,460	125,280
Profit per staff member £	76,774	64,585	155,505	28,689
Index relative to investment trusts = 1.00	0.490	0.415	1.00	0.184

(Source: PricewaterhouseCoopers, 1998)

All of these factors need to be favourably disposed for one firm to perform above the sectoral average. If the firm has a bias towards retail funds and Investment Trust funds, and the funds under management per employee (in £ million) are above the sector average, and this combines with a relatively low internal costs structure and this will deliver a relatively higher (than the sector) profit margin on income.

We start by considering the composition of funds under management between three broad categories: institutional funds, retail funds and private funds (see Table 6.18).

Most of the major players have a split portfolio between institutional funds and retail funds with a small per cent of funds held and managed for private clients (see Table 6.19). Some companies like MAM and Perpetual specialize and run a heavily biased fund composition, with Perpetual a specialized retail fund management business.

It is clear that a strong bias towards retail funds can enhance fee income to the fund management firm because, on average, fee income from managing retail funds exceeds that of institutional and private clients (see Table 6.20). The difficulty is that fund management firms need to manage a portfolio of funds to spread risk.

It is also interesting to note that the sector average of funds under management per employee has not increased significantly since 1993. That is, funds under

Table **6.18:** Composition of funds under management

	Institutional	Retail	Private
AMVESCAP	39	59	2
Edinburgh	32	65	3
Schroders	59	30	11
Aberdeen	39	59	2
MAM	78	8	14
M&G	32	68	0
Perpetual	0	100	0
Ivory and Sime	32	66	2
Sector Average	53	39	8

(Source: PricewaterhouseCoopers, 1998)

Table **6.19:** Fee income and type of fund

	PWC Benchmarks		
	Institutional	**Retail**	**Private**
Management Fees % FUM	0.20	0.80	0.27
Other	0.01	0.10	0.08
Total	0.21	0.90	0.35

(Source: PricewaterhouseCoopers, 1998)

Table **6.20:** FUM per employee £ million

	1993	**1997**
AMVESCAP	36	37
Edinburgh	30	36
Schroders	64	63
Aberdeen	17	36
MAM	80	77
M&G	16	24
Perpetual	11	17
Ivory and Sime	26	24
Sector Average	43	46

(Source: Company Report and Accounts)

management (FUM) per employee have increased by a mere 7 per cent on average and after taking into account inflation then we would conclude that there has been a real drop in the value of FUM per employee.

We can so far conclude that the competitive pressures are forcing fund management businesses to cut margins for managing funds and that it is difficult to structurally adjust the composition of funds under management into retail funds that are also a highly competitive business segment. Firms in the sector have not been able to transform the scale of funds under management per employee either from managing a greater volume of FUM per employee or reducing the employment base in relation to the FUM.

In order to try and cut operating costs fund management companies are moving away from actively managed funds towards tracker type funds that require less 'management' and attract lower fees.

Restructuring and the fund management business

Many fund management firms are quoted PLCs and as such are under the same pressure to enhance shareholder value and EVA[TM]. In an environment where cost recovery and cost reduction cannot rapidly transform results and shareholder value the sector is actively restructuring through Mergers and Acquisitions (M&A).

Table 6.21 illustrates that the restructuring involves the consolidation of assets under management into a smaller number of players and these bids are for small as well as large companies. In the last two to three years £245.5 billion of funds under management have been consolidated into fewer players. The cost of these deals ranges from between 0.7 to 3.1 per cent of funds under management.

These are not small deals because we must remember that in general terms the average fund management business obtains fees of roughly 1 per cent of funds under management. So investment in M&A represents anywhere between two to three years of total fund management fee income. The deals are expensive because they require the take-over bidder to pay the market price for the business, that is the market price of the shares and not the historical cost of assets in the balance sheet. PricewaterhouseCoopers estimate that the cost of these deals is even greater at ten times the average company income stream.

> Such has been the demand for investment businesses that sellers have been able to achieve prices averaging around 2.7% of the value of assets under management typically representing over ten times the annual revenue stream.
>
> *(PricewaterhouseCoopers, 1998)*

The productive and financial logic of restructuring

The logic behind these mergers is often explained as 'it helps an organization achieve a critical mass', 'it brings together complementary assets' or 'provides an immediate track record in a new market'. Size and sheer scale is also important and this is often expressed as gaining 'economies of scale', as output expands so unit costs fall. In addition to cost reduction potential the merged firm(s) also has a larger fund

Table **6.21**: Restructuring M&A and the UK fund management sector

Date	Acquirer	Target	Funds Under Management (FUM)mill	Bid (m)	Bid/FUM %
Feb 96	Edinburgh FM	Dunedin	£4,600	£83	1.8
Feb 96	NatWest	Gartmore	£24,900	£472	1.9
Nov 96	INVESCO	AIM	$57,100	$1,600	2.8
Sept 97	Permier AM	Fleethorpe and Fleetlynx	£90	£3	3.1
Nov 97	Ivory and Sime	FPAM	£7,900	£132	1.7
Nov 97	Merrill Lynch	MAM	£104,000	£3,100	3.0
Dec 97	Aberdeen AM	Prolific	£8,400	£56	0.7
Dec 97	Old Mutual	Capel Cure Myers	£5,000	£65	1.3
Feb 98	AMP	Hendersons	£14,300	£382	2.7
Mar 98	AMVESCAP	LGT	$65,000	$1,300	2.0

management base giving it a larger lump of capital on which to provide clients with an improved service and greater spread of investment products.

The question that needs to be asked is 'to what extent do mergers improve financial performance?'

Let us again start from the PricewaterhouseCoopers report. This report observes that in general terms the results of merger within the fund management business have been disappointing. We summarize their findings in Figure 6.4.

It is clear from the PricewaterhouseCoopers study that well over three-quarters of merger deals did not recover the costs of the deal and the implication is that rationalization of activities and costs savings have not been generally sufficient to pay for the deal. The delay in recovering the costs of the deal will be prolonged where firms are unable to make large cost savings and productivity improvements. Remember Lord Hanson always tried to recover the cost of the deal by breaking up the acquired business and selling the parts for more than the cost of whole deal.

This delay in recovering the costs of the deal may well be further prolonged by the fact that the PricewaterhouseCoopers report observes that just 50 per cent of respondents had not been able to reduce their cost base after the merger.

The other admission referred to in the PricewaterhouseCoopers report relates to whether or not mergers have improved shareholder value. Eighty-three per cent of firms in the fund management sector, and involved in a merger or take-over, note that they have not been able to improve, or only marginally improve, shareholder value (see Figure 6.5). This is in a business sector that thrives on the idea that organizations need to promote strategies improve shareholder value. A senior partner of Stern

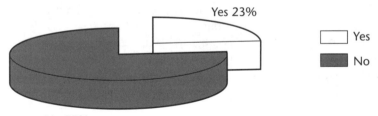

Figure **6.4:** Costs recovered from deal?

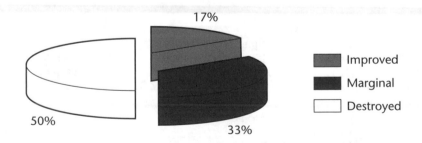

Figure **6.5:** Fund management companies: have mergers and acquisitions improved shareholder value?
(Source PricewaterhouseCoopers, 1998)

Stewart recently observed that firms that destroy shareholder value are in need of 'drastic surgery'. In the PricewaterhouseCooper's survey 50 per cent of merged fund management companies admitted to the fact they had destroyed shareholder value.

The problem is that when a company acquires another business it must pay the current market price for the business, that is, the market value of the share capital. The difference between the net book value in the balance sheet and the market price is often written off by the acquiring company and is termed 'goodwill'.

In the post-M&A accounts of the new combined business, the balance sheet value of capital employed is inflated by the addition of new assets purchased at the market value of the equity. The inflated capital employed in the balance sheet operates to suppress the rate of return on capital unless earnings are transformed or the cost base of the combined business reduced. In the absence of market growth, rationalization of employment is necessary in order to normalize the return on assets employed so increasing the EVA^{TM} in relation to capital employed.

Rationalizing physical employment often transforms earnings because labour costs are by far the most important internal cost. This fact is also true for fund management firms because they operate with a labour's share of value added of between 60 to 70 per cent and in this respect they resemble an average UK manufacturer (see Table 6.22).

The operating characteristics of the merged businesses may be such that rationalization of the employment base is limited. The two merged companies may operate in two entirely different geographic markets or the overlap between products/services is limited.

In relation to M&A, as it relates to the fund management sector, Pricewater-houseCoopers observe that after discounting for growth in the merged firms in their sample, they see little evidence of cost reduction in employment costs as a percentage of FUM, 'Removing the free effect of market growth on this ratio (costs in relation to funds under management) reveals only a small residual decrease in the true unit costs'.

To further illustrate this particular problem we look at the case of AMVESCAP. This fund management company is the product of a merger in 1997 between two companies. AMVESCAP has its origins in the Investment Counselling Division of the Citizens and Southern National Bank (CSNB) in Atlanta. In 1971 INVESCO was incorporated as a subsidiary of CNSB. In February 1997 AIM and INVESCO merged to establish AMVESCAP. AMVESCAP has its headquarters in London although some 85 per cent of FUM are located in the USA. The consideration for the merger was shares

Table **6.22:** Labour's share of value added and cash generated per employee. (Average 1994 to 1998)

	Labour's Share of Value Added
Merrill Lynch (USA)	70
Schroders (UK)	60
AMVESCAP (UK)	54
Flemings (UK)	60
United Asset Management (USA)	66

(Source: Datastream/ICV)

and £372 million in cash. Assets under management of the combined business are now roughly £200 billion (see Figure 6.6).

In line with the rough doubling of funds under management, the merger revenues (fees) for managing the assets also doubled and operating profit increased by a factor of three on the 1996 level. However the Return on Capital Employed has dropped off substantially after the merger after a period during which the ROCE had been rising steadily (see Figure 6.7).

In 1996 the ROCE peaked at 22 per cent, a considerable margin over and above the UK Industrial and Commercial Company weighted average cost of capital of 12 per cent. Up to 1996 EVA™ (ROCE per cent minus WACC 12 per cent multiplied by Capital Employed) had increased to £32 million but has since halved after the merger. Putting it another way the merger has technically destroyed shareholder value using the EVA™ metric.

Even though the merger has resulted in a reduction of EVA™, overall the consolidated business has an increased lump of profits available for distribution to the shareholders in the form of dividends. AMVESCAP shareholders do benefit from the fact that dividends distributed from earnings have increased.

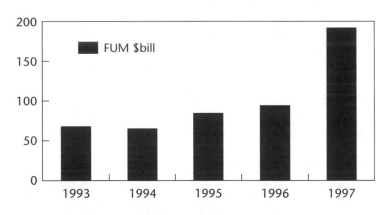

Figure **6.6:** AMVESCAP FUM $billion

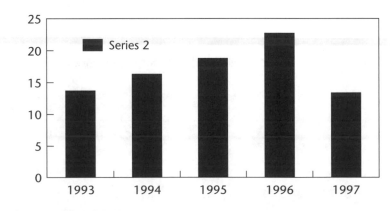

Figure **6.7:** AMVESCAP ROCE

Strategically, although AMVESCAP is not generating the lump of EVA^{TM}, it is keeping financiers happy with increased dividends and interest margin and is in a position where it can raise more funds for further acquisitions and augment the lump of profit available for distribution.

The paradox of this case is that quoted fund management companies are locked into an expectations cycle that is essentially one of their own making. Fund managers drive expectations through their trades in company equity and these expectations often run ahead of the real performance of the business. This performance is separately determined by a complex set of relations in which the market, internal operating ratios, and balance sheet capitalization often frustrate outcomes for shareholder value.

Fund management firms, like their counterparts in the rest of the corporatized quoted sector of the economy turn towards restructuring through merger take-over and rationalization as a means to satisfy their own shareholder interests. In this respect we come full circle because fund management expectations as to future returns establish the precondition for rationalization and restructuring of the fund management sector.

The actions of the fund management sector are of wider strategic significance because they manage such a large and increasing value of equity (see Table 6.23).

In the UK eight fund management firms manage roughly £670 billion of share capital and this is equivalent to twice the value added (net output) generated by the UK Industrial and Commercial sector.

In aggregate, the consolidation of business capital within the quoted corporatized sector takes us into a world where the market value of shareholder funds are concentrated in fewer larger corporations. Economies of scale in relation to the management of funds takes us further along the road towards 'passive' rather than active management of funds. The concern is that managing the sheer scale of these funds requires quasi indexation because co-ordination of the portfolio of FUM becomes all that more difficult when more people are involved. As trading become semi-automatic the possibility is that the bubble will burst when expectations run ahead of earnings to a point where liquidity is not sufficient to maintain the appreciation in capital values.

The economic consequences of such a collapse would be similar to those experienced in Asia and especially Japan. Real wealth effects are important because income from capital assets feeds household consumption and expenditure. In 1971 UK household income from private pensions and annuities amounted to 5 per cent of total UK household income (£16 billion in 1995 prices) and this had risen to 11 per cent by 1995 (£66 billion in 1995 prices).

Table **6.23:** Top 100 international fund management companies by country of registration: funds under management in $ billion

	Japan	USA	UK	Europe	Other	Total
Total Funds Under Management	4019	6210	1072	3427	1366	16094
No. of Firms	22	36	8	27	7	100

(Source: HSBC Company Securities, 1998)

Workshop questions/exercises

Q1 What do you understand by the process of a separation of ownership and control?

Q2 To what extent are managers free from shareholder influence in relation to the process of corporate resource planning and control?

Q3 What are the main sources of corporate finance? To what extent are UK Industrial and Commercial Companies self-financing?

Q4 It is argued that the stock market is increasingly disconnected from the real economy and business performance. To what extent do you agree with this position?

Q5 What factors operate to limit a firm's ability to deliver a return on capital employed (ROCE) that exceeds a 12 per cent cost of capital?

Q6 Briefly describe the following:
(a) Market Capitalization;
(b) Economic Value Added (EVA^{TM});
(c) Dividend Yield;
(d) Return on Capital Employed.

Q7 Why do fund management companies find it difficult to realize a strong return on capital employed (ROCE) even after pursuing a mergers and acquisitions strategy?

References

Berle, A. and Means, G. (1932) *The Modern Corporation and Private Property*, London: Macmillan.

Bond, S. and Devereux, M. (1988) 'Financial Volatility: The Stock Market Crash and Corporate Investment', *Fiscal Studies*, April.

Deutsche Bundesbank (1988) *Monthly Report*, Frankfurt, April.

Dyson, A. (1988) 'Balancing the investment risk', *Pensions Management*, May, pp. 7–8.

Financial Times (1998) *Financial Times Guide: The Future for European Pensions*.

Hayes, R.H. and Abernathy, W.J. (1980) 'Managing our way to economic decline' *Harvard Business Review*, July–August, pp. 67–77.

Hayes, R.H. and Garvin, D.A. (1982) 'Managing as if tomorrow mattered' *Harvard Business Review*, May–June, pp. 70–79.

HSBC Securities (1998) UK Fund Management: Major Themes, HSBC, June, London.

Klammer, T. (1973) 'The association of capital budgeting techniques with firm performance'. *The Accounting Review*, April, pp. 353–364.

Mayer, C. (1988) 'New issues in corporate finance', *European Economic Review*, June.

PricewaterhouseCoopers (1998) *Pursuing Profitability: Variations on a Theme – A Comparative Analysis of Financial and Operational Performance within the Fund Management Industry*, London.

Savage, D. (1978) 'The channels of monetary influence: a survey of the empirical evidence', *National Institute Economic Review*, February.

Stock Exchange (1998) *Fact File*, London Stock Exchange.

W.M. Company (1997) *A Comparison of Active and Passive Management in Major Equity Markets*, August, London.

CHAPTER 7

The political environment

In this chapter we discuss the impact of the political environment on business. It is clear that the political environment can passively or actively support business. A *laissez-faire* free market approach to political economy takes a back seat approach to the management of the economy. Arguing the case for unrestricted labour and capital markets within which prices adjust to clear markets.

This classic approach to government within the economy was criticized by Keynes in the 1930s who argued for a more interventionist approach to secure full employment. Most of the advanced economies practise a variable mix of free market and government intervention. In Japan the state (through its agencies such as MITI) plays an active role in resource management and planning. Much the same is also true of the Malaysian and Korean economies.

In the so-called mixed economies governments have traditionally intervened in the economy through fiscal and monetary policies. These policies are designed to control inflation, interest rates, exchange rates, etc. The impact of such policies on business is clear. An adverse movement in the exchange rate could undermine export competitiveness and high interest rates undermine price competitiveness. However it is the case that within Europe governments are ceding control over traditional macro-economic policy instruments and embracing a more liberal free market approach. The free movement of capital and labour within deregulated markets is seen as the route towards facilitating international competitiveness. Regulation is seen as stifling business efficiency and frustrating productivity-led growth.

Privatization and the removal of the state from the provision of public sector products and services goes hand in hand with deregulation as a central political objective in the advanced mature economies. In our case study on pensions we review the implications of privatizing pensions provision in old age. Privatizing welfare in this case, it is argued beneficially, shifts the burden of funding to the individual and

(continued on next page)

(continued from last page)
away from the state. The roundabout repercussions of such a policy could also be negative. Privatizing pensions will have implications for the distribution of income for retired households and may negatively impact on consumption where many retired households depend upon a state minimum provision. Privatizing pensions will intensify the demand for equity that could further push up share prices and the required return on investment in the corporate sector.

It is important to view government as a superstructure that acts to redistribute income from one household to another to underwrite the provision of products and services in which the private sector would find it difficult to make a surplus e.g. universal education, health and social welfare services. Within this framework government policy sustains household demand through a series of policies that redistribute income.

Introduction

The classical political economists, writing in Britain at the start of the Industrial Revolution, stressed the need to free business from the constraints of feudal tradition and regulation if capital accumulation was to flourish. To this day, many companies remain suspicious of anything they perceive as political interference. Yet the business community has never favoured pure *laissez-faire*, in the sense of an absence of government involvement in the economy. Even in mid-nineteenth-century Britain, when free market capitalism was at its most triumphant, companies relied on government for the laws they needed to establish private property rights, support the creation of a compliant labour force and ensure the enforceability of contracts.

In the twentieth century, business has looked to government for the provision of necessary services which the market has been unable to provide (basic sanitation and universal education, for example), and for favourable macro-economic conditions (low inflation and exchange rate stability, for example). In many developing countries, business/government partnerships and protectionist trade policies have been promoted as effective ways of breaking out of underdevelopment and penetrating markets dominated by companies based in richer countries. Initiatives to promote political objectives such as full employment, income redistribution, minimum wage levels, or limits on working hours, have in general been less popular with business. Even in these areas, however, some companies have been supportive, not least because they see such policies as reducing the risk of social unrest, or they want protection from rivals who would otherwise be able to derive a competitive advantage from lower labour costs or inferior working conditions.

Public services

Many European countries built up substantial public sectors after the Second World War, encompassing industries like energy supply, transport and communications as well as education, social services and health. Towards the end of the twentieth century, however, the boundary between public and private sectors, in almost all these countries, shifted in favour of the latter. Often, privatization was based on neo-liberal beliefs that the private sector is inherently more efficient than the public sector in providing services, and that any public interest considerations can better be addressed by regulation (setting performance standards or imposing price controls, for example) than by public ownership. In some cases, the main motivation was to finance tax cuts, or to reduce public sector borrowing.

In determining which public services could be privatized, a key factor has been their capacity to generate cash surpluses from which shareholder claims for dividends can be met. This capacity is greatest where the purchase/sales ratio and labour's share in value added are both low. Ideological proponents of privatization have claimed that private ownership will generate superior efficiency, benefiting employees, customers, suppliers and shareholders alike. Britain is an interesting test case, as privatization was pursued particularly energetically here in the 1980s. Although each service that was privatized had its own special characteristics, the general pattern in mature commodity markets like power utilities (coal, electricity, and gas), where there were few opportunities for demand growth, was less to generate new income than to redistribute existing income from employees to shareholders (Froud *et al.*, 1996).

What remained in the public sector was services whose capacity to generate cash was limited, but where significant positive externalities were involved (see Key Concept 7.1). The price of private education, for example, would be beyond the reach of all but the richest families, but there are significant advantages for the economy as a whole in having a universal education system, funded from general taxation, which can ensure that all recruits into the labour market have basic literacy and numeracy skills. In services such as this, the main emphasis of recent reforms has not been privatization, but the development of Performance Indicators to encourage a more effective use of tax revenues.

Traditional public sector management practices concentrated on budget allocations, devoting little attention to how efficiently or effectively resources were utilized. Performance Indicators, in contrast, focus attention on the outputs of services (patients treated by the health service, for example, or students taught by the education service) and on outcomes (health or education standards, for example). In this way, it is suggested, they measure how well a public sector agency is performing, they improve accountability, and they stimulate managers to enhance performance.

In practice, the use of Performance Indicators has been far from straightforward. Taking secondary education in England and Wales as an example, the main emphasis in the 1990s was on publishing information on

---

KEY CONCEPT 7.1
Externalities

Externalities are positive or negative impacts on people who are not parties to the transaction.

When you smoke a cigarette in a public place, for example, you create external nuisance and health costs for other individuals who have to breathe in the smoke. Similarly, when a firm pollutes a river, it creates external costs for people downstream who use that river for their drinking water.

When, on the other hand, a firm offers its employees training in transferable skills, it creates external benefits for the local economy as a whole, because it expands the pool of skilled labour from which all firms can recruit. Similarly, if a fishing boat limits its catch to sustain fishery resources, it creates benefits in terms of sustained harvests for all fishing boats in future years.

Externalities represent a misallocation of resources, because producers of negative externalities do not have to take account of the external costs of their activities, while bestowers of external benefits are not rewarded for this. Generally speaking, unregulated markets over-produce goods and services which create harmful externalities, and under-produce goods and services which create beneficial externalities.

To compensate for such market failures, neo-classical economics suggests that action should be taken to 'internalize the externality'. Taxes can be imposed where producers create negative externalities, for example, while subsidies can be given to reward the creation of positive externalities. Alternatively, where positive externalities are involved, a public body can provide the service, financing and distributing it according to politically determined criteria.

---

the proportion of the pupil intake who pass examinations. For example, the 'percentage of 15 year olds with 5 or more GCSEs at grades A–C' (the most widely quoted indicator) is something that can easily be measured, but indicators such as this, which reduce education to examination success, do not reflect the full range of educational objectives. Even if the reductionism of an exclusive focus on examination results is accepted, there is no necessary link between how well a school is doing and the examination performance of its pupils, given that social background is such an important influence on the latter. A school situated in a well-off suburb may have better examination results than one in a deprived inner city area, but how much this is due to the quality of teaching, and how much to social conditions, cannot be read off from the published statistics.

The problems do not stop there. Indicators based on examination results are published in the form of school league tables, and parents are encouraged to use them as a basis for choosing which school they want their children to enter. As a result, the 'best performing' schools become oversubscribed, whilst morale in the 'worst performing' schools deteriorates. Resource allocation and teacher remuneration are partly determined by measured performance, creating an in-built temptation for over-subscribed schools to exclude from their intakes children who they perceive to be unlikely to succeed at examinations. Theoretically, publication of performance indicators acts as a spur for 'under performing' schools to take steps to improve future performance, but in practice the most common outcomes have been a concentration of attention on those pupils most likely to achieve the specified grades, and the establishment of a vicious circle which further widens inequalities between disadvantaged and advantaged pupils.

A different set of issues is raised by the provision of road space. Most roads are in the public sector because, although roads are an essential part of any country's transport system, there are practical difficulties in charging according to use. Tolling has been used in some countries for motorways, where there is a limited number of entry and exit points, but revenues can rarely cover the full costs, as high charges would divert traffic onto minor multi-access roads, where tolling would be prohibitively expensive to administer. As a result, road construction and maintenance are usually financed out of general taxation. Fuel duties are often used to ensure that the amount motorists pay in taxes covers not only the direct costs of road maintenance, but some of the indirect costs – from accidents, noise, and damage to health and the environment also. What they do not take into account, however, are the costs of congestion – costs which road users impose on other road users, through increasing their travel times, as a result of using roads at times when they are already congested.

Table 7.1 shows one estimate of the relationship between external costs (not borne by the individual user) associated with road use and taxes paid, for the UK in 1993. Estimates such as this require financial valuations of health and environmental costs which are not conventionally measured in market prices. The estimated cost of deaths from accidents and air pollution, for example, is based on an assumed value of a human life of £2 million, which is derived from questionnaire surveys of people's willingness to pay for hypothetical reductions in risk. Clearly the precise results of such calculations are debatable, but alternative assumptions would not significantly alter the finding that UK road taxes correspond to less than a half of the external costs of road use. This raises significant problems for resource allocation. As traffic congestion intensifies, so do the logistics problems of business, particularly in sectors which rely on just-in-time delivery. New investment based on 'predict

Table **7.1:** UK external road transport costs and tax revenues, 1993

	£ billion
Road damage costs	1.5
Air pollution and global warming costs	19.8
Accident costs	2.9–9.4
Noise costs	2.6–3.1
Congestion costs	19.1
Total external costs	45.9–52.9
Road taxes (fuel and vehicle duties)	16.4

(Source: Maddison *et al.*, 1996)

and provide' (the UK government's approach in the 1980s) would be enormously expensive, simply because without demand restraint, traffic growth forecasts are so large, and it might also do little to ease congestion in the long run, because new capacity would generate further new traffic.

It is sometimes suggested that raising fuel duties so that they covered the full external costs of road use would be an effective way of rationing demand to make better use of existing road space. This might be suitable for health, environmental and accident costs, but it would not be appropriate for congestion costs, which only apply to certain roads at certain times of day. To use fuel duties to reduce these costs would be a particularly blunt instrument, and it would raise important equity considerations, particularly in relation to low-income rural motorists, who often have no alternative to using a car for work or shopping journeys, but who may never drive on congested roads.

An alternative treatment of congestion, which has been introduced in Singapore and Norway, and is being actively explored in many other countries, is congestion charging. Recent interest has been stimulated by technological advances which now make it possible to automatically debit road users with a charge for entering a defined area. Theoretically, charges can be varied according to the current level of congestion, but in practice they vary in a pre-determined way according to the time of day, to make them more acceptable to users.

Claims have been made that congestion charging will produce health and environmental benefits, as well as reducing the amount of congestion. Here, much will depend on how the revenues are spent. In Norway, charge revenues have gone towards the finance of new road construction, which encourages growth in road traffic, with negative health and environmental impacts. If the revenues are used to finance improvements in public transport, as is currently proposed in Britain, then local air pollution within the charge area should improve, as commuters shift from private to public transport (which has less emissions per passenger kilometre). In the long-term, however, charging could encourage jobs and shops to move outside the charge area, intensifying social disadvantage for low-income residents of inner city areas, and encouraging longer car journeys in the suburbs. Negative health and environmental impacts would be greatest if, as is often suggested, congestion charges were accompanied by a reduction in fuel duties. In this case, although car trips within charge areas might be reduced, the overall distance travelled by car, and the related pollution effects, would almost certainly increase (Neale, 1995).

Managing the economy

At the end of the Second World War, governments throughout the developed world assumed a responsibility for promoting macro-economic conditions which they thought would ensure full employment, not least because they believed that their failure to address the problem of mass unemployment in the inter-war years had threatened the survival of the capitalist system by undermining social stability and promoting international conflict. In the 1970s, as memories of mass unemployment subsided, the emphasis shifted from ensuring full employment to countering inflation, but national governments continued to assume that, by delivering appropriate macro-economic policies, they could play a crucial role in creating the conditions for business to prosper. In this early post-war period, the economic theories which guided macro-economic policy assumed that national economies were relatively closed. As international trade and investment expanded in the late twentieth century, however, national-level macro-economic policies became increasingly constrained by the international environment in which they operated.

Industrial policy

In Japan, industrial intervention by government played an important role in the country's post-war development. The key institution here was MITI, the Ministry of International Trade and Development. Back in 1949, when MITI was first established, the consensus view was that it would be pointless for Japan to develop a car industry, as this would be unable to compete effectively with North American and West European firms. MITI's counter argument was that car industry development should be given high priority, and that the infant car industry should be protected from foreign investment and car imports. With these policies, MITI suggested, the Japanese car industry could develop a competitive advantage in the long term, with positive knock-on effects for the capital equipment industry. The MITI view prevailed, with consequences that are familiar to us all.

MITI continued, for much of the second half of the twentieth century, to identify development priorities in terms of long-term market (and value added) possibilities rather than short-term financial costs. It was able not only to determine priority sectors for long-term development but also to use its powers to control imports and foreign investment, and to influence the allocation of bank loans, to co-ordinate private businesses towards these strategic objectives.

Elements of the MITI approach were adopted by other East Asian economies in the last quarter of the twentieth century. Neo-classical development economics has been highly critical of the inefficiencies of import-substitution industrialization as practised in Latin America in the 1970s, and has emphasized the superior economic performance of the more export oriented approach adopted in East Asia in the 1980s. Export orientation was identified in this theory with 'openness' to foreign trade and investment, and neo-liberal macro-economic policies that controlled inflation but intervened only minimally to regulate market forces.

Close examination of the newly industrializing economies (NIEs) of East Asia revealed a rather different picture, however – 'By the late 1980s irrefutable evidence that most NIEs did not conform to the neo-liberal characterisation. They were aggressively picking or creating "winners" at the industry (and even firm) level by intervening in trade, credit allocation, technology imports and local technology diffusion and creation, education and training, export activity, and so on' (Lall, 1996). In South Korea, for example, the government actively intervened on a number of different levels to encourage the restructuring and new investment that it believed was necessary for world export market success. It permitted inward foreign direct investment only when there was no other way of obtaining a desired technology or gaining access to world markets.

Keynesian demand management

Although some Western economies (most notably France) experimented with interventionism, industrial policies were never pursued as consistently or energetically as in East Asia. In the UK and USA, government policies in the third quarter of the twentieth century were influenced by a selective interpretation of Keynes' *General Theory of Employment, Interest and Money*. Keynes, writing in 1936 at the end of the Great Slump, rejected the orthodox neo-classical assumption that market forces would guarantee full employment (by letting wages fall if there were more people looking for work than there were jobs available, encouraging employers to take on more labour). He was mindful of the political infallibility of massive wage cuts in a modern economy, and he also pointed out that even if wages did fall, prices might fall as well, leaving real wages unchanged and removing any incentive for employers to take on more labour.

Keynes also suggested that even if real wages did fall, employment would rise only if the positive effects on labour costs outweighed the negative effects on product demand. An inverse relationship between wages and jobs might apply at the level of an individual firm, where it would be legitimate to assume an insignificant impact on demand for that firm's products. At the level of the national economy, however, a fall in wages would result in a decline in consumption expenditure, and thus a decline in aggregate demand (see Key Concept 7.2). Wage cuts, which might theoretically create jobs at a micro level, could destroy them at a macro level.

In place of the neo-classical emphasis on self-clearing markets, Keynes suggested that output and employment were determined by the level of effective demand. The main components of effective demand behaved independently of each other, and there was no reason to suppose that they would interact in such a way as to guarantee full employment. Consumption expenditure, he argued, is determined primarily by income, with the average propensity to consume (the proportion of personal disposable income that is consumed rather than saved) tending to fall as incomes rise over time. Investment expenditure, on the other hand, is determined by expected rates of return in relation to the costs of raising capital. Keynes emphasized the volatile nature of business expectations. Business confidence might be stable over long periods of time, but then be shaken by a surprise event such as a collapse in share values brought about by the bursting of a speculative

KEY CONCEPT 7.2
Aggregate and effective demand

Aggregate demand (sometimes called aggregate expenditure) is a schedule which shows how the volume of expenditure in an economy varies with the level of income. Effective demand is a point on this schedule which represents the actual value at a particular time of the sales which firms anticipate.

There are four components of aggregate demand: consumption expenditure on domestic products by households (C); investment expenditure by firms (I); government expenditure (G); and net exports, or exports minus imports (X–M). In the diagram below, we assume that I,G, and X are autonomous (i.e. they are determined independently of current domestic income), but that C and M increase as domestic income increases.

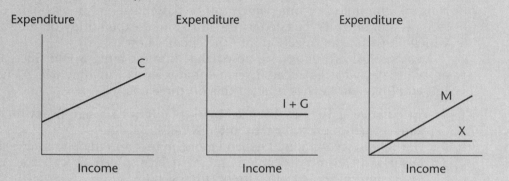

Components of Aggregate Demand

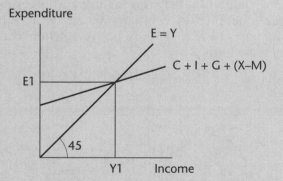

A simplified aggregate demand schedule, made up from these components, is shown above. Adding I and G to C shifts the aggregate demand schedule upwards, while adding net exports changes its slope as well. Expenditure on imports increases with domestic income, so the slope of the open aggregate demand schedule (AD) is flatter than that of the domestic consumption schedule (C).

The 45 degree line E = Y shows the amount of expenditure which is needed to sustain a given level of income, so the point where AD intersects this line, at an effective demand of E1, represents an 'equilibrium' national income of Y1. As Keynes emphasized, there is no guarantee that this 'equilibrium' will be sufficient to guarantee full employment.

bubble. Investment spending might then decline, depressing effective demand and thus future output and profit levels, even if interest rates fell to zero.

The impact of a change in effective demand on levels of economic activity can be illustrated by a simple model of a macro-economy which focuses on the circular flows of income between firms and households (see Figure 7.1). Imagine at this stage an economy with no foreign trade and no government expenditure or taxes. Households receive incomes from firms (mainly wages and salaries, but also profits and rents) in return for factor services (mainly labour, but also capital and land). Some of this income is saved, but most is passed back to firms in the form of consumption expenditure, in return for products. Household savings represent a leakage from this circular flow, as they reduce the consumption expenditure which is passed on to firms, and thus the amount of income which can be passed back to households. Firms' receipts are, however, boosted by the investment expenditure of other firms, which constitute an injection into the circular flow.

Neo-classical orthodoxy supposed that interest rates would fluctuate to ensure that savings balanced investment at a level of income which ensured full employment. Keynes rejected this on three counts:

1 Speculative activity in financial markets might be a significant independent influence on short-term interest rates.
2 Household savings might depend more on incomes than on interest rates.
3 Business investment decisions might reflect subjective expectations of future returns more than current interest rates.

Instead, he suggested that it is changes in income, not interest rates, which bring about equilibrium between savings and investment.

Take, for example, an economy which is at full employment with a national income (Y) of £1 million per year, where consumption expenditure (C) assumes the form

$$C = £100,000 + 0.75Y.$$

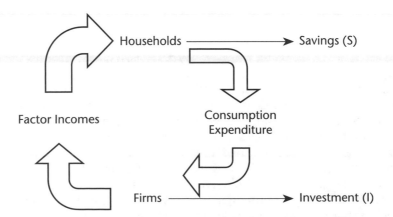

Figure **7.1:** The circular flow of income in a closed economy with no government

At full employment, C is £850,000 per year, and households save £150,000 per year – investment spending (I) needs also to be £150,000 per year to maintain full employment. Suppose now that businesses become pessimistic about future returns, and cut their investment spending to £100,000 per year, so that firms' receipts fall by £50,000. Household income will also fall by £50,000, inducing a cut in consumption expenditure. Y will continue to decline, until it reaches a new equilibrium at £800,000, where savings have fallen until they equal investment spending at £100,000. Note that a fall in investment spending, if sustained, brings about a greater fall in national income, and therefore employment. In this example, the multiplier (the relationship between the change in national income and the change in expenditure which brought it about) is 4 (200,000/50,000).

A more realistic version of the circular flow diagram is shown in Figure 7.2. Here receipts from exports and government spending are shown as injections into the circular flow of a national economy, while imports and tax payments are leakages. Keynes, writing at a time when two-way trade in manufacturing products between industrialized economies was less significant than it is today, paid little attention to the potential role of imports in allowing the benefits of increased effective demand to leak abroad, reducing the size of the domestic multipier. What he stressed was the positive role the public sector could play in maintaining effective demand at the full employment level. He argued that fiscal policy should be used to redistribute income from richer to poorer households, to counter the tendency of the average propensity to consume to fall as incomes rise. Coupled with this, he suggested an interventionist approach where governments would agree with the business

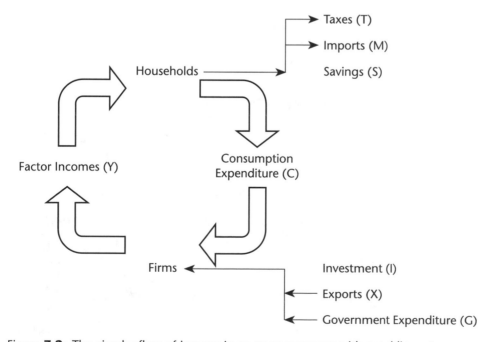

Figure **7.2:** The circular flow of income in an open economy with a public sector

sector a stable level of private sector investment which would guarantee full employment. And finally, to supplement these long-term measures, governments could use their own spending and taxation and try to balance short-term fluctuations in effective demand, borrowing to finance increases in public spending at times when private sector spending was deficient.

Many post-war Western governments followed Keynes, with varying levels of commitment, in giving priority to full employment. They rejected his suggestions that they should assume greater control over investment spending, however, and gave little emphasis to income redistribution. Instead they preferred to use fiscal policy (the general relationship between government spending and tax revenues) to influence the overall level of effective demand. If private sector spending was insufficient to ensure full employment, for example, a government might plan to either boost its own spending or reduce taxes. Initially, this would require increased borrowing to finance the deficit, but eventually incomes and consumption expenditure would rise, increasing tax revenues again.

In practice, demand management was never an exact science. Fiscal changes took time to work through to private sector spending decisions, and sometimes measures that were designed to even out economic cycles in fact exaggerated them, because the time lags had been underestimated. What can be said was that, in general, businesses believed that governments would not allow mass unemployment to reappear, and that this helped keep confidence at a high level, sustaining the post-war investment boom until the early 1970s. Unemployment, during this period, averaged less than five per cent of the workforce in every major developed economy except Italy (see Table 7.2). This, in turn, made employees feel more secure about their jobs, encouraging them to continue spending a high proportion of their incomes even as these rose over time. A virtuous circle was set up, with high levels of investment and consumption spending reinforcing each other.

Neo-liberalism

Keynes had been a leading representative of what has been called 'liberal collectivism' (Cutler *et al.*, 1986) committed to the maintenance of the

Table **7.2:** Percentage unemployment in major industrial economies, 1952–91

	1952–60	1961–67	1968–73	1974–79	1980–86	1987–91
W. Germany	3.9	0.8	0.9	3.6	5.9	5.7
France	2.0	1.4	2.5	4.5	8.6	9.6
Italy	7.6	4.5	5.8	6.6	8.9	10.6
UK	1.4	1.7	2.6	4.4	10.6	8.8
USA	4.5	4.9	4.7	6.7	7.8	5.7
Japan	2.0	1.3	1.2	1.9	2.5	2.4

(Source: Ormerod, 1994)

political and economic freedoms of democratic capitalism, but believing that some state intervention is needed to maintain the social cohesion on which its survival depends. Liberal collectivism played an important role in the economic and social policies of many post-war governments, but from the 1970s a more individualist neo-liberal philosophy, which emphasized curtailing the economic role of the state, became the predominant influence on government policies.

The long post-war economic boom was brought to a halt by the successful action in 1973 of OPEC (the Organisation of Oil Exporting Countries) in cutting oil supplies. This quadrupled the world market price of oil, triggering the global recession of 1973–75. Unusually in this recession, not only did unemployment increase dramatically (see Table 7.2), but so did inflation (see Table 7.3). Despite the obvious role of changed world commodity prices in the inflation of the 1970s, neo-liberals blamed Keynesian demand management for the crisis, and pushed for different macro-economic policies which emphasized strict monetary controls to bring down inflation, and reductions in the economic role of government to promote enterprise. Neo-liberals accepted increased unemployment in the short term as the price which had to be paid for bringing inflation under control, while arguing that in the long term new jobs would be created by the creation of an 'enterprise culture' and greater labour market flexibility.

A key neo-liberal proposition, put forward initially by Friedman (1977), is that there is a unique level of unemployment at which inflation is zero. Friedman called this rate the 'natural rate of unemployment'; a subsequent refinement of Friedman's analysis identifies a non-accelerating inflation rate of unemployment (NAIRU) at which the inflation rate is stable. Friedman's 'natural rate' is shown by U_n in Figure 7.3. If a government uses Keynesian demand management policies to bring unemployment down to the full employment level (U_f), Friedman suggested, its borrowing requirements will bring about an inflationary expansion in the supply of money, creating a positive inflation rate of P_1. Initially, there is a simple trade-off between actual inflation and unemployment (called the Phillips Curve, after the economist who first popularized it in 1958). Although there is now positive inflation, people continue to expect zero inflation, and the economy moves along the Phillips curve from position A to position B.

Table **7.3:** Annual percentage inflation in major industrial economies, 1952–91

	1952–60	1961–67	1968–73	1974–79	1980–86	1987–91
W. Germany	1.2	2.7	4.2	5.5	3.5	2.1
France	4.4	3.4	5.7	10.1	8.7	3.1
Italy	2.4	4.2	4.9	15.1	12.7	5.6
UK	2.8	3.2	6.4	14.4	7.6	5.4
USA	1.4	1.7	4.8	7.8	5.9	4.3
Japan	2.7	5.6	6.5	9.5	3.1	1.9

(Source: Ormerod, 1994)

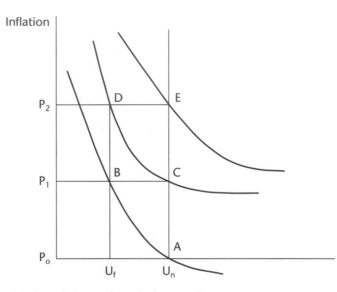

Figure **7.3:** Friedman's 'natural rate' of unemployment

The core of Friedman's argument against Keynesian demand management was an assertion that attempts to reduce unemployment below the 'natural rate' could not be sustained because they would generate inflationary expectations. If a government persists in trying to keep unemployment at U_f, he suggested, then people will come to expect an inflation rate of P_1, and the Phillips curve will shift outward, with the economy reaching a new equilibrium at C. Here, unemployment has returned to the 'natural' rate, and actual and expected inflation are again equal, but this time there is positive inflation P_1. If the government continues to boost aggregate demand, then this will move the economy along the new Phillips curve to D, reducing unemployment but raising actual inflation still further. Again, inflationary expectations adjust upwards, resulting in another outward shift in the Phillips curve, and a new equilibrium at E.

In effect, Friedman suggested a long-run relationship between inflation and unemployment which is vertical at the 'natural rate' of unemployment. According to this theory, monetary expansion can only increase real output in the short term. In the long term, its sole impact is on inflation. The conclusion is stark – any sustained attempt by a government to reduce unemployment below its 'natural rate' is doomed to failure, and can only result in accelerating inflation, the end point of which is a collapse in people's confidence in money.

Elegant though Friedman's 'natural rate' was as a theory, there was little empirical evidence to support it, either at the time or subsequently. Comparison of Tables 7.2 and 7.3, for example, suggests that the relationship between unemployment and inflation varies significantly from one period to another and one economy to another, reflecting different capacities to react to external shocks like the oil price rises of the 1970s more than differences in inflationary expectations resulting from macro-economic policy shifts. In addition, looking at changes over time within a given economy, reduced unemployment does not appear to be inevitably accompanied by increased inflation – at times, reduced unemployment may be accompanied by reduced inflation, or increased unemployment by increased inflation.

If Friedman's assessment of the relationship between inflation and unemployment had little empirical foundation, his policy prescription of strict control of money supply to squeeze inflationary expectations out of the system, was equally problematic. This can be seen most clearly in Britain in the early 1980s, when government policies were determined by strict monetarist criteria. Here the Thatcher government announced that levels of output and employment were outside its control, and concentrated its macro-economic attention on a medium-term financial strategy which targeted reductions in the growth of broad money and in public sector deficits (see Key Concept 7.3). In an attempt to meet its targets for reduced growth in the supply of broad money, the Bank of England pushed interest rates up to very high levels, believing that this would restrain business and consumer borrowing, and hence the ability of the banks to create new deposit money. In practice, however, the effect of higher interest rates on money supply was difficult to predict. Firms in financial difficulties, for example, had little choice but to increase their bank borrowing to meet higher interest rates

---

KEY CONCEPT 7.3
Public sector deficits and broad money

Public sector deficits are financed largely by selling interest-bearing securities to the banking system or the general public. If a government sells securities redeemable at short notice (e.g. Treasury Bills in the UK) to the banks, it effectively obtains bank deposits in return for assets which form part of the banks' liquid reserves. As the government spends this money, recipients deposit it with the banks again. This increases bank liquidity, encouraging the banks to expand their lending, which in turn creates new deposits. As bank deposits are the main means of exchange in a modern economy, they are included in 'broad' definitions of money supply (though precise demarcation of what constitutes 'broad money' is impossible, as many financial deposits are at the same time interest bearing assets and potential means of exchange).

If a government finances a public sector deficit by issuing long-dated gilt edged securities however, bank liquidity is not increased, and there is no impact on money supply. If the deficit to be financed is large, and the government wants to avoid expanding money supply by concentrating on sales of medium and long term debt, the government can, however, become very dependent on the goodwill of financial markets. To sell more securities, a government usually has to offer higher yields, which has the effect of raising long-term interest rates generally. In addition, if financial institutions are opposed to the direction of government policy, as in the UK in 1976, they can put pressure on the government to change its policies, simply by postponing their purchases of government securities.

on existing loans, so the rise in interest rates had the perverse effect of increasing bank lending.

Despite the new policies, and record interest rates, UK monetary growth continued to exceed the targets, and the government embarked on a process of severe public sector expenditure cuts to bring down its borrowing requirement. Inflation eventually fell in the mid-1980s, but more as a result of declining world commodity prices than successful monetary controls. If the impact of strict monetarist policies on the UK rate of inflation in the early 1980s was ambiguous, the outcome for output and jobs, particularly in the manufacturing sector, was not. High interest rates attracted short-term international funds into sterling, raising its exchange rate and making it more difficult for UK businesses to protect their home markets from import penetration or to maintain their share of export markets (already depressed by world recession). Domestic demand was hit by the public expenditure cuts, and low levels of product demand and high interest rates combined to discourage new investment. Company profitability hit a post-war low, and many firms went into liquidation. Manufacturing output fell by 15 per cent between 1979 and 1982, and almost 1.5 million manufacturing jobs were lost. Registered unemployment more than doubled, and in 1983, for the first time in centuries, the UK imported more manufactured goods than she exported.

A third way?

By the late 1990s, strict monetarism had become unfashionable again. Macro-economic policies continued to give priority to low rates of inflation, but instead of targeting money supply, governments now tended to target inflation directly, allowing short-term interest rates to vary in relation to current performance against the target. In the UK, for example, the newly-elected Blair government in 1997 announced a target inflation rate of 2.2 per cent, appointed an independent Monetary Policy Committee chaired by the Governor of the Bank of England, and charged this Committee with determining each month the level of interest rates which they deemed necessary to keep inflation to the government-determined target. When current inflation exceeded the target, as in 1997–1998, interest rates would be pushed up, and when it fell down to the target again, as in late 1998/early 1999, then interest rates would be cut.

As in the mid-1980s, falling inflation in 1998/9 reflected more the behaviour of world commodity prices than the efficacy of domestic monetary policy. The world market price of crude oil, for example, fell below $10 per barrel in December 1998, its lowest level in real terms for 50 years. Historically low levels of inflation, seen by neo-liberals as creating the conditions for sustained economic development, brought their own problems. In Japan, for example, deflation (falling prices) characterized many sectors of the economy. Here, savings with financial institutions were discouraged by negligible returns, whilst consumers were encouraged by the prospect of prices being lower in the future than they are at present to postpone discretionary purchases. Low demand meant firms had little incentive to invest, while price cutting to achieve cost recovery on past investment became self-defeating as it made postponement of purchases appear to be even more potentially profitable for the consumer.

Despite its rhetorical proclamation of a 'Third Way' between the harshness of neo-liberalism and the instability of 'boom and bust' Keynesianism, the 1997 Blair Government in the UK did little to change neo-liberal economic priorities. As short-term interest rates rose in 1997–98 in pursuit of a single policy objective, to hit the inflation target, so did the exchange rate of sterling appreciate against other currencies, hastening a cyclical downturn in manufacturing. The new government announced a series of measures to improve the employability of the young unemployed, lone parents, and people with disabilities, but, by adopting 'prudent' fiscal rules to prevent the funding of current spending by government borrowing, it ensured that little could be done to expand the number of job vacancies that they could fill.

As we saw in Chapter 3, most of the increase in the GDP of the UK over the last quarter of the twentieth century went to the top two quintile groups of the population. This resulted in a situation where effective demand depended to a great extent on discretionary expenditure by cash-rich and time-poor households, which could easily be cut in a downturn (Froud *et al.*, 1999). Instead of the scenario envisaged by Keynes, where investment, affected by shifts in business confidence, was the most volatile component in effective demand, output and jobs have become more vulnerable to changing patterns of consumption by high income households. Discretionary consumption, like investment, depends on confidence in what the future will bring, and nowadays this can be affected by movements in house or share prices as well as by changed labour market conditions. The case for public spending to prevent a cyclical downturn in output and jobs has never been stronger, but it has been ruled out by government insistence on fiscal 'prudence', regardless of the state of the economy.

Labour market and social security policies

The social cohesion sought by liberal collectivists in the mid-twentieth century was seen to depend not only on government commitment to full employment, but also on support for collective bargaining institutions which would promote job security at the level of the individual business, and on the creation of a 'welfare state' which would provide adequate living standards for people who were excluded from employment (whether temporarily, as a result of short-term sickness or unemployment, or permanently, as a result of retirement). Collective bargaining would, it was proposed, ensure decent working conditions, for most working-age males at least, while fears about job insecurity, sickness, or poverty in old age could be allayed by entitlements to a social fund made up of contributions from employees, employers, and general taxation. Although, in practice, the achievements of the welfare state fell short of its ideals, the liberal collectivist principle of social insurance formed an integral part of the post-war social settlement in Britain and elsewhere in Europe.

As neo-liberalism became more influential in the 1980s, its proponents not only shifted the main emphasis of macro-economic policy from full employment to price stability, but they also pushed for fundamental changes in labour market regulation and in the organization of welfare. High 'natural' rates of unemployment, they suggested, were caused by labour market rigidities which hampered competitiveness by slowing the adjustment of pay and employment to changed product market conditions. To remedy this, labour law was amended to place greater restrictions on trade union activity and to relax constraints on the ability of employers to dismiss workers. At the same time, steps were taken to promote more decentralized pay bargaining and more 'flexible' work patterns (part-time and temporary employment, self-employment, and sub-contracting, for example). Such measures were often presented as 'deregulating' labour markets, but in reality what occurred was the replacement of one form of regulation by another. As Standing (1997) has stressed:

> Nobody should be misled into thinking that the rolling-back of protective and pro-collective regulations constitutes 'deregulation'. What supply-siders have promoted is pro-individualistic (anti-collective) regulations, coupled with some repressive regulations, intended to prevent people from making particular choices or to encourage, facilitate or promote other forms of behaviour.

The results, in many cases, included increased job insecurity, poorer working conditions, higher levels of long-term unemployment, and an increased incidence of low pay.

The post-war welfare system was increasingly seen by neo-liberals not only as a wasteful form of public expenditure, but as a barrier to labour market flexibility, discouraging the unemployed from taking low-paid jobs. So real benefit rates were cut, and reforms were introduced which undermined the emphasis given by collective liberalism to social solidarity between the well-off and the less well-off. Instead of a universal system of benefits, in which every citizen had a stake, the well-off were encouraged to provide for themselves through private insurance schemes, while state provision became increasingly focused on means tested benefits for the poor. Neo-liberals argued that these changes improved the cost-effectiveness of social security programmes, by targeting public expenditure on those in most need. In practice, however, standards of provision often declined, and neo-liberal policies were accompanied, as we saw in Chapter 4 by a significant widening of inequalities in living standards between rich and poor.

The Third Way in labour market and social security reform, promoted particularly by the Clinton Administration in the USA and the Blair government in the UK, keeps many of the elements of a neo-liberal approach, while introducing new programmes which aim to enhance skill levels and transfer more people from welfare into work. Entitlement to welfare payments for people of working age, it is now argued, should no longer be based solely on need (unemployment, for example, or disability or single parenthood). Instead, receipt of welfare benefits should be conditional on evidence that the claimant is actively seeking employment, for which the government will offer appropriate support (training, work experience, or childcare, for example) and financial reward (minimum wage levels and lower starting rates of income tax, for example). Welfare-to-work programmes, it is claimed, tackle the personal demoralization which results from welfare dependency by improving the employability of claimants, and they improve economic performance by both reducing public expenditure on social security and raising the productivity of the potential labour force.

It is too early to assess the effectiveness of recent welfare to work initiatives, but, without macro-economic policies to increase output and jobs, it is hard to see that measures to improve the employability of social security claimants can do much to improve their employment, except by displacing people who now have jobs. If they are applied insensitively, programmes which make benefits conditional on active job seeking can all too easily increase the number of people living in poverty. In the US state of Wisconsin, regarded by many as the model for welfare to work initiatives, the 'Wisconsin Works' programme cut numbers on welfare by 75 per cent in its first year of operation (1997/98). Yet most of the people leaving welfare either did not find jobs, or obtained jobs which were low-paid and insecure; as a result, their living standards, and those of their families decreased dramatically.

The Third Way emphasis on enhancing skill levels of benefit claimants as a way of improving their access to job opportunities is linked to a focus on skills enhancement for employees generally as a route to improved international competitiveness. It has long been recognized that there are significant positive externalities involved in training provision (see Key Concept 7.4). Where transferable skills are involved, for example, firms in a market-based system will be unwilling to make adequate training provision, for fears that 'free-riding' competitors will poach their skilled workers rather than invest in training themselves. Differences in government support for vocational training and post-school education can result in significant national differences in the proportion of the workforce possessing skill qualifications, as Table 7.4 illustrates.

The UK expansion of higher education and post-school vocational education shown in Table 7.4 reflects concerns, widely held in the 1980s, that low levels of work-based training and post-school education in the UK

Table **7.4:** Proportion of employees with recognized post-school qualifications

	Higher level		Intermediate level	
	1978–79	**1993**	**1978–79**	**1993**
UK	7%	13%	22%	31%
USA	16%	22%	11%	18%
Germany	7%	11%	59%	61%

(Source: Crafts and O'Mahony, 1999)

were a major contributor to poor economic performance. Government measures to boost provision, some had argued, would improve international competitiveness, by encouraging a shift into higher value added production. It has since become clear that whilst enhanced skills may be a necessary condition for such a shift, they are far from sufficient, and that qualifications are in any case not necessarily synonymous with skills. Indeed, there is considerable evidence that product market strategies which emphasize standardized, low value-added production act independently of labour skills (Keep and Mayhew, 1999). The implication is that measures to enhance skill levels in isolation from changes in wider systems of production and marketing are doomed to fail.

Current UK government policy appears to move beyond a narrow focus on skills supply, by promoting collaborative partnerships to encourage the creation of innovating clusters of knowledge-based economic activity (Department of Trade and Industry, 1998). Again, however, market conditions are downplayed, and it is assumed, unrealistically, that the specific conditions of Silicon Valley in California can be transplanted to all sectors of the UK economy. Under the Third Way, developed economies are invited to escape from the trap of intensified competition with low-labour-cost countries in price-sensitive markets for low-value-added products. Enhanced skill levels, it is suggested, will enable them to shift their output to more sophisticated products whose quality will justify a premium price and support higher levels of pay. Expanded output of such products will, however, generate higher levels of value added only when there is a similar expansion in market demand. What is not addressed in this Third Way discourse is where, globally, the required increases in demand for high value-added products are to come from.

Global economic management

National economic policies cannot be considered in isolation from each other. As we saw in Chapter 1, business operations are becoming increasingly international in their scope, and patterns of international exchange are becoming increasingly complex. Multinational corporations are now a feature not just of the extractive and manufacturing sectors, but increasingly of many service industries as well. International trade is no longer just an exchange of manufactured goods produced in one part of the world for raw materials provided by another. Developed countries with similar social settlements exchange similar manufactured goods between each other, as their businesses compete with each other in seeking out new export markets to facilitate cost recovery. In situations where product markets are differentiated and fixed costs of production are high, businesses need buoyant export markets to compensate for lost market shares at home, and where product life cycles are short, they need increased exports to maximize returns from the sales of existing products which are needed to finance new product development.

Alongside a rapid expansion of two-way flows of products between developed countries, businesses based in low-labour-cost countries are now using their cost advantage to export to the developed countries, while businesses based in developed countries are setting up plants in low-labour-cost countries, or out-sourcing many of their components or products there, in order to pursue cost reduction. Flows of international finance are becoming similarly complex. Manufacturing enterprises in low-labour-cost countries, for example, may use the more sophisticated financial services of the developed countries, whilst at the same time finance capital based there is looking for investment opportunities in developing markets, as fund managers seek new opportunities to diversify their portfolios and improve their returns.

Much recent debate has focussed on the significance of 'globalization'. Some argue that developments such as those outlined above have created a situation in which global market forces have transcended the power of national governments to regulate them. Others quote statistics suggesting that the world economy was more integrated a century ago than it is today, and highlight persisting differences in national conditions which still have a profound influence on business policies, even with the most international of companies. What is sometimes forgotten on either side of this debate is that international companies operate within a distinctively global political framework which both influences and is influenced by national politics, and which has, in recent years, been instrumental in promoting a neo-liberal agenda which encourages deregulation of flows of money, products and investment across national boundaries.

The international monetary system, which was established at the Bretton Woods conference in 1944, was designed to avoid the 'beggar-thy-neighbour' policies of the inter-war years, when governments tried (and failed) to solve problems arising from the world recession in isolation from each other by using exchange controls and competitive devaluations in such a way as to discourage trade, reward destabilizing financial speculation, and export unemployment from one country to another. Bretton Woods was the international expression of the principles of social solidarity which were so central to liberal collectivism; as Keynes, the leader of the British delegation to the conference, remarked in his closing speech: 'We have been learning to work together. If we can so continue, this nightmare, in which most of us here present have spent so much of our lives, will be over.'

What the delegates at Bretton Woods attempted to create was a supra-national framework which could guide national policies in such a way as to encourage trade and growth, and avoid recession. This new framework, it was hoped, would provide the appropriate international context in which domestic policies to promote full employment could be most effective. The dollar was convertible into gold at a fixed price of $35 per ounce, and other currencies were given a par value against the dollar. Monetary authorities were obliged to use their gold and foreign currency reserves to maintain the market value of their currency within one per cent of the par value. Par values could be adjusted from time to time, but only in the case of a 'fundamental disequilibrium' between imports and exports; competitive devaluations were to be avoided.

The International Monetary Fund (IMF) was formed to act as a sort of central banker for the world economy. The IMF held a pool of currencies and gold deposited by member countries, from which it could extend short-term credit to countries whose currencies were under pressure, helping them to maintain stability in their exchange rates. A sister institution, the World Bank, was given responsibility for making available long-term capital which could be used to supplement private international investment for post-war reconstruction (and later for Third-World economic development). Proposals for an International Trade Organisation which would link trade liberalization to minimum labour standards were, however ditched, following US opposition; in its place a General Agreement on Tariffs and Trade (GATT) was formed, with the more limited aim of just reducing trade barriers.

To maintain exchange rates at their par values, it was essential that national governments stuck to the new rules. Keynes proposed that the IMF should impose stiff financial penalties on countries which ran up large deficits on the current accounts of their balance of payments (see Key Concept 7.4), and also on countries which ran up large surpluses. Adjustment, he suggested, should be by surplus countries expanding their aggregate demand, rather than deficit countries contracting theirs. The US delegation rejected this, and in practice the burden of adjustment fell solely on the deficit country. The Central Bank in a deficit country might initially respond to a rise in imports by using its gold and foreign currency reserves to

---

KEY CONCEPT 7.4
Balance of payments accounts

A country's balance of payments is an accounting record of all transactions between its residents and residents of other countries in a given period, usually a year. The visible balance (sometimes called the trade balance) shows the value of exports less imports of physical goods (food, raw materials, and manufactured products or components). The current account balance brings together this, the services balance (exports less imports of banking, travel, etc.), and net income from foreign investments (interest, profits and dividends).

When there is a surplus or deficit on the current account, this must be covered by an equal and opposite deficit or surplus on transactions in external assets and liabilities (capital flows). These include foreign direct and portfolio investment, banking transactions, and government asset transactions (including the use of official reserves).

Following the principles of double entry bookkeeping, a country's overall balance of payments should always balance, as all transactions involving the exchange of one currency for another are balanced by transactions of equal value in the opposite direction (although incomplete information, particularly in relation to short-term capital flows, requires statisticians to include a 'balancing item' to cover errors and omissions).

The terms 'deficit' or 'surplus' in relation to a country's balance of payments will therefore always refer to a part of the balance of payments accounts, usually the current account balance.

buy its own currency in the foreign exchange markets, to counter downward pressure on its exchange rate. In the event of a continued drain of reserves to support the exchange rate, the authorities had to take action to reduce imports and increase inflows of private capital (by raising interest rates, for example). If the country had to approach the IMF for support as lender of last resort, then the IMF would insist on stringent adoption of such deflationary measures as a condition of the loan.

The 1997 current account balances, and their components, of the UK, USA, Germany and Japan are shown in Table 7.5.

The Bretton Woods' system never worked exactly as its founders intended. Structural differences between economies made it difficult to hold exchange rates at fixed levels, and international inequalities widened as stronger economies were free to accumulate reserves while growth in weaker economies was periodically brought to a halt as they were forced to restrain domestic demand to limit their current account deficits. The IMF and World Bank did not have sufficient financial resources to play the roles they were given at Bretton Woods, and in practice the USA, as the most powerful post-war economy, managed the system. This worked all the time that the US current account was in surplus, but in the 1960s the US economy moved into deficit. The USA was able to exploit its position as the dominant country in the international system and avoid the pressures to deflate which applied to other deficit countries, enabling it to embark on a costly war in Vietnam. Its monetary authorities became less and less able to satisfy foreign demands for dollars, however, and the dollar became increasingly vulnerable to speculative attack. In the early 1970s, the USA gave up its battle against the speculators. Convertibility of the dollar was abandoned, and its exchange rate against other currencies was devalued, bringing the fixed exchange rate regime to an end.

In the regime which followed, exchange rates were determined mainly by market forces. Monetary authorities attempted to inject some stability into a turbulent situation, by using reserves or manipulating interest rates, but on the whole the last quarter of the twentieth century was a period of sometimes dramatic changes in exchange rates. Neo-liberals argued that exchange rate flexibility would enable international prices to adjust to national differences in costs, thus maintaining purchasing power parity in the face of differential inflation rates (see Key Concept 7.5). In practice, however,

Table **7.5:** Current account balance of payments, 1997 ($ billion)

	UK	USA	Germany	Japan
Trade balance	−20	−200	+67	+83
Services balance	+19	+107	−33	−54
Interests, profits, dividends	+11	−8	−2	+56
Current account balance (as % of GDP)	+11 (+0.9)	−155 (−1.9)	−5 (−0.2)	+94 (+2.2)

(Source: National Institute Economic Review)

KEY CONCEPT 7.5
Purchasing power parity

If trading partners experience different rates of inflation, nominal exchange rates would have to change for real exchange rates to be maintained at a constant level. Thus if, over a period of ten years, the price of goods in the UK rose by 100 per cent, but the price of goods in Germany remained unchanged. Then to maintain the same rate of exchange between UK goods and German goods, the exchange rate of the £ against the D-mark would have to halve.

Purchasing power parity theory suggests that exchange rates change to maintain the purchasing power of each currency so that in periods where inflation is rising faster in the UK than in other countries, the exchange rate of the £ will fall, and vice versa. In the long term, exchange rates do tend to move in the direction that purchasing power parity theory suggests (though not necessarily to the extent that the theory would predict). Over shorter time periods, however, other influences predominate, and the activities of foreign exchange speculators are often the most significant determinant of changes in exchange rates.

---

exchange rates were more volatile than the purchasing power parity approach suggested, particularly in the short term. This reflected an increased demand for foreign exchange to acquire foreign assets, encouraged by liberalization of capital markets (see Chapter 6). Demand for foreign assets is determined more by expectations of future performance than by experience of past inflation, and this will often cause market exchange rates to diverge from the purchasing power parity rate. The divergence is intensified if financial institutions use their market power to shift funds between currencies in order to speculate against countries which the market judges to be 'weak'; monetary authorities, in such situations, have frequently been unable to counter the weight of speculative activity.

It is sometimes suggested that since the collapse of fixed exchange rates in the early 1970s, the IMF has had little role to play in the international monetary system. In fact the IMF continues to co-ordinate monetary policies on a world-wide basis, by intervening directly at times of crisis (such as during the Latin American debt crisis of the early 1980s), and by ongoing surveillance of each country's economic policies and performance, which constrains national government policy both directly and indirectly (through its effect on market sentiment). The main problem is not that there is no policy co-ordination, but that the co-ordination which is exerted is often inappropriate.

The IMF, and its sister organization the World Bank, have moved away from the collective liberalism that was espoused at Bretton Woods, and consistently promoted a neo-liberal perspective on economic development, both in their lending conditions and in their ongoing surveillance. Liberalization of foreign exchange controls and exchange rate flexibility are strongly encouraged, for example, while public sector borrowing and state enterprise are equally strongly discouraged. Removal of trade barriers is a frequent feature of both IMF and World Bank loan conditionality. This has been given the sanction of international law since 1995, when the GATT (whose reputation for endless discussion had earned it the nickname of the 'General Agreement to Talk and Talk') was replaced by the much tougher World Trade Organisation (WTO). Under WTO rules, where national governments cannot reach agreement over trade disputes, a free-trade solution can be imposed. This applies even in situations where trade barriers have been raised to support health or foreign aid policies, as for example with the European Union ban on imports of growth-hormone-injected beef, or with its support for small-scale banana growers in Africa and the Caribbean.

The assessments made by the IMF, World Bank and WTO are presented as guides to sound government, and are justified by appeals to economic theories such as the law of comparative advantage (see Key Concept 7.6).

KEY CONCEPT 7.6
Comparative advantage

Ricardo's theory of comparative advantage states that it is differences between countries in the relative production costs of commodities which determine patterns of specialization and trade, not absolute cost differences. Suppose, to take Ricardo's example, Portugal can produce a unit of wine with 80 hours of labour, and a unit of cloth in 90 hours, while the UK can produce the wine in 120 hours and the cloth in 100. Portugal has, on these figures, an absolute advantage in both wine and cloth, but the UK could not import both on a long-term basis, for it would have nothing to offer in exchange. Profitable trade can take place on the basis of the different relative costs, however. In Portugal one unit of wine exchanges for 8/9 units of cloth, while in the UK it exchanges for 12/10 units of cloth and so Portugal has a comparative advantage in wine and the UK in cloth. If Portugal produces two units of wine and the UK two units of cloth, then the same total output in the two countries can be produced in 30 less hours. Provided a mutually acceptable basis for exchanging Portuguese wine to UK cloth can be found, both countries will benefit from specialization and trade.

| | Before Specialization | | | After Specialization | | |
	Wine	Cloth	Total	Wine	Cloth	Total
Portugal	80	90	170	160		
UK	120	100	220	–	200	
Total			390			360

It is often argued that comparative advantage theory provides a justification for policies which promote free trade. The theory assumes full employment, however, limiting its applicability in the real world, and it says nothing about the distributional consequences of a move from protection to free trade, which can be considerable.

Little account is taken of the limited applicability of comparative advantage in the modern world, or of the damaging effects of dogmatic application of neo-liberal policies on social and environmental settlements. In the Latin American debt crisis of the early 1980s, for example, the IMF's main concern was to avoid defaults which might provoke a worldwide banking crisis. It used its influence to persuade the creditors to reschedule their debts, in return for which it imposed tough austerity programmes on the debtor countries. Most of the costs of adjustment fell on these debtor countries, even though the debt problem was largely caused by factors outside their control (a combination of rising interest rates and declining export markets in the 1979–82 world recession). Within the debtor countries, it was the poorest citizens who suffered most. Failure to alleviate the debt service burden was environmentally destructive, too, as it encouraged debtor countries to destroy valuable rainforest in order to speed up the development of cash crops to boost export revenues.

One of the core beliefs of the IMF and World Bank has been that a combined liberalization of trade, capital markets, and foreign exchange will provide the most effective framework to encourage economic development and enhance world prosperity. The limits of this belief were cruelly exposed in the East Asian crisis of 1997–98, when financial panic spread from one country to another, resulting in massive falls in both asset values and real output, and threatening a worldwide recession. East Asia was, in the 1980s and early 1990s, the most dynamic region of the world economy. Years of rapid economic growth, coupled with a gradual liberalization of local financial markets and a desire on the part of fund managers in the developed economies for international diversification of their investment portfolios, encouraged huge net private capital inflows into the region in the early 1990s, peaking at about $20 billion in July 1997. Only a small proportion of these inflows took the form of direct investment. Most was short-term portfolio investment and commercial bank lending, and much of this was channelled, via domestic banking systems, into speculative property development.

Many East Asian governments calculated, correctly, that their economies would be more attractive to foreign investors if risks from devaluation were minimized by pegging their currencies to the US dollar. When the exchange rate of the US dollar rose against the Japanese currency from 94 yen in 1995 to 130 yen in 1998, East Asian governments struggled to stabilize their own exchange rates against the dollar, which made their exports increasingly uncompetitive, particularly in relation to China. Current accounts started showing huge deficits, and in summer 1997 Thailand was forced to devalue its currency, which led to a massive withdrawal of foreign short-term capital, a local stock market collapse and a massive contraction in domestic output. The devaluation produced panic amongst foreign investors elsewhere in the region, leading to further withdrawals of funds and successful speculative attacks against the currencies of Malaysia, Indonesia, and the Philippines, with equally damaging effects on stock markets and output levels (see Table 5.13).

The East Asian experience, and the subsequent spread of a similar destructive cycle (capital inflow followed by currency speculation and then stock market crash and major recession) to Russia and Brazil, led many bankers, economists, Finance Ministers, and even currency speculators, who formerly advocated financial liberalization, to question neo-liberal orthodoxy and argue for a return to foreign exchange controls. The IMF, in contrast, saw the East Asian crisis as a product not of capital liberalization, but of exchange rate rigidity and ineffective financial sector regulation. The answer, it suggested, was increased 'transparency' in fiscal and monetary policy on the part of national governments, coupled with greater powers for the IMF itself to intervene to promote free capital movements and strengthen financial sector supervision. With this level of disagreement between the key players, conditions were far from favourable for the 'new Bretton Woods' now being called for by advocates of the Third Way.

Regional economic integration

In an era when the ability of national governments to assert their own political priorities has been eroded, and the power of non-elected supra-national agencies to dictate the policy agenda has been enhanced, it is perhaps not surprising there have been moves to create regional alliances which might open up an intermediate policy space which can be used for the mutual advantage of their members. Most such alliances take the form of free trade areas, confining their attention to the removal of trade barriers between member countries. NAFTA, the North American Free Trade Area, formed in 1993 by the USA, Canada and Mexico, is the most prominent of these.

The European Union (EU), which at present consists of 15 European countries, goes much further than the abolition of trade barriers. At its start in the 1950s, when only 6 countries were involved, the main aim was to set up a customs union, where not only would visible trade barriers between members be abolished, but there would be a common external tariff on imports from the outside world. In the Single Market programme of 1987–1992, the emphasis was on stimulating capital mobility within Europe by the removal of non-tariff barriers (physical, fiscal, and technical) to internal trade. In the 1990s, there was a new shift towards Economic and Monetary Union (EMU), to remove remaining barriers to capital mobility resulting from exchange rate variability. In 1999, 11 of the 15 member countries joined a single currency, the Euro, and allowed their monetary policies to be co-ordinated by a single European Central Bank (ECB). Ultimately, the aim of many EU members is greater political integration, organized on federal lines.

The development of regional integration projects like the EU results, over time, both in the expansion of member countries' foreign trade, and in the diversion of trade from non-member countries to member countries. The extent of this trade-diversion effect for the UK, since it joined in 1973, is shown in Table 7.6. The potential advantages for member countries of economic and monetary integration depend not just on trade effects or the encouragement given to the creation of integrated European businesses, but also on the development of a large, relatively self-sufficient economy, similar

Table **7.6:** Area composition of UK trade 1973–97 (% total)

	Exports			Imports		
	1973	**1992**	**1997**	**1973**	**1992**	**1997**
EC	36	56	56	36	52	54
Other developed economies	40	24	24	39	32	29
Oil exporting countries	6	6	6	9	2	2
Rest of the World	18	14	14	16	14	15
Total	100	100	100	100	100	100

(Source: UK Annual Abstract of Statistics, 'Red Book')

in both size and economic power to that of the USA. For many member countries, too, EMU seemed to offer, for the first time in their recent histories, a possibility of macro-economic policies which are oriented more to their domestic needs than to exchange rates and the balance of payments. Their ability to take advantage in practice of this theoretical possibility was, however, constrained by the operational structure of EMU, which reflected the circumstances of its formation.

Under the 1992 Treaty on European Union, the ECB was to be independent of political influence, and to have price stability as its prime objective. Countries needed to satisfy certain convergence criteria in order to be eligible for membership of EMU. These criteria were drawn along conventionally neo-liberal lines, which stressed the importance of low inflation and strict limits on the size of government budget deficits. Most EU countries had to drastically reduce the size of their government budget deficits in order to satisfy the convergence criteria, placing severe constraints on the adoption of Keynesian demand management policies to tackle unemployment rates which were, by now, significantly higher than in the USA or Japan. Inflation generally fell, but in many cases unemployment rates increased still further, at a time when unemployment in the USA was falling (see Table 7.7). This situation is likely to continue with the evolution of EMU if member governments adhere to the Stability and Growth Pact they agreed in 1997. One requirement of the Pact is that member governments exercise fiscal

Table **7.7:** Unemployment and inflation rates 1993–98

% unemployment	1993	1994	1995	1996	1997	1998
Germany	7.9	8.4	8.2	8.9	10.0	4.2
France	11.7	12.3	11.7	12.4	12.4	10.9
Italy	10.3	11.4	11.9	12.0	12.1	12.2
UK	10.5	9.6	8.7	8.2	7.0	4.7
USA	6.9	6.1	5.6	5.4	4.9	4.5
Japan	2.5	2.9	3.1	3.4	3.4	4.5

Table **7.7:** Unemployment and inflation rates, 1993–98 (*continued*)

Annual Inflation	1993	1994	1995	1996	1997	1998
Germany	4.5	2.7	1.8	1.5	1.8	0.9
France	2.1	1.7	1.7	2.0	1.2	0.7
Italy	4.2	3.9	5.4	3.8	1.8	1.7
UK	1.6	2.5	3.4	2.4	3.1	2.6
USA	3.0	2.6	2.8	2.9	2.3	1.6
Japan	1.2	0.7	−0.1	0.1	1.7	0.4

Note: Germany, France and Italy were the three major founders of the Euro-zone in 1999. The UK met the convergence criteria, but decided not to join at this stage, partly because the UK business cycle was out of phase with that in other EU countries.
(Source: OECD Economic Outlook)

restraint to avoid any government budget deficits in the medium term (i.e. over the course of a business cycle). This allows for counter-cyclical fiscal policies, but precludes any attempt at demand management to alleviate longer-term unemployment.

Case study: Retirement pensions

> The European pensions market is undergoing a period of rapid change. The financial pressures of an aging population combined with governments' need to cut spiraling welfare budgets are the chief driving forces fuelling the trend towards greater private pension provision.
>
> *(Financial Times, 1998: The Future for European Pensions)*

Within Europe it is argued that pensions provision should be increasingly privatized because state schemes are becoming too costly to maintain as the population in retirement expands. Maintaining incomes in retirement is not just a political debate but it is an economic and social issue. Those who have retired are generally living longer and they are active consumers of food, durable goods and services and so sustain business activity and active employment for those in non-retired households. The political issue raised by the privatization of pensions relates to the degree to which it is politically acceptable to tax those in employment to maintain incomes of those in retirement. In the UK a flat-rate (or earnings-related in some cases) state pension is provided to underwrite the incomes of those in retirement. It has been argued that this redistribution of income from those economically active to those in retirement is necessary because a minimum social welfare floor is required for those in retirement.

On average between one-fifth and one-quarter of the population in Europe are dependent rather than economically active (that is the population aged 65+ as a proportion of the population aged 15–64 see Table 7.8). The financial impact on the state of a collectively funded system not only depends upon the demographics in

Table **7.8:** Dependency ratio in Europe

Country	Population mill	Dependency Ratio %
Belgium	10.2	24.2
Denmark	5.3	22.4
Finland	5.1	20.9
France	58	22.7
Germany	82	21.7
Italy	57.4	23.2
Netherlands	15.6	18.8
Norway	4.4	25
Portugal	9.9	22.4
Spain	39.3	23.5
Sweden	8.9	28.6
Switzerland	7.1	22.4
UK	59	24.6

(Source: William M Mercer Company)

terms of the dependent population but the terms and conditions on which the state provides a pension to its citizens on retirement.

Some state schemes are more generous than others with high replacement ratios that is the ratio of average per head pension income to average per head income in work. The average Italian worker having put in 40 years of full-time work would expect to receive up to 80 per cent of their last 5 years' average income in work index linked to prices. In Germany after 40 years of contribution for a full pension the replacement rate (earnings in retirement as a per cent of those in work) could be as much as 60 per cent. The actual rate shown in Table 7.9 is 52 per cent.

The UK, by way of contrast, has a maximum theoretical replacement rate in the state scheme of 20 per cent of career income but is actually averaging just 18 per cent, which is the lowest replacement rate in Europe. Compare this replacement rate with that of France at 60 per cent, some three times higher. Maintaining the incomes of those households in retirement has always been justified on the basis that it makes positive economic sense because high incomes maintain a positive multiplier effect through expenditure in household goods and services.

The question that increasingly arises within Europe is 'to what extent should the incomes of those in retirement be underwritten by the state through a tax on those in work?'

The greatest problems arise in countries like France, Germany and Italy (as one might expect given the replacement rates) where replacement rates are high and have been the hallmark of the post-war social settlement of these countries. In Italy and France some minor adjustments have been undertaken to cut state pension provisions but social resistance to change is high. According to the FT Pension Survey 'Germany also has a serious problem. The state scheme is in deficit and more than half of the liabilities of company pension schemes are not backed by assets.'

Table **7.9:** Government pension schemes

Country	Period for Full Pension Years	Actual Average Replacement rate %	Indexation
USA	35	39	Prices
Japan	40	20	Net wages
Germany	40	52	Net Wages
France	38	60	Prices/Gross Wages
Italy	40	54	Prices
UK	50	18	Prices
Canada	40	29	Prices
Sweden	30	39	Prices

(Source: IMF Occasional Paper No 147 Dec. 1996 'Aging Populations and Public Pension Schemes')

In Eastern European countries the retreat of the state from pensions provision has been swift both because the state can no longer underwrite the schemes and privatized business could not take the burden. These countries have undertaken reforms similar to those of the Chile that of moving towards private individually funded schemes.

Generally it is argued that in order to underwrite the pensions social settlement the state will need to fund pensions through extra borrowing as the support ratio falls. Consider the case of Japan, a country not that generous in terms of its pensions replacement rate. Here demographic adjustments are such that without tax increases or an alteration in the conditions of state provision government debt as a per cent of GDP is expected to rise to 140 per cent by 2040 from the 1994 position of roughly 40 per cent. In the UK, the least generous in terms of maximum replacement rate, the cost of state pension provision represents 4.5 per cent of national GDP compared to 13.9 per cent in Italy. The UK funded system is not expected to strain government finances (see Figure 7.4).

Reform of pensions will take the form of shifting the burden from the state to the individual. The state, it is argued, should encourage saving for old age and provide incentives. For example in the UK Trust Law is used to promote occupational pension schemes and this is backed up with tax incentives and tax relief. More recently New

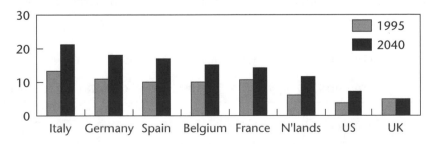

Figure **7.4:** Pensions as a percentage of GDP
(Source: Goldman Sachs (1997) *The Global Pension Time Bomb and its Capital Market Impact*)

Labour has announced its Individual Savings Accounts (ISAs) to encourage individuals to save for retirement. Occupation pre-funded pension schemes in the UK are segregated into those that are 'defined benefit' (also known as final salary) and 'defined contribution' (also known as money purchase). On retirement the former is linked to the employee's final salary up to a maximum of two-thirds and the latter is used to fund the purchase of an investment annuity.

Even though UK occupational pension schemes have been described as one of this century's great success stories, with assets worth £600 billion, it is noteworthy that some 60 per cent of the low-income retired UK households receive little income from their occupational pension (see Table 7.10).

Most commentators agree that if tax increases are not acceptable to those in work and governments find it politically difficult to raise funds to cover the cost of pension provision, the outcome seems to be the adoption of private individually funded schemes. Currently in Europe (the EU) the assets of funded pensions were ECU 1,074 and the coverage rate was 22.6 per cent of the retired population. To increase coverage to 30 per cent and 70 per cent would require a 5- and 16-fold increase in the value of assets under management. It is also generally argued that these assets would need to be predominantly held in securities/equity funding in order to produce the necessary long-term return on funds. In the US the national government provision is substantially invested in US Treasuries and is intended to pre-fund the US pension system. Given the demographic adjustments the fund could be insolvent by 2030 (HSBC Securities 1998). The alternative, it is argued, is for rises in taxes accounting for one-quarter of payroll in the US or privatization or a combination of the two. In Japan the public schemes are under stress from the fact that (as we have already noted) by 2025 over 25 per cent of the population will be over 65 and the present system does not have enough funds to meet current liabilities. In addition corporate schemes are also facing funding problems with many large corporate pension funds recording shortfalls of up to 40 per cent and unable (given the equity and bond market condition) to fund the 5.5 per cent annual return set by regulatory authorities.

The move from state to private pensions shifts the burden on to the individual. It is also the case that most of the funding requirement for underwriting these pensions will need to come from domestic and global securities. Goldman Sachs calculate that the extra demand for pension fund assets will be split as shown in Figure 7.5.

On the demand side demographics ageing population(s) will combine with the politics of neo-liberal welfare economics to increase the requirement for pension fund assets. On the supply side, this demand will need to be met with an increased supply of securities that is itself dependent upon the expansion of the corporate sector and

Table **7.10:** Source of income for UK retired households, 1995

£ per annum	Quintile 1	Quintile 2	Quintile 3	Quintile 4	Quintile 5
Occupational and Private					
Pension Income	385	928	1,388	3,340	9,647
Investment Income	304	328	408	1,015	4,311

(Source: UK Family Expenditure Survey)

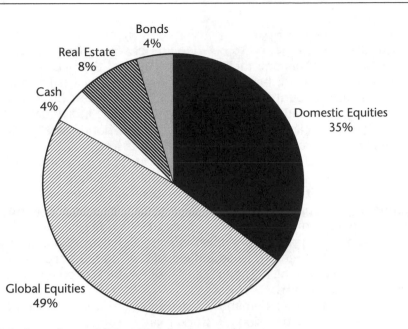

Figure **7.5:** Extra demand for pension fund assets, by category

stability of financial markets. Risk is shifted from the state to the individual where the problem of capital market instability is a real one. The individual may find their investment for retirement subject to stock market fluctuations and variable annuity interest rates.

These risks obviously depend firstly on the assets structure of pension funds (see Table 7.11).

We can already observe that in the US and UK, where private pension fund management is already well developed, equity makes up a much larger proportion of total assets held. The UK case is also rather exceptional in that some three-quarters of assets are held in equities.

Table **7.11:** Asset structure of pension funds

Country	Equity	Fixed Income	Real Estate	Other	Total Assets
UK	77.6	13.9	4.8	3.7	100
Germany	7.7	74.1	6.5	11.7	100
France	13.6	38.0	8.1	40.3	100
Italy	7.7	63.0	21.0	8.3	100
Spain	5.0	76.0	1.0	18.0	100
Japan	36.0	61.8	0.9	1.3	100
USA	54.7	29.5	10.5	5.3	100

(Source: Goldman Sachs, HSBC)

By way of contrast the major EU partner pension-fund managers prefer to locate assets in bonds with the USA positioned somewhere in between, probably reflecting the fact that many individuals manage their own portfolio and the bias is towards a fixed-return financial asset as a risk hedge. In Japan the preference is for domestic bonds and bonds generally account for up to 61.8 per cent of assets holdings.

In either case the risk of fluctuations in return is a real one. The individual is always warned that the stock market 'can go up as well as down' and bond market rates can go up or down affecting the income from a pension-fund asset.

Shifts in government policy away from state provision of pensions towards the private provision of income in retirement is one that will generally affect the social settlements of Europe. The liberal-economic framework that underpins European political and economic development is consistent with this movement. A reasonable pension income in retirement is important because this feeds through into consumption expenditure and positive multiplier effects. A shift from a collectivized state provision of income in retirement to an individualized funded pension scheme transfers risk and uncertainty into the household and thus will impact on consumption and expenditure levels and patterns.

On the supply side the increased demand for pension fund assets and especially equity funds further fuels the expansion of stock market capital gains. We have discussed the implications of the disconnection between stock market expectations and business behaviour in Chapters 5 and 6. It is likely that we will see further intensified restructuring in the corporate sector as firms try to deliver the required return on investment and demands for increased shareholder value from pension fund managers. The impact of this on the corporate sector is uncertain but likely to involve adjustments in the composition of employment and income from employment that are adverse.

Our case study on pensions serves to illustrate the impact of neo-liberal free market economics on income provision in retirement. It renounces the Keynesian collectivist position that was argued on the basis of beneficial roundabout implications. Shifting the burden of pension-fund provision from the state to individual has roundabout implications for the retired household as well as the corporate sector. These are likely to be negative in economies that suffer from slow and cyclical growth patterns and have a highly skewed distribution of income within the household population.

References

Crafts, N. and O'Mahony, M. (1999) 'Britain's productivity performance', *New Economy*, **6** (1), pp. 3–16.

Cutler, T., Williams, K. and Williams, J. (1986) *Keynes, Beveridge and Beyond*, London: Routledge.

Department of Trade & Industry (1998) *Our Competitive Future: Building the Knowledge Driven Economy*, London: Stationery Office.

Friedman, M. (1977) 'Inflation and Unemployment', *Journal of Political Economy*, **83** (3).

Froud, J., Haslam, C., Johal, S., Shaoul, J. and Williams, K. (1996) 'Stakeholder Economy?: from utility privatisation to New Labour', *Capital and Class*, **60**, pp. 119–134.

Froud, J., Haslam, C., Johal, S., Leaver, A., Williams, J. and Williams, K. (1999) 'The Third Way and the Jammed Economy', *Capital and Class*, **67**, pp. 155–165.

HSBC Securities (1998) 'UK Fund Management: Major Themes', London: HSBC.

Keep, E. and Mayhew, K. (1999) 'The assessment: Knowledge, skills and competitiveness', *Oxford Review of Economic Policy*, Vol. 15, pp. 1–15.

Lall, S. (1996) *Learning from the Asian Tigers: Studies in Technology and Industrial Policy*, Basingstoke: Macmillan.

Maddison, D., Pearce, D., Johansson, O., Calthrop, E., Litman, T. and Verhoef, E. (1996) *The True Costs of Road Transport*, London: Earthscan.

Neale, A. (1995) 'How green are congestion charges?: economic instruments and sustainable transport', *International Journal of Urban and Regional Research*, **19** (3), pp. 447–455.

Ormerod, P. (1994) 'On Inflation and Unemployment', in J. Michie and J. Grieve Smith (eds.) *Unemployment in Europe*, London: Academic Press.

Standing, G. (1997) 'Globalisation, labour flexibility and insecurity: the era of market regulation', *European Journal of Industrial Relations*, **3** (1), pp. 7–37.

Essential reading

Froud, J., Haslam, C., Johal, S., Leaver, A., Williams, J. and Williams, K. (1999) 'The Third Way and the Jammed Economy', *Capital and Class*, **67**, pp. 155–165.

Neale, A. (1995) 'How green are congestion charges?: economic instruments and sustainable transport', *International Journal of Urban and Regional Research*, **19** (3), pp. 447–455.

CHAPTER 8

The natural
environment

In this chapter we observe that economic activity can be sustained over time only if its use of natural resources is limited to the rate at which they can be regenerated. This can be seen most clearly in relation to the harvesting of renewable natural resources, as in forestry or fishing.

Consequently it is important to encourage business policy and strategies towards dematerialization. This is a deliberate reduction in material intensity per unit of GDP. This normally lessens the energy required to manufacture and use products. It would involve the substitution of lighter for heavier materials in existing products (for example increased use of aluminium and plastics instead of steel in car design); miniaturization of products (for example the development of laptop computers capable of doing similar work to the personal computers of a decade earlier); the direct replacement of products by services (for example the development of voicemail as a substitute for telephone answering machines); the structural shift at a macro level from manufacturing to services (see Chapter 3).

It should be noted that, as defined, dematerialization does not necessarily imply a decline in materials consumption. If GDP is rising at a faster rate than materials input per unit of GDP is falling, then total materials consumption will continue to rise. It is argued by many that the introduction of tough environmental legislation will increase costs and reduce price competitiveness on the internal market place. Firms in relatively deregulated regions would be at an advantage against firms that need to invest heavily in clean technology or product development.

Michael Porter has argued, against conventional business wisdom, that tough environmental regulation can boost international competitiveness, by encouraging resource-saving or product-enhancing innovation, and creating early-mover advantages in international markets. To foster the sort of innovation which would deliver increased competitiveness as well as improved environmental quality, he suggests, regulation would need to focus on outcomes rather than technologies, leaving it to businesses to determine how best to achieve continuous improvement in environmental quality.

Introduction

We turn now to business strategies in relation to the natural environment. This is an aspect of business analysis which has received little attention until recently, but which is becoming increasingly significant, for corporate policy as well as for national and international regulation.

All economic activity relies on the natural environment, both as the supplier of its raw materials and as the dumpsite for its waste. At an early stage of economic development, skills in the wise use of natural resources were central to a community's ability to sustain itself over time. Industrialization brought new opportunities for expanding the scope of production and consumption, but also new environmental threats, including air pollution, water contamination, and deforestation. Often, these threats were tolerated as a necessary price that had to be paid for economic progress, but as industrial systems developed, they became less acceptable.

Over time, local communities become less resigned to poor air and water quality, and more effective in pressing for improvements. As global industrial activity expands, global environmental problems begin to emerge. These include global warming (produced largely by the 'greenhouse effect' of burning fossil fuels such as coal and oil) and depletion of the ozone layer (resulting from release into the stratosphere of CFCs, chemical products which were widely used in the late twentieth century as inexpensive aerosol sprays, coolants, insulating materials, and solvents).

Local pollution can sometimes be ignored, because only a limited number of people are affected by it, but there is no escape from global environmental problems. Everyone is affected by the rising sea levels and climate change that result from global warming, and by the increased risk of skin cancer associated with stratospheric ozone depletion. Companies may resist taking responsibility for such issues, but they face international political pressure which can only increase as the problems intensify.

Sustainability

Economic activity can be sustained over time only if its use of natural resources is limited to the rate at which they can be regenerated. This can be seen most clearly in the relation to the harvesting of renewable natural resources, as in forestry or fishing. If a fishing community catches fish at a faster rate than new fish are spawned, then stocks will decline, reducing the size of catches in years to come. Advances in fishing technology, such as using electronics to locate shoals and dragnets to harvest them, can increase catches in the medium term, but in the longer term they just accelerate the rate at which stocks are depleted, ending, if unchecked, in a situation where there are no more fish to catch (as occurred in 1992 with Newfoundland cod in the North East Atlantic). In the case of deforestation, there are damaging effects not only on future timber production, but also on local climate, soil erosion and flooding, as well as on global climate (forest growth takes excess carbon dioxide from the atmosphere and stores it as wood, reducing global warming).

In agriculture, production methods which can be sustained over many decades may become unsustainable in the longer term. Early in the second millennium BC, for example, Bronze-Age farmers in Dorset on the south coast of England broke with Neolithic custom to descend from the open chalk uplands and settle in the dense woodland of the Poole Basin. They and their descendants cleared large areas of trees, and ploughed the sandy soils to grow crops and graze animals. As more and more of the tree cover was removed, the rains washed away the nutrients, and the soil became acidified. Heather, gorse, and bracken flourished, and agriculture became increasingly difficult to sustain. By the middle of the first millennium BC, much of the area was depopulated, and all that remained of the Bronze-Age farming communities were their burial mounds. Subsequently this heathland landscape – the 'Egdon Heath' of Hardy's novels – became an excellent habitat for birds and reptiles, but it was viewed by the human populations of the surrounding areas as a wasteland, useful only as rough grazing and a source of fuel, and its few remaining inhabitants were labelled as 'heathen'.

In the late twentieth century, new farming methods, based on the application of chemical inputs, the development of high-yielding varieties and, most recently, the genetic modification of crops, have resulted in massive increases in agricultural productivity. Again, however, there are environmental costs, which in the long term have negative impacts on production as well as on biodiversity. Widespread pesticide use, for example, initially increased yields by killing pests and reducing the damage to crops they caused. Only those pests which had a genetic resistance to the pesticides survived, and as they reproduced, crop damage increased once more. The response of the agro-chemical industry was to encourage more frequent spraying, which involved higher costs to farmers, health problems for farm workers, contamination of drinking water supplies, accumulation of pesticide residues in the food chain, and destruction of the pests' natural predators. The pest population continued to evolve greater resistance to pesticides, with the end result that, half a century after the introduction of modern pesticides, the proportion of crops which are lost to insects had not changed. Now, crops like soya and oilseed rape are being genetically modified to make them resistant to herbicides, with the danger that the new genes will migrate to wild relatives of these crops, risking the creation of new 'superweeds' which may become capable of resisting natural controls.

Within the manufacturing industry, increased skill in the capture and application of fossil energy has been critical for the rises in productivity and incomes brought about by industrialization. High rates of consumption of fossil fuels pose significant sustainability issues for the sector. There are two problems here. First, there is resource availability. Geologically, new supplies are being formed at such a slow rate that, from a human perspective, fossil fuels can be regarded as a non-renewable resource. Known global coal reserves would, at current consumption rates, last beyond the next century, but recoverable supplies of natural gas might become exhausted sometime in the second half of that century (i.e. C2100). In the case of oil, although new sources are being discovered all the time (around the Caspian Sea and in Scotland's 'Atlantic Frontier', for example), most industry analysts predict that global supplies will start to decline sometime in the first quarter of the new century.

The second and more immediate problem with fossil fuels relates to pollution, and to the greenhouse gases that are produced when they are burnt (especially carbon dioxide). The problem is most severe in the case of coal, the most abundant resource. Concerns about global warming led governments at the 1997 Kyoto summit to agree legally-binding reductions in greenhouse gas emissions by industrialized countries of about 10 per cent between 2000 and 2010. These target reductions are likely to be intensified as the century progresses, requiring either a reduction in economic activity or a combination of:

(i)   dramatic improvements in energy efficiency;
(ii) a shift from coal to natural gas and renewable energy sources (nuclear power poses its own sustainability problems in terms of the storage of radioactive waste);
(iii) a significant dematerialization of economic output (see Key Concept 8.1); and
(iv) design improvements which extend the life or recyclability of products.

Service industries generally have less of a direct environmental impact than other sectors, but even here, business strategies can have important implications for sustainability. Many service businesses make extensive use of material products, and their purchasing policies often pay little regard to environmental considerations. In large firms, for example, IT hardware is frequently scrapped when new equipment with a slightly enhanced technical

---

KEY CONCEPT 8.1
Dematerialization

Dematerialization is a reduction in material intensity per unit of GDP. This normally lessens the energy required to manufacture and use products. Dematerialization has four main sources:

1. Substitution of lighter for heavier materials in existing products (e.g. increased use of aluminium and plastics instead of steel in car design).
2. Miniaturization of products (e.g. the development of laptop computers capable of doing similar work to the personal computers of a decade earlier).
3. Direct replacement of products by services (e.g. the development of voicemail as a substitute for telephone answering machines).
4. The structural shift at a macro level from manufacturing to services (see Chapter 3).

It should be noted that, as defined, dematerialization does not necessarily imply a decline in materials consumption. If GDP is rising at a faster rate than materials input per unit of GDP is falling, then total materials consumption will continue to rise.

specification becomes available. Many service providers are also responsible for significant road transport impacts, which are not only a major source of local air pollution, but are also becoming the main contributor to global warming in developed economies. Table 8.1 shows the situation with regard to emissions of carbon dioxide (the main greenhouse gas) in the UK. Here, overall emissions have declined since 1970 as a result of de-industrialization and a shift in power generation from coal to gas, but emissions from road transport doubled between 1970 and 1976, as improvements in fuel efficiency were swamped by the increase in road traffic.

Retailers opening new out-of-town shopping facilities, for example, play a major role in encouraging greater car dependence by their customers. Even teleworking (the use of IT and telecommunications to work from home), whose 'green' credentials have been widely proclaimed in recent years, can have damaging effects on sustainability. In the short term, by cutting the need to travel to work, it has a positive environmental impact. In the longer term, however, there is evidence that it encourages employees to move out to rural areas, where their families become more dependent on long car journeys for their shopping, schooling, and leisure activities.

Sustainable development

Sustainability issues first appeared on the business agenda in the late 1980s, with the popularization of the concept of sustainable development (see Key Concept 8.2). In a comparatively short space of time, this has been adopted as a target objective by environmental groups, business corporations, national governments and international agencies alike. Where in the 1970s environmental groups and business organizations were united only in their belief that environmental protection was incompatible with economic growth, the new discourse of sustainable development has encouraged a measure of shared interest in the evolution of innovative business solutions to environmental problems.

A practical outcome of adopting sustainable development as a policy objective has been an emerging understanding that it is better, both

Table **8.1:** Carbon dioxide emissions by source, UK (million tonnes of carbon)

	1970	1980	1990	1996
Industrial Combustion	66	43	37	38
Power Stations	57	58	54	43
Commercial & Public Services	9	9	8	11
Domestic	26	23	22	25
Road Transport	16	21	30	31
Other	10	11	8	6
Total	184	165	159	154

(Source: UK Digest of Environmental Statistics)

KEY CONCEPT 8.2
Sustainable development

There are many different definitions of sustainable development. The most widely quoted is that of the 1987 Brundtland Report: 'development which meets the needs of the present without compromising the ability of future generations to meet their own needs' (World Commission on Environment and Development, 1987). To maximize political support, this definition is deliberately vague about what constitutes 'needs', and how many 'future generations' should be considered. The natural environment is valued not for itself, but in terms of its ability to meet human needs. The apparently contradictory requirements of sustainability and development are bridged by an appeal to social justice, coupling a greater priority for meeting the present needs of the world's poor with a greater emphasis on inter-generational equity. An implication of the latter is that in situations where there is significant depletion or regeneration of natural capital, investment appraisal techniques which discount future values may be inappropriate (see Table 6.1 exhibit and calculation).

ecologically and economically, to anticipate environmental problems and prevent them at source, than to wait for disasters to occur and then try to clean up after them. Attempts to operationalize more precisely what sustainable development might mean in practice have not been particularly successful. A major issue is that most ecosystems are too complex for us to be able to predict what changes are sustainable over long periods of time, so that we will only know what has been sustainable after the event. Ambiguities in definition, too, allow different organizations to interpret sustainable development in different ways. Business interest, for example, has concentrated much more on pollution prevention and energy saving (where there may be immediate financial returns) than on product life extension or poverty reduction.

The life cycle approach

One practical technique which has been helpful in focusing business attention on the longer-term environmental consequences of its operations is Life Cycle Assessment, or LCA (see Key Concept 8.3). LCA was first developed by Coca-Cola in 1970 to evaluate the resource and pollution implications of different types of soft drink container. Since then it has been widely used as a basis for improving environmental performance.

Packaging is one of the main areas in which LCA has been applied by companies. For many products some packaging is needed for protection from damage, particularly during transit, but excessive packaging can be extremely wasteful in its use of resources and at the disposal stage. In 1990, Procter & Gamble, the detergent manufacturer, used LCA to investigate alternative

---

KEY CONCEPT 8.3
Life cycle assessment (LCA)

LCA (sometimes known as 'cradle-to-grave analysis') starts by identifying physical resources used and wastes generated at each stage in the life cycle of a product – raw material extraction, processing, transport and distribution, use and disposal or recycling/ reuse. An analysis is then made of the negative and positive impacts on the environment at each stage of the product's life cycle. Finally, possibilities for improving environmental performance are identified. These might involve seeking alternative supply sources, redesigning the product, process or packaging, or taking back products at the end of their life and reusing components or materials.

Interpreting LCA results is not always straightforward, and the opportunities to make selective use of LCA data to support spurious 'green' claims for products are considerable. The cost of tracking every element of a complex product would be prohibitively expensive, so boundaries have to be set – by selecting particular stages of the life cycle for detailed analysis, for example, or using industry average data (which may disguise large inter-plant differences in actual environmental performance). Impacts may vary according to where the product is consumed. Often, too, solution A may be better than solution B at one aspect of environmental performance, but worse at another – if opinions differ as to how these aspects should be weighted, it may prove impossible to judge which solution offers the best environmental performance overall.

---

packages to the large plastic bottles in which it supplied its fabric conditioner. They found that if they produced a more concentrated product and supplied it in small refill pouches made from much lighter plastic, they could cut both energy demand and waste generated by around 80 per cent over the life cycle as a whole. It was clear that improved environmental performance would be accompanied by significant cost savings. Procter & Gamble decided to pass these on as price reductions to consumers, which encouraged rapid market take-up, despite some initial consumer resistance to having to transfer the product from one container to another. The refill concept was extended to liquid detergents, and copied by other mass-market producers. Within three years, 80–90 per cent of liquid detergent sales were of refill packs rather than new bottles.

More radical packaging solutions, like consumers refilling their bottles from a container at their local shop, which would have produced still higher environmental performance, were not considered. Within the limited scope of the exercise, however, using LCA identified an improvement which offered clear advantages along every major dimension of environmental impact – energy use, air emissions, water emissions and solid waste. Interpretation of LCA data has been much less straightforward in the case of detergent products themselves, however. This is illustrated by recent controversies about the use of phosphates as a 'builder' to maintain the pH (alkalinity) of wash water at a level which maximizes the ability of other ingredients to remove dirt and stains. When phosphates are drained into the water system, they contribute to eutrophication, algal growth which consumes oxygen and in extreme cases cause aquatic life to die (as at Lake Erie, on the US/Canadian border, in the 1960s). Concerns about eutrophication of rivers and lakes has led some countries to ban or restrict phosphates in detergents.

Landbank, the environmental consultancy, compared the life cycle environmental impacts of phosphate in relation to zeolite, the main alternative builder. A panel of scientific experts was asked to give weights to different environmental impacts, to allow aggregation. The main impact, for each builder, was judged to be not at the disposal stage, but during the extraction, processing and transport of the raw materials. Discharges of gypsum into the Atlantic Ocean from the Moroccan plant which processed the raw phosphate were found to cause extensive damage, for example, while the opencast mining of bauxite (from which zeolite is manufactured) caused similar damage in Australia; in each case, large quantities of carbon dioxide were emitted as energy was expended to process the raw materials and transport them to the detergent manufacturers. Comparing equal amounts of detergent, phosphate builders were judged to be almost 40 per cent more damaging over the life cycle than zeolite. It was assumed, however, that consumers use more zeolite-built than phosphate-built detergent per wash, to compensate for inferior wash performance in hard water areas, rendering the overall difference in environmental impact insignificant (see Table 8.2).

As with all LCA studies, the conclusion that phosphate-based detergents are no more environmentally damaging than zeolite-based alternatives involves a considerable element of subjective evaluation. In particular, the assumption that consumers would use 43 per cent more zeolite-built detergent than phosphate-built was not based on any research into consumer behaviour. Many independent commentators suspected that the report's scope, data and conclusions were biased to favour the product of its sponsor, Albright & Wilson (the world's leading phosphate producer). These suspicions were heightened when a follow-up study concluded that installing advanced wastewater treatment systems would halt eutrophication more effectively than banning phosphate detergents, as detergents accounted for only about 20 per cent of the total phosphates passing through sewage works. This study was commissioned by Kemira, the Finnish chemicals business which manufactures phosphates and supplies wastewater treatment systems.

It is not just manufacturers who make use of a life cycle approach. B&Q, the leading UK DIY retailer, has an environmental policy which aims to

Table **8.2:** Life cycle impact scores* of alternative detergent builders

	Equal amount basis	Equal performance basis**
Phosphate based	107	107
Zeolite based	77	110

*based on median weights given to various pollutants by an expert panel
**assumes 1 kg of zeolite needed to give same wash quality as 0.7 kg of phosphate
(Source: Landbank Environmental Research and Consultancy (The Phosphate Report, 1994))

improve the environmental performance of all the products it stocks as well as of its own retailing operations. It has modified the life cycle concept to identify, for wood products and paints in particular, what environmental improvements it can promote. Using a Supplier Environmental Audit to improve environmental performance up the supply chain has been the key here. In 1992–3, all B&Q suppliers were asked questions to elicit their awareness, policies and action in relation to different environmental issues. Supplier responses were rated on a scale from A ('... a systematic, mature, and well-documented environmental programme is in place. Suppliers have developed innovative responses to environmental issues.') to E ('... suppliers expose B&Q to severe liability') and F (failure to provide requested information). In 1994, B&Q contacted the 65 per cent of its suppliers who were rated at grade D or below, requiring them to achieve at least grade C ('... have identified key issues ... and have a framework policy in place which commits the company to achieving broad objectives') by the end of the year. Ten companies were delisted for failing to achieve this target.

Public concern about the destruction of tropical rainforests led B&Q in 1990 to discuss with environmental groups and the timber trade ways of ensuring that the products it sold were sourced from well-managed forests. This coincided with efforts by the World Wide Fund for Nature (WWF) to work with timber traders and retailers to improve forest management on a global basis, with the aim of protecting biodiversity, and to set up an independent certification scheme, the Forest Stewardship Council (FSC). WWF found that retailers like B&Q were more responsive than producers to its concerns about deforestation, and it worked to mobilize their buying power to bring about change. For B&Q, committed as it was to the principle of Supplier Environmental Audit, the development of independent certification by the FSC was seen as helpful both in reducing the burden on the business of having to scrutinize timber sources in 50 different countries and in calming consumer worries about spurious green claims for timber products. In 1995, B&Q became the first retailer in the world to set a target that all of its timber supplies should have FSC certification before the end of 1999.

Eco-innovation

Many of the businesses that have made extensive use of LCA have gone on to promote eco-efficiency (see Key Concept 8.4). Substantial improvements in eco-efficiency can be brought about by adopting fairly simple modifications to existing products and processes, but already some managers are suggesting that business needs to be more pro-active in meeting the environmental challenges of the twenty-first century while preserving company profitability. Claude Fussler, a vice president of Dow Europe, is a prime example; his text exhorts business leaders to innovate with 'outstanding implementation of radical ideas which will meet future needs' (Fussler, 1996). These 'radical ideas' could result in significant improvements to existing products ('hypercars' capable of doing several hundred miles per gallon, for example)

KEY CONCEPT 8.4
Eco-efficiency

The term eco-efficiency is used by the World Business Council on Sustainable Development (WBCSD) to describe 'the delivery of competitively priced goods and services that satisfy human needs and bring quality of life, while progressively reducing ecological impacts and resource intensity throughout the life-cycle, to a level in line with the earth's carrying capacity' (Schmidheiny, 1992). This concept (often abbreviated to 'producing more with less') is used to promote win-win solutions that can produce more value added for business while reducing its environmental impact. Widespread application of current best practice could, it has been suggested, bring about a fourfold increase in resource productivity, allowing a doubling of material living standards while halving resource use (von Weiczsäcker *et al.*, 1997).

The WBSCD, and the 120 international companies which comprise its membership, see eco-efficiency as the main contribution that business can make to sustainable development. Eco-efficiency has the advantage of being easily incorporated into existing corporate strategies; this can, however, have the effect of encouraging businesses to over-simplify the environmental problems they face, and downplay the social dimensions of sustainable development.

---

or replacement products/services that meet the same need with greater eco-efficiency (more user-friendly public transport systems, for example, or Internet shopping/home delivery services to reduce the need to travel).

Much of the emphasis in case histories of eco-innovation is on shifting pollution reduction efforts from end-of-pipe controls to minimizing waste at source. Pollution control can be traced through three distinct stages of historical development. Initial efforts can be characterized as 'dilute and disperse' – installing taller chimneys, for example, so that smoke is sent up into the atmosphere rather than choking the community that surrounds the factory. What goes up, however, must at some point come down. The solution to one environmental problem (e.g. poor local air quality) becomes the source of a new one (e.g. the acid rain which forms when sulphur dioxide from factory chimneys and power plants combines in the atmosphere with nitrogen oxides from vehicle exhausts, and then descends to destroy forests and lakes hundreds of miles away).

In the second stage, end-of pipe controls are evolved to address these problems, often in response to tighter regulation. Flue gas desulphurization can be introduced into coal-fired power stations, for example, and car exhausts can be cleaned by the addition of catalytic converters. Again, however, one problem is solved, only for another to be created. The filters used in FGD, for example, require large inputs of limestone, reduce combustion efficiency, and produce large quantities of solid and liquid waste. In the third stage, products and processes are redesigned to minimize the resources they consume and the waste they generate, through the adoption of 'Clean Technology' (see Key Concept 8.5). Theoretically, by

KEY CONCEPT 8.5
Clean technology

Clean Technology (sometimes called Cleaner Technology, or Clean/Cleaner Production) is defined by the United Nations Environmental Programme (UNEP) as 'the continuous application of an integrated preventative strategy to processes and products to reduce risks to humans and the environment'. It contrasts with end-of-pipe controls which are add-on devices to clean up riskier processes or products.

The advantage of Clean Technology for the environment is that it avoids the displacement of environmental damage from one medium to another. The selling point for business is that, in principle, it can reduce production costs, instead of increasing them. This is illustrated in the diagram below.

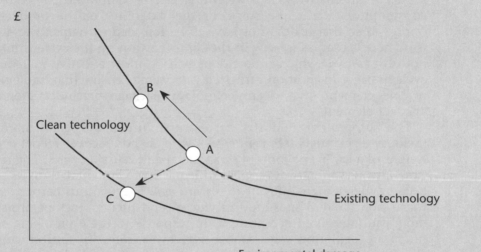

The existing technology curve shows the existing trade-off between cost and environmental damage. Applying end-of-pipe controls reduces environmental damage, but it involves increased cost for the business, resulting in a movement up the curve, from A to B. The clean technology curve shows the situation after introduction of an innovation which reduces waste at source, improving the trade-off between environmental damage and cost. Bringing in the new technology makes it possible to reduce both environmental damage and cost, by shifting from A to C.

anticipating potential problems and preventing their occurrence, clean technology both improves environmental performance and reduces business costs, though in practice this win-win scenario may be difficult to achieve.

Clean technology can take a number of different forms. At its simplest, end-of-pipe waste can be fed back into the production process, or marketed as a saleable product in its own right. More complex conversions of waste into raw materials or useful products are possible, as in 'industrial ecology' networks. At Kalundborg in Denmark, for example, community pressure to reduce local pollution resulted in the establishment of an elaborate system of linkages, centred on the local oil refinery, coal-fired power station, and pharmaceuticals plant (see Figure 8.1). In Japan, MITI sees initiatives which plan inter-industry material flows for zero emissions as a potential source of competitive advantage in the twenty-first century, and it is sponsoring research to identify clusters of industries where one industry's waste can be matched with another's input requirements, so as to eliminate waste from the cluster as a whole (Pauli, 1998).

We saw in Chapter 4 that the greatest scope for cost reduction is at the design stage, and the same applies to improvements in environmental performance. Products can be re-designed to minimize impacts over the life cycle as a whole, for example, by ensuring that materials or components are recycled. Alternatively, lightweighting can be employed to reduce energy consumption at the use stage, or the durability of the product can be improved so that it does not have to be replaced so frequently. A practical issue here is that, as we saw in the earlier section on life cycle thinking, it is not always clear which innovations will be most effective in reducing life cycle impacts. In addition, structural factors may ensure that implementation of one element of a clean technology package precludes progress with another element.

The European car industry, for example, inhabits a sector matrix which includes dismantlers (see Figure 4.4), who already recover 75 per cent of the weight of a car in the form of scrap metal and reusable parts. The remaining 'shredder waste', however, creates major environmental impacts, and will become increasingly difficult to discard as EC regulations barring hazardous waste from landfill sites are introduced, and incinerator operators become more cautious about accepting it. In response to these problems, manufacturers are exploring ways to boost recovery rates, by introducing design changes which will make it easier to identify and dismantle different

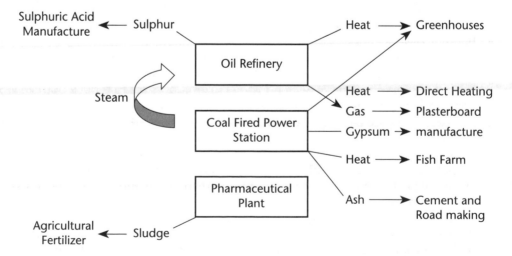

Figure **8.1:** Industrial ecology links at Kalundborg, Denmark

components and materials for reuse or recycling, and by training dismantlers in more sophisticated recovery techniques. At the same time, manufacturers are experimenting with lighter materials than steel, such as aluminium and plastics, to improve the fuel efficiency of their products in response to a 1998 Voluntary Agreement between themselves and the European Commission for a 25 per cent cut in carbon dioxide emissions from new cars by 2008.

Profitability for dismantlers depends crucially on the price they can obtain for recovered materials, which depends in turn on world market prices for raw materials. These plummeted in 1998, to such an extent that the value of recovered materials from an average end-of-life car in Britain dropped to around £20, which only just covered recycling costs. Design initiatives on recyclability could improve dismantler profitability by reducing labour costs, but lightweighting initiatives might have the opposite effect, by reducing the content of steel, which has a much higher scrap value than plastics. In addition, measures to extend the durability of the product would also lower profitability, by reducing the throughput of end-of-life cars. Whether or not the manufacturers can secure the co-operation of the dismantlers in improving materials recovery will depend in large measure on the implications of these different design choices and global market trends. Illustrating the decisions about life cycle environmental performance cannot be taken in isolation from their effects on economic conditions within the sector matrix that is needed to deliver that performance.

More generally, promotion of clean technology by bodies like UNEP is often premised on an assumption that only ignorance prevents businesses from realizing the win-win scenario illustrated in Figure 8.1. Structural barriers to clean technology diffusion are, however, substantial. The more complex solutions require new engineering skills, high capital outlays, long payback periods and, in some cases, new types of relationship between enterprises, which most businesses will not contemplate without significant market reward or regulatory pressure. This will particularly be the case where financial environments are dominated by short-termism. Environmental consultancy, too, is highly fragmented, and firms in the sector are renowned for preferring to recommend off-the-shelf clean-up packages than to customize clean technology solutions specific to the conditions under which their clients are operating.

Environmental regulation and market incentives

Michael Porter has argued, against conventional business wisdom, that tough environmental regulation can boost international competitiveness, by encouraging resource-saving or product-enhancing innovation, and creating early-mover advantages in international markets (Porter, 1991; Porter and van der Linde, 1995). To foster the sort of innovation which would deliver increased competitiveness as well as improved environmental quality, he suggests, regulation would need to focus on outcomes rather than technologies, leaving it to businesses to determine how best to achieve continuous improvement in environmental quality.

Regulation

Environmental regulations vary from country to country, and they change over time. In most cases, however, there has been little emphasis on innovation. The traditional approach in Britain, for example, was to set up different agencies to regulate different types of pollution (air, land and water). Inspectors negotiated standards with companies behind closed doors, on a case-by-case basis which took into account local environmental conditions, the availability of pollution control techniques, and the financial cost of installing them. This approach ignored linkages between different types of pollution – the water pollution that is created by filter sprays which remove dust and gases from chimneys, for example. Critics maintained, too, that inspectors gave more weight to the negative implications of tighter controls for company balance sheets than to the positive effects on environmental quality, so that regulation was applied with an extremely light touch on the whole.

In the 1990s, the British approach was modified to emphasize integrated pollution control by a single body, the Environment Agency. The Agency has a statutory responsibility for working in partnership with industry, and the onus is on companies to determine the Best Practicable Environmental Option (BPEO) for their discharges, the aim being to minimize overall environmental impacts across air, water, and land, while avoiding 'excessive costs'. Under BPEO, alternative options have to be assessed, and environmental impacts are supposed to be more important than financial calculations. Experience to date suggests, however, that 'practicable' usually means lowest cost, provided minimum environmental standards are met.

Pollution control in Germany has traditionally given less emphasis than in Britain to economic factors. New production processes have to employ the Best Available Technology (BAT), regardless of its cost, or of local environmental conditions. Although application of BAT ratcheted up environmental standards at a much quicker rate than in Britain, the emphasis on availability encouraged adoption of end-of-pipe controls rather than clean technology solutions, and industry argued vehemently, in the depressed economic climate of the 1990s, for a reduction in the costs of regulation.

In the USA, regulators have been prepared to adopt 'technology forcing' standards, particularly with car exhaust emissions, which require companies to go beyond best available technologies to achieve higher environmental standards. As in Germany, however, the main emphasis has been on end-of-pipe controls, and industry has argued that ambitious environmental targets impose excessive cost; in the 1980s the US Federal Government slowed down the introduction of new environmental regulations by insisting that they need to be supported by a comparison of costs and benefits. Japan has also put more emphasis than Britain or Germany on improving the technology of pollution control, and comes closest to Porter's insistence that regulation should be designed to promote innovation. A key policy instrument here is open dialogue between regulators, polluters, and environmental technology providers, to disseminate rising standards as rapidly as possible.

In all these countries, the emphasis in the difficult market conditions of the 1990s was more on deregulation than on the introduction of new regulatory frameworks to stimulate innovation. This decade also saw moves, particularly in the European Union, to promote market incentives for environmental innovation, like eco-labelling and eco-taxation (Neale, 1997b).

Eco-labelling

Eco-labelling is aimed at creating demand pressure for environmental innovation, by giving consumers reliable information about environmental performance. Under the European Union scheme introduced in 1993, Life Cycle Assessment (LCA) is used to identify the most significant environmental impacts for a product group, and to establish criteria which must be satisfied before a particular product can be awarded an eco-label. The scheme is a voluntary one, and the criteria are such that only about 10–15 per cent of a product group could qualify for an award.

The idea was that environmental innovation would be encouraged by rewarding manufacturers with product differentiation based on independent verification of above-average environmental performance, and at the same time giving consumers reliable information about environmental performance. In practice, the scheme has had very little effect, as the process of setting criteria has been extremely time consuming, and even in those product groups for which criteria have been established, few producers have bothered to apply for the eco-label.

In the laundry detergent product group, for example, Procter & Gamble, the leading producer and one of the pioneers of business use of LCA, refused to apply on principle. They argued that it was pointless rewarding manufacturers for low ingredient eco-toxicity, as the environmental impact of consumers using too high a wash temperature was greater. Instead, they joined other mainstream detergent manufacturers in sponsoring an alternative voluntary code of practice which sets much less ambitious environmental performance targets. At the 'green' end of the spectrum, Ecover, the Belgian firm which produces vegetable-based products to ensure rapid biological degradation after disposal, has also not applied for the eco-label, because it fears customers will think that its environmental performance was no better than products based on petrochemical ingredients that take much longer to biodegrade, which could also qualify.

Eco-taxation

Eco-taxation refers to the use of the tax system to discourage environmental damage. It can be *ad hoc*, as with taxes on petrol, or part of a broader strategy, sometimes called ecological tax reform, of shifting the structure of taxes away from 'positives' (e.g. income or jobs) towards 'negatives' (e.g. resource use or pollution). The main theoretical case for ecological tax reform is that it provides economic incentives for producers and consumers to reduce their environmental impacts. Unlike regulatory controls, which provide no reward for doing better than environmental standards, eco-taxes encourage improved environmental performance whatever its existing level. Some environmental economists argue that economic valuation techniques, such as contingent valuation (see Key Concept 8.6), should be used to determine tax levels. In practice, however, tax rates are usually determined by political calculations, the aim being to bring about price adjustments which shift producer and consumer behaviour towards a politically determined standard rather than to seek some economically 'optimum' measure of externality (see Key Concept 7.1) based on a hypothetical willingness to pay.

Much of the effectiveness of eco-taxes depends on how they are designed, and how the revenues will be spent. If innovation is to be encouraged, it makes sense to introduce an eco-tax at a low initial level (so as not to harm competitiveness and the ability to finance environmental innovation), but to announce, in advance, year-on-year increases (to signal clearly the need to take avoiding action while giving sufficient time to adapt, and to allow the environmental effectiveness of the tax to increase without sacrificing revenue yield). If the revenue raised is offset by reduced taxes on labour, then most econometric models suggest that the net effect on aggregate employment should be positive, but alternative uses of the revenue (to reduce value added tax, for example) might have a negative net effect.

Account needs to be taken, too, of local circumstances and income distribution effects. In principle, the extension in 1994 of Value Added Tax to domestic energy in Britain should have encouraged household investment in better insulation and more energy-efficient heating. Because insulation standards were so low, however, higher energy prices adversely affected the living standards of low-income households and, without any compensating increase in social security benefits, their ability to afford these investments was reduced. Arguably, it would have been more effective to announce a firm intention to introduce the tax in the future, while offering grants and

KEY CONCEPT 8.6
Contingent valuation

Contingent valuation is the most widely used of the techniques which have been developed to estimate what the market value of an environmental asset would be if people had to pay for it. At its simplest, people are interviewed to establish their willingness to pay for preservation of the asset, an average value is calculated, and this is multiplied by the numbers benefiting from the asset. Contingent valuation has been useful in situations where an asset's value reflects popular taste (a picturesque view, for example). It is of little use in situations where consumers have no direct perception of the value of an environmental asset (rainforest, for example) or of the effect of an environmental problem (carbon dioxide emissions, for example).

subsidies for energy-efficiency measures to give low-income households a realistic opportunity to reduce their energy consumption before the new tax came into effect.

In the European Union, the main push for ecological tax reform came with the Commission's 1992 proposal for an EU-wide energy tax (weighted according to the carbon content of the fuel), as the main instrument for stabilizing carbon dioxide emissions under the 1992 Climate Change Convention. The proposal, which was to apply to all but the most energy-intensive industries, provoked widespread disagreement and it was eventually dropped after opposition from the Spanish government (seeking to protect its coal industry), the UK government (objecting to what it saw as a step towards a unified EU tax system), and business pressure groups (concerned about possible effects on competitiveness in relation to the rest of the world). Variants of the carbon and energy tax have been introduced by member governments in Sweden, Denmark and the Netherlands, however, and the EU-wide tax proposal may need to be resurrected now there are legally-binding targets, following the 1997 Kyoto agreement, to cut greenhouse gas emissions by 2010.

Experience in those European countries that have introduced a variant of the carbon/energy tax suggests that it can bring environmental benefits without damage to jobs or living standards. Structural conditions affecting elasticities of demand for energy are critical here. This illustrates a more general point that eco-taxation may be a necessary condition for improved environmental performance, but it is far from sufficient. What it provides is a financial incentive for eco-innovation, by imposing a cost penalty on environmental damage that can only be reduced by limiting that damage. There is no guarantee, however, that all producers and consumers will respond in the desired way to the changed price signals, and much will depend on willingness to invest in innovative solutions rather than absorb the costs of the tax.

For companies, organizational structure and institutional context are key intervening variables. If, in large firms, branch managers must obtain head office clearance to finance the installation of major pollution control devices or energy-efficient motors, they may prefer instead to pay higher charges and 'hide' them within current cost budgets, particularly if the payback period is more than three years. Similar outcomes may result when small firms are unwilling to seek external funds to finance the capital expenditure, because of high interest rates for example. For consumers, too, investment costs are an important consideration. Many householders, for example, may be reluctant to install effective insulation or to purchase energy efficient appliances, because they are unable to afford the initial cost, even though they would benefit financially in the long run.

Environmental accountability

Although it has become fashionable in recent years to argue that modern business has many stakeholders, including employees, regulators, customers, community and environmental groups, the structure of corporate governance still gives primacy to one stakeholder group, the shareholders, who provide its equity capital. Companies have a statutory responsibility to account to their shareholders for the use made of their funds and reporting systems have evolved which measure financial performance in terms of profit and loss, balance sheets, etc. Within these systems, environmental performance is considered only in so far as it is reflected in current financial results. Some countries are beginning to explore ways that larger companies might be required to report their environmental performance on a consistent basis, but meanwhile companies themselves are exploring different ways of communicating their environmental policies. The result, at the start of the twenty-first century, is a confusing array of environmental reporting initiatives, with little consistency of approach.

Environmental Management Systems (EMS)

Since the 1980s an increasing number of companies, particularly in industries where there are significant environmental risks, have set up Environmental Management Systems, not just to focus management attention on the environmental regulations they need to comply with, but to minimize the risks of expensive environmental disasters and to identify profitable opportunities for environmental improvement beyond compliance. In many cases, companies have sought independent verification of their systems, which they can use to signal their environmental commitment to interested stakeholders (particularly insurers, purchasers with their own environmental policies, and ethical investment funds).

In the European Union, the Eco-Management and Audit Scheme (EMAS) was introduced in 1995, as a voluntary scheme covering industrial sites. In order to apply for certification, a company must have a company-wide environmental policy, and undertake a comprehensive environmental review to identify its key environmental impacts. There should be clear targets for improved environmental performance at the site, and a programme for achieving them, with regular monitoring of progress. Every year, the company must publish an environmental statement, summarizing the most significant environmental impacts at the site, and reporting progress towards its targets, which is verified by an accredited independent environmental verifier.

There are a number of problems with EMAS as it stands. Only 1,500 sites had been registered in the first three years of the scheme's operation, and most of these were in Germany, where verification procedures are less stringent than elsewhere. The fact that targets are self-selected means that they do not always address the environmental issues that stakeholders would identify as most significant, and the emphasis is always on improving present performance rather than achieving environmental standards. This, coupled with the variable quality of environmental statements, makes it difficult to use EMAS to compare the environmental performance of sites, even within the same industry. The focus on site-level performance disguises damage that may be occurring elsewhere in the supply chain, and may give a misleading picture of performance in the organization as a whole. And although the regulation which set up the scheme recommended that company environ-mental policies should 'take account of possible clean technologies', in practice the emphasis on incremental improvement and self-selected targets does little to encourage the fundamental innovation that these technologies would often require.

If the operation of EMAS leaves much to be desired from an environmental point of view, then ISO 14001, the global environmental management standard introduced in 1996, raises deeper concerns. Take up has been much more rapid than with EMAS – more than 4,000 certificates had been issued in the first 18 months of the scheme's operation (although half of these went to companies in just three countries, Japan, the UK, and Germany). A big part of the scheme's popularity with business is due to the ease with which it can be obtained. When the standard was designed, a prime consideration, stemming from the International Organisation for Standardisation's commitment to removing trade barriers, was to make it as inclusive as possible. In addition, US business lobbying ensured that no information would be disclosed that might increase liabilities in relation to US environmental law. As a result, there is no requirement for a company to make public anything other than a general statement of its environmental policy. There must be a system in place which sets targets and monitors their achievement, but all that needs to be verified is that the system operates as stated – any external auditing that takes place is of the system, not of performance, even against the company's self-selected targets.

Possession of an ISO 14001 certificate says nothing about a company's environmental performance, but just confirms that there is an EMS in place. Despite this weakness, companies, particularly in the chemicals industry, are arguing increasingly vehemently that ISO 14001 certification should become a licence for self-regulation, exempting them from regulatory controls.

Engaging stakeholders

Alongside the evolution of EMS, many large corporations are now exploring ways of more effectively communicating their environmental performance to stakeholders. A popular way of doing this is through the vehicle of an annual environmental report. Many early examples were little more than PR exercises, designed to present the company's environmental impacts in the most favourable light. Recently, however, a number of companies have produced something more substantial, modelled on the statutory financial report and accounts. Now, companies are beginning to release relevant information on their environmental performance, and in some cases to provide a balanced and externally attested review of progress in achieving environmental targets. Few companies address sustainability issues in their environmental reporting, however, and, as with EMAS statements, the quality of the reports is very variable, and it is often impossible to use them for analysis of comparative environmental performance.

Another recent innovation is to develop communication as a two-way process, by actively involving stakeholders in the assessment of environmental performance, so that they can contribute to improving the organization's environmental decision making. This approach was developed initially as part of the 'Responsible Care' programme adopted by chemical industries worldwide to improve their community relations in the wake of the 1984 Bhopal disaster. It is based on a recognition that stakeholders may not share company management's priorities in terms of environmental management. Rather than assuming the company knows best, or following a 'decide-announce-defend' sequence, the aim is to encourage open discussion of options before coming to a decision, so that everyone concerned has a better awareness of the issues involved. The company still makes the final decision, but the dialogue means that its managers are better informed, and adverse publicity is limited.

Stakeholder engagement can extend to corporate strategy issues, as with the Eastern Group, a leading integrated energy supplier in the UK. In 1996, Eastern Group managers met with representative stakeholders, using a dialogue process managed by the Environment Council, a UK charity which facilitates environmental mediation. The process identified carbon dioxide emissions from power generation as the key sustainability issue facing the company, and development of renewable energy supplies as the most appropriate solution. Following the dialogue process, Eastern Group decided to establish targets of generating 10 per cent of its electricity from renewable sources by 2010, and an additional 10 per cent of its energy from gas-fired combined heat and power plants by 2010. It also introduced an 'EcoPower' tariff, whereby its electricity customers can choose to pay a supplement to an independent fund (matched pound-for-pound by the company) which supports investment in additional renewable energy projects.

Business environmental performance in developing countries

In 1992, the World Bank was embarrassed by the leaking to the *Economist* of an internal memo from its Chief Economist, Laurence Summers ('Let them eat pollution', 8 February 1992). In this memo, Summers suggested that more could be done to encourage the migration of dirty industries to developing countries. There were three parts to his argument. First, he suggested, the costs of pollution can be measured in terms of earnings forgone as a result of ill-health, which will be lowest in low-wage economies. Second, the costs of pollution are non-linear, with local environments able to cope with small amounts of pollution at little cost, but the costs rising dramatically once critical thresholds are crossed – from this perspective Africa becomes, as Summer put it, 'vastly under-polluted'. Third, there is a high income elasticity of demand for a clean environment, because people place more value on this as their incomes rise. On all three counts, Summer argued, shifting pollution from high-income countries (with over-loaded environments) to low-income countries (with environments which are under less stress) will reduce the total costs of pollution.

Leaving aside the dubious ethics of Summer's first point, with its implication that human life is more valuable in the USA or Japan than in Mexico or China, there is little empirical support for his argument. The cities in developing countries that are the most feasible sites for new industrial development already suffer the worst air pollution in the world, as a result of lax regulation of industrial emissions, massive traffic congestion, and adverse local climatic conditions. The World Bank's own World Development Report for 1992 presented data which showed that urban concentrations of suspended particulate matter (the aspect of air pollution which poses the greatest risk to human health) in low-income countries were twice those in middle-income countries, and six times those in high-income countries. Usually, too, it is the poor in developing countries who are the most vocal in their opposition to 'dirty' industrial development. Political and business elites may see the development of pollution havens as a source of competitive advantage in the global market place, but it is the poor who have to live with the local pollution, and it is their livelihoods which suffer most from the ill-health this brings in its wake.

Local pollution

While Summer's positive case for relocating polluting industries from developed to developing countries lacks credibility, there is little doubt that lax environmental regulation in many developing countries has encouraged lower environmental standards on the part of companies there, and some migration of environmentally damaging activities from developed countries. In East Asia, tighter regulation of pollution from heavy industries in Japan in the early 1970s led some companies to re-locate elsewhere in the region, rather than incur the costs of cleaning up their processes. Mitsubishi Corporation's shift of its ore-processing operations to the Asian Rare Earth joint-venture near Ipoh in Malaysia illustrates some of the damage that can result. Here radioactive waste from the new plant was dumped along roadsides and in rivers, resulting in significant clusters of leukaemia, with miscarriage and infant mortality rates three times the national average, provoking lawsuits from local villagers. In the early 1990s, after facing adverse international publicity, the company reduced its share in the joint venture, to limit its legal liability, but it showed little willingness to pass on its expertise in pollution prevention, and eventually the plant was shut down.

Damage from unsustainable development is perhaps greatest in resource-based industries like forestry. Although two-thirds of the land area of Japan remains forested, Japanese trading companies (including another division of Mitsubishi Corporation) have turned to tropical forests in the region for low-cost timber, making Japan the world's leading importer of tropical timber. Expansion of logging operations has brought wealth to plantation owners and political leaders in countries like the Philippines, Thailand, Malaysia and Indonesia, as well as to the trading companies. The rate of deforestation has, however, been unsustainable, and has caused enormous damage to ecosystems. Local impacts have included climate variability which alternates between flooding and drought, widespread soil erosion and frequent land-slides, and threats to the survival of indigenous people and wildlife species. There are trans-boundary effects, too, when fires which have been lit to clear land for plantation development get out of control, releasing massive amounts of stored carbon (contributing to global warming) and creating widespread smoke pollution. This occurred most dramatically in 1997, when fires on the Indonesian islands of Sumatra and Kalimantan produced a thick haze which suffocated much of Indonesia, Malaysia and Singapore for several months.

Differences in environmental regulation between developed and develop-ing countries raise important issues for multinational companies, even when there is no conscious decision to exploit these differences. Union Carbide Corporation, for example, set up an Indian subsidiary in the early 1970s, not to take advantage of low-cost production but to meet demand for pesticides from local farmers using new high-yielding varieties of wheat. Revenue predictions for the plant it built at Bhopal were rarely achieved, however, as farmers were unable to afford purchases of the pesticide in drought years, and cost-cutting measures taken in the early 1980s to protect plant profitability resulted in safety lapses and a string of minor accidents. The 1984 explosion, which remains the world's worst ever industrial disaster, occurred when water entered a tank storing methylisocyanate (MIC), one of the highly toxic ingredients used in manufacturing the pesticide. Pressure built up to such an extent that toxic fumes were released into the local atmosphere, killing around 10,000 people, and disabling around half a million.

Union Carbide claimed that it was not responsible for the disaster, on the grounds that the plant's design was sound, that local management was responsible for poor operating procedures, and that the Indian government was responsible for lax regulation and for the siting of the plant in a densely populated area. The company also put forward a theory that sabotage by an unidentified former employee with a grudge against the company had caused the disaster. Many of these claims did not stand up to closer investigation. The plant's storage tanks were designed for much cooler climatic conditions than in India, and the refrigeration unit had been turned off to save costs. Much of the equipment was badly maintained, again to save costs. Corporate headquarters in the USA knew about these defects, as company policy required detailed safety reports to be submitted every quarter, to ensure compatible operating standards. Above all, it became clear that Union Carbide had taken little account in its decision making of the social and political conditions in which its Indian subsidiary was operating, and which made the 'accident' possible. The company's share price plummeted as shareholders realized the scale of the disaster, anticipating huge compensa-tion claims and the company found itself having to take on a huge burden of debt to protect itself against a hostile take-over bid, while fighting in the courts to deny liability. In the late 1980s, while survivors struggled to obtain some compensation, the company had to dramatically downsize its operations to remain in business.

Global issues

Developing countries do not suffer solely from intense local pollution – they are also highly vulnerable to global environmental problems. High-income economies can to some extent buy themselves out of the consequences of climate change, by constructing higher sea walls to protect their coastal areas from rising sea levels, for example (although even the Netherlands, which has considerable expertise in reclaiming land from the sea, finds it more cost-effective to try to slow global warming than to adapt to it). Low-income economies cannot afford this option, however, and the consequences of even small rises in sea levels can be catastrophic for them, as low-lying countries like the Maldives or Bangladesh are already starting to discover.

International measures to limit global warming also have significant economic implications for developing countries. Average carbon dioxide emissions from low-income economies, per head of population, are one-ninth of those from high-income economies, reflecting much lower levels of industrial development. Per unit of GDP, however, they are five times as great, reflecting lower levels of energy efficiency (see Table 8.3). This raises major problems for international negotiations on measures to reduce global warming. Uniform targets to reduce greenhouse gas emissions from present levels would condemn low-income economies to permanent underdevelopment, and starve them of the funds they would need to improve their energy efficiency. On the other hand, targets related to population would require massive reductions in emissions from high-income countries. It is hardly surprising, then, that emission control and forest preservation have become bargaining counters in geopolitical negotiations over debt relief, trade, and development aid as well as climate change.

At the 1997 Kyoto climate summit, developing countries refused to agree to controls on their greenhouse gas emissions, arguing that this would block their attempts to raise their living standards. The USA refused to agree to the Protocol requiring developed countries to accept legally-binding reduction targets, unless the developing countries accepted some restraint in their emissions. At the end of the summit, a compromise was reached, setting up a 'Clean Development Mechanism' (CDM), under which developed countries could relax their targets if they agreed to finance programmes to improve energy efficiency in developing countries. Under CDM, high-income

Table **8.3:** Global carbon dioxide emissions

	Total (bn tonnes)		Per capita (tonnes)		Kg per 1987 $ of GDP	
	1980	1995	1980	1995	1980	1995
Low-income economies	2.0	4.5	0.9	1.4	4.2	3.4
Middle-income economies	2.8	7.1	2.9	4.5	1.7	2.6
High-income economies	8.88	11.1	12.0	12.5	0.9	0.7

(Source: World Bank (World Development Indicators))

economies would effectively be able to 'trade' emissions reductions abroad against their domestic targets, reversing the emphasis of Summer's infamous pollution export proposal. The details of how CDM would be implemented have yet to be worked out, and it remains to be seen what effect it would have on global emissions, how many dollars would be transferred from rich to poor countries, and what effect, if any, this would have on the living standards of the poorest people in low-income economies.

Case study: 'Corporate greening' – the case of Shell

Shell is a multi-national grouping of companies with a unique structure. It was formed in 1907 by an alliance between the Royal Dutch Petroleum Company, based in the Netherlands, and the British-based 'Shell' Transport & Trading Company. The two companies retained their separate identities and shareholdings, but merged their operations to share joint risks and proceeds (60 per cent to Royal Dutch, 40 per cent to 'Shell'). The alliance linked Royal Dutch's oil fields in South East Asia with the transport and trading expertise of 'Shell', to challenge the global dominance of the US-based Standard Oil. Royal Dutch and 'Shell' have remained as separate parent companies of the Shell Group, which now consists of numerous operating companies which extract, transport, refine and retail oil and provide other energy services throughout the world, and service companies which provide business support and technical guidance from the centre.

The Shell Group is the largest business organization in Europe, and until 1998 it jockeyed for position with Exxon (a descendant of Standard Oil) as the largest of the oil majors of the world. In the 1990s, it featured regularly as one of the ten companies most admired by the UK senior directors surveyed each year by *Management Today* and as the leading company for shareholder value on the London Stock Exchange, as measured by the calculations of Market Value Added (MVA) published annually in *The Sunday Times.* As with the other oil majors, the profits Shell has made over the years have been ploughed into the acquisition of retail sites, enabling it to market what is essentially a commodity as a branded product, and to respond to the challenge of cut-price supermarket petrol by itself diversifying into convenience shopping on the forecourt.

Return on Average Capital Employed (ROACE) is Shell's chosen indicator of current financial performance; this is affected by cyclical upstream earnings from exploration and production (where most of its value added is created), which reflect fluctuations in world market prices (see Table 8.4). Compared with the other oil majors, Shell achieved the highest Total Shareholder Return (dividends plus capital gains) over the period 1988–97, but in 1996–98 its ROACE fell to bottom place. To improve its relative position, the Group embarked on a massive restructuring programme to strip out excess capacity, with the aim of boosting ROACE to at least 15 per cent by 2001. This target (set in 1997) was based, however, on an assumed world oil price of $18 per barrel, and its achievement was threatened by an unprecedented combination of adverse circumstances in 1998. Shell was hit harder than its rivals by the 1998 collapse

Table **8.4:** Return on average capital employed and crude oil prices, 1990–98

Year	ROACE by Shell (%)	Brent crude ($ per barrel, av.)
1990	11.6	23.7
1991	7.9	20.0
1992	9.0	19.4
1993	7.9	17.0
1994	10.3	15.8
1995	10.7	17.1
1996	12.0	20.5
1997	12.0	19.1
1998	2.8	12.8

(Source: Shell Annual Reports)

of East Asian markets and by its above-average dependence on high-cost offshore oil supplies in a period of unusually depressed oil prices. At the same time, its competitive position within the oil industry was threatened by the massive mergers which created Exxon/Mobil (now much bigger than Shell) and BP Amoco. In the last quarter of 1998, when oil prices dipped briefly below $10 per barrel (their lowest level for 30 years, and significantly below the cost of off-shore extraction), Shell's net income became negative, dragging its ROACE for the year as a whole to below 3 per cent.

Social responsibility and environmental management

The different parts of the Shell Group have jealously guarded their autonomy, and decision making within the organization has involved more decentralization than is usual in big business. Sometimes decisions taken by local managers have produced harmful consequences for the group as a whole. In the early 1970s, for example, the Shell Operating Company in Italy made corrupt payments to politicians. Over the same period, the Operating Company in South Africa was breaking sanctions against supplying oil to the illegal regime in Rhodesia (now Zimbabwe). In each case, apparently, local managers took these initiatives without informing the centre, but Shell's reputation world-wide suffered.

To avoid a recurrence of similar problems, while preserving its tradition of local autonomy, the Group set out in 1976 a *Statement of General Business Principles*, which gave explicit guidance to managers on appropriate business behaviour. These Principles adopted, uniquely for big business at that time, a stakeholder perspective, recognizing four 'inseparable' areas of responsibility – not just to shareholders, but to employees, customers and society as well.

It might seem unlikely that a company producing and marketing fossil fuels could be sincere about improving environmental performance, but alongside its *Business Principles*, Shell was developing scenario planning as an integral part of its strategy formulation. Alternative scenarios (coherent pictures of possible alternative futures) were presented to managers to challenge their assumptions and get them addressing potential problems before they became live issues in the outside world. By the mid-1980s, Shell was using scenarios to explore potential threats and opportunities from the activities of environmental groups. This encouraged the extension of its health and safety systems to include environmental management issues, a greater emphasis on the natural gas part of its business (natural gas being less polluting than oil or coal), and diversification into renewable energy development. Shell also became one of the founder members of the World Business Council for Sustainable Development (WBCSD).

Despite an apparent sensitivity to environmental concerns, unusual in the industry, Shell at this stage had quite a narrow interpretation of environmental policy. Operating companies started producing annual environmental reviews for group use in the early 1990s, for example, but their main concerns were about compliance with prevailing regulations rather than eco-innovation, and the results were not published. The discussion, deliberation and consensus building that went on within the company did not extend much beyond its boundaries, and Shell managers determined what the key environmental issues were, and how these might be resolved, with little reference to the stakeholders identified in its *Business Principles*. As a result, little account was taken of the contested nature of the environments in which the company operated (Neale, 1997a).

1995: Brent Spar and Nigeria

The drawbacks in Shell's insular approach to environmental management were highlighted in 1995 by its failure to understand public concerns about its decision to dump Brent Spar (a redundant North Sea oil installation) at sea, and about its involvement in environmental degradation and human rights abuses in Nigeria. In each case, the company discovered that compliance with lax regulatory standards was not enough, and that modern mass communications could bring poor environmental performance in remote exploration and production locations to the attention of a world-wide audience, affecting global retail sales.

Although Shell's share of Nigerian oil output has declined since the country's independence from colonial rule in 1960, Nigeria remains a major source of crude oil for the company, generating about 12 per cent of its global output. Nigerian oil is especially valued for its low sulphur content, which makes it easier and less costly to refine than oil from other sources. If the product is relatively clean, however, the same can not be said about conditions in the Niger Delta where the oil is extracted. Overland pipes carry the oil close to villages and spills, whether from corrosion or sabotage, have been frequent, damaging the subsistence crops and fishing waters on which the inhabitants depend. More than three-quarters of the gas which is brought up with the oil is flared, causing massive local air pollution; in addition the quantities of carbon dioxide and methane released from the Nigerian oilfields make them the single most important source of global warming in the world.

Poor environmental performance by the oil industry in Nigeria reflects the interconnectedness of government and company policy. Shell operates in Nigeria as a joint venture with other oil companies, the most significant being the state-owned Nigerian National Petroleum Corporation (NNPC). Expenditures have to be agreed by all partners, and delays by the NNPC in advancing its 55 per cent share have made the funding of new investment a major problem. This has been partly offset by the lax pollution controls successive military governments have used to encourage oil production, which allow the companies to cut back on maintenance expenditure and upgrading of equipment. Military elites have used the oil revenues to fund patronage systems to maintain their power, while providing little compensation for the 7 million inhabitants of the Delta.

For much of the period in which Shell has been producing oil in the Niger Delta, few people outside the area were concerned about conditions there. This changed in the early 1990s, when various Delta communities, in particular the Ogoni, demonstrated publicly against environmental destruction, and called for an international boycott of Shell products. The protests were brutally suppressed by the military, but damning reports from Amnesty International, Greenpeace, WWF and the World Bank, adverse publicity co-ordinated by The Body Shop, and an award-winning TV documentary on Britain's Channel 4, brought criticism of Shell's involvement to a world-wide audience. In 1995, the military authorities arrested Ken Saro-Wiwa and eight other Ogoni leaders and hanged them, despite pleas from all over the world for their release. Shell was widely condemned for appearing to do nothing to save them.

Brent Spar raised more straightforward issues for Shell than its Nigerian operations, but they were no less damaging for the company's reputation. The Spar was installed in 1976 as a storage buoy for North Sea oil from the Brent Field, which Shell UK operated in a joint venture with Esso. Back then, the main aim was to bring the oil ashore quickly, and oil installations were designed with little consideration for end-of-life disposal issues, even though international law required redundant structures to be dismantled onshore. It was only in 1991, when the Spar was decommissioned, that Shell UK addressed the technical problems of how to bring it ashore without rupturing the structure.

Shell UK spent the next three years studying different disposal options, to determine the 'Best Practicable Environmental Option' (BPEO), as required by the UK regulatory authorities. Two options for Brent Spar – horizontal dismantling for onshore disposal and deep sea dumping – were assessed in detail. Shell's consultants suggested that environmentally there was little to choose between the options, but that on-shore disposal costs would be four times those of deep-sea dumping. Shell UK convinced themselves and the UK government that dumping was the BPEO and did not feel a need to test this against outside opinion, beyond minimum legal requirements. The UK government was particularly concerned that if onshore disposal was chosen, it would have to bear most of the cost (as the company could offset this against Petroleum Revenue Tax).

In ignoring outside opinion, Shell UK alienated the scientists who were most familiar with the proposed dump site in the Atlantic Ocean, the engineering contractors who wanted to explore how the Spar might be brought safely onshore, Britain's North Sea neighbours who had little sympathy for the primacy of financial calculations over the precautionary principle in the UK government's BPEO procedure, and Greenpeace, who had a long history of campaigns against ocean dumping.

It was Greenpeace's intervention in 1995 which was to prove a turning point for Shell. The organization was particularly concerned that Shell's Brent Spar disposal would be used as a precedent to re-assert the legitimacy of dumping at sea and in April 1995 its activists occupied Brent Spar. They mounted a massive media campaign, inviting reporters on board and providing European television companies with dramatic anti-Shell video footage. Shell found it hard to justify its dumping decision in public debate. The Greenpeace message was clear – companies should not use the sea as a dumpsite, and should take responsibility for their own waste. Shell spokespeople, in contrast, kept repeating that they had satisfied legal requirements to determine the BPEO, without realizing that this was a concept which had little meaning for most of their audience, particularly outside the UK.

Opinion polls showed that few people in Northern Europe supported the Shell case. Many motorists boycotted Shell products, and Shell sales in Germany fell by 20 per cent. Political pressure was put on the UK government by the German government, and Novo Nordisk, the Danish pharmaceuticals company and a co-member of the WBCSD, publicly challenged Shell to justify its decision making. Dissident Shell shareholders added to the opposition, calling for more rigorous external monitoring of environmental performance. Underlying all these actions was a feeling that Shell and the UK government were taking the easy option with Brent Spar, for short-term financial reasons, and riding roughshod over public opinion.

There was also unease among Shell UK's European partners. Deutsche Shell in particular criticized Shell UK for failing to anticipate the adverse market consequences of not communicating the reasoning behind its decision to dump Brent Spar. After intensive discussions within the Shell Group in June 1995, Shell UK announced that it was abandoning the dumping operation.

Transformation?

Brent Spar and the Nigerian crisis coincided with the first stages of a massive organizational change at Shell. A Group senior management meeting in 1994 decided that the company was too bureaucratic and inward-looking, and that a 'transformation' in its structure and culture was needed if it was to remain competitive in the years to come. Shell UK's decision-making over Brent Spar was seen as typifying the drawbacks of the old 'never apologize and rarely explain' approach, based as it was on assumptions that disposal was a purely technical issue, and that there was no need to listen to public opinion (Neale, 1999).

Shell UK was encouraged to open up its decision making. It announced an international competition to generate alternative solutions, and worked with the Environment Council to devise a Dialogue Process in which representative stakeholders, in London, Hamburg, Amsterdam and Copenhagen, evaluated different disposal options. Shell UK took account of views expressed in the Dialogue seminars, that more emphasis should be given to waste minimization, and it submitted a new decommissioning plan which involved cutting up the Spar and reusing the sections as a quay extension near Stavanger in Norway. The revised plan met with widespread public acceptance, and it offered significant environmental advantages over both options previously considered, at a cost midway between the two. A new UK government agreed that this was the BPEO, and implementation started in 1998.

In the more complex Nigerian situation, Shell's transformation was less thorough. The company responded to criticisms that it had colluded in the hanging of the Ogoni leaders by insisting that it had exerted 'quiet diplomacy' to secure clemency for them (although not their release). To have done any more, it argued, would have involved unwarranted interference in the affairs of a sovereign state. Soon after the hangings, Shell had to make a decision as to whether to agree with the Nigerian Government to proceed with a long-delayed liquefied natural gas project. Shell decided to go ahead, on the grounds that there would be enormous environmental benefits from the reductions in flaring-off which the project would make possible, as well as expanded revenues from LNG exports. Coming so soon after the Ogoni hangings, however, Shell's decision seemed to many critics to be further evidence of its support for the military regime, and consumer boycotts of Shell products intensified, particularly in the USA. The Group has since announced that it will not enter joint venture agreements where the partners do not share similar business principles, but existing joint ventures which conflict with Shell's business principles, such as those in Nigeria, still remain in place.

At Group level, an innovative website was constructed to promote debate about wider responsibilities (www.shell.com), and the *Business Principles* were revised to incorporate concerns about human rights and sustainable development. Unlike its US-based rivals, Shell supported targets for reduced greenhouse gas emissions at the 1997 Kyoto Climate Summit, and it set up a new core business, Shell International Renewables, to promote solar power and other renewable energy sources, with a five-year investment budget of $500 million. The Group also committed itself to have independently certified environmental management systems in place at all major installations by 2001.

Significant efforts have been made to improve environmental and social accountability. In 1998 Shell published its first annual social accountability report (*The Shell Report*), to monitor the extent to which the business principles are adhered to in practice. This report encourages debate on a range of environmental and social issues, including equal opportunities, human rights, corruption and political activities as well as health, safety and environmental management, and there are plans to develop, for future reports, independently audited sustainable development accounts which measure 'total net value added' by adjusting EVA^{TM} and MVA values to take account of environmental and social impacts. Also in 1998, the annual Health, Safety and Environmental Report presented, for the first time, independently verified global data on HSE performance throughout the group.

As an integrated oil major, managing the full range of operations from oil exploration to forecourt petrol sales, and selling oil products in most of the countries in the world, Shell is more dependent on customer goodwill than is the case with oil producers that concentrate on upstream activities. Global consumer research carried out by the company in 1997 found that 'people are just as concerned about the corporate behaviour of a company as they are about the convenient location of its sites' (*Shell World*, February 1998). Shell continues to argue that, with many aspects of environmental performance, if standards vary between different parts of the world then company policy should reflect that. Yet, as 1995 showed, consumers, and the environmental groups that influence them, will often judge a company, wherever it operates, according to the standards that apply where they live, so that a good corporate reputation in one part of the world may be damaged by poor environmental performance in another.

Shell has, since 1995, been making significant moves in the direction of responding to what its stakeholders are saying about its environmental performance, and looking ahead to providing more sustainable energy services in the twenty-first century. It remains to be seen whether, in the depressed market conditions at the turn of the century, the company will continue along this path, or be diverted by short-term financial pressures onto a different one.

Workshop questions relating to case study

Q1 To what extent might life cycle thinking at the start of Shell's operations in Nigeria and the North Sea have helped the company avoid some of its environmental problems in the 1990s?

Q2 Why do you think that Shell was more prepared to change its mind over Brent Spar than over Nigeria?

Q3 What conclusions would you draw from this case about the relationship between a company's preparedness to listen to its stakeholders, its capacity for eco-innovation, and its public reputation?

Q4 In the light of this case, assess the arguments for and against the proposition that multinational companies should adopt global best practice throughout their operations, and not vary their standards according to local circumstances.

Q5 Using current Shell reports (available on www.shell.com), assess the group's financial and environmental performance since 1998.

To what extent do you think that continuation of Shell's innovations in environmental policy will depend on improved financial performance?

Q6 What practical problems would you foresee in measuring 'total net value added', as proposed in *The Shell Report – 1998*, and how might they be resolved?

How relevant and credible do you think such a measure would be for assessing company environmental and social performance?

References

Fussler, C. (1996) *Driving Eco-Innovation: A Breakthrough Discipline for Innovation and Sustainability*, London: Pitman.

Neale, A. (1997a) 'Organisational learning in contested environments: lessons from Brent Spar', *Business Strategy and the Environment*, **6** (2), pp. 93–103.

Neale, A. (1997b) 'Organising Environmental Self-regulation: Liberal Governmentality and the pursuit of Ecological Modernisation in Europe', *Environmental Politics*, **6** (4), pp. 1–24.

Neale, A. (1999) 'Coming out of their Shell', in Charter, M. and Polonsky, M. (eds.) *Greener Marketing*, Sheffield: Greenleaf.

Pauli, G. (1998) *UpSizing: The Road to Zero Emissions*, Sheffield: Greenleaf.

Porter, M. (1991) 'America's green strategy', *Scientific American*, April, p. 96.

Porter, M. and van der Linde, C. (1995) 'Green and Competitive: ending the stalemate', *Harvard Business Review*, Sept–Oct, pp. 120–134.

Schmidheiny, S. (1992) *Changing Course: A Global Business Perspective on Development and the Environment*, Cambridge, Mass: MIT Press.

von Weiczsäcker, E., Lovins, A. and Lovins, H. (1997) *Factor Four: Doubling Wealth, Halving Resource Use*, London: Earthscan.

World Commission on Environment and Development (1987) *Our Common Future*, Oxford: Oxford University Press.

Essential reading

Porter, M. and van der Linde, C. (1995) 'Green and Competitive: ending the stalemate', *Harvard Business Review*, Sept–Oct, pp. 120–134.

Neale, A. (1997) 'Organising Environmental Self-regulation: Liberal Governmentality and the pursuit of Ecological Modernisation in Europe', *Environmental Politics*, **6** (4), pp. 1–24.

Internet resources

The following websites will be useful for updates on issues raised in this chapter:

www.ends.co.uk (ENDS Report)

www.cutter.com (Business and the Environment; Environment Watch Western Europe; Global Environmental Change Report)

www.asianenviro.com (Asian Environmental Review)

www.zeri.org (Zero Emissions Research Initiative)

The ENDS website maintains a useful range of links to other relevant sites.

Many company websites include sections on their environmental policy. For cases featured in this chapter, see:

www.diy.co.uk (B&Q)

www.ecover.com (Ecover)

www.eastern.co.uk (Eastern Group)

www.mitsubishi.co.jp (Mitsubishi Corporation)

www.pg.com (Procter & Gamble)

www.shell.com (Shell International)

www.unioncarbide.com (Union Carbide)

Statistical appendix

GDP by kind of activity in current prices 1970 to 1994

Japan

	Agriculture	Mining	Manufacturing	Electricity Gas and Water	Construction	Wholesale and Retail Trades	Transport and Communication	Finance Insurance and Real Estate	Community and Social Services	Government Services	Total
Bill yen											
1970	4463	621	26340	1557	5662	10504	5022	9306	7033	4642	75150
1975	8130	776	44250	3002	14324	21904	9541	20549	16251	13128	151855
1980	8876	1345	71682	6400	21181	31261	16071	36941	28165	20531	242453
1985	10214	959	94673	10305	25381	42836	21087	49330	46391	26285	327461
1990	10921	1122	121219	11242	43428	58358	28475	72338	63624	32688	443415
1994	10149	1027	117151	13356	51644	60770	30656	85648	80452	37783	488636
Percentage shares											
1970	5.94	0.83	35.05	2.07	7.53	13.98	6.68	12.38	9.36	6.18	100.00
1975	5.35	0.51	29.14	1.98	9.43	14.42	6.28	13.53	10.70	8.65	100.00
1980	3.66	0.55	29.57	2.64	8.74	12.89	6.63	15.24	11.62	8.47	100.00
1985	3.12	0.29	28.91	3.15	7.75	13.08	6.44	15.06	14.17	8.03	100.00
1990	2.46	0.25	27.34	2.54	9.79	13.16	6.42	16.31	14.35	7.37	100.00
1994	2.08	0.21	23.98	2.73	10.57	12.44	6.27	17.53	16.46	7.73	100.00

Employment by kind of activity in current prices 1970 to 1994

Japan

	Agriculture	Mining	Manufacturing	Electricity Gas and Water	Construction	Wholesale and Retail Trades	Transport and Communication	Finance Insurance and Real Estate	Community and Social Services	Government Services	Total
000s											
1970	570	240	12010	290	3400	5580	2880	1480	4200	3150	33800
1975	590	160	12040	320	4020	6150	3030	1780	5180	3650	36920
1980	570	150	12070	350	4480	7280	3260	2030	6290	3910	40390
1985	1146	121	13169	347	4524	8862	3166	2361	8616	3935	46247
1990	948	97	13819	396	5084	9163	3255	2725	10532	3942	49961
1994	910	82	14155	427	5878	9584	3395	2751	12466	4008	53656
Percentage shares											
1970	1.69	0.71	35.53	0.86	10.06	16.51	8.52	4.38	12.43	9.32	100.00
1975	1.60	0.43	32.61	0.87	10.89	16.66	8.21	4.82	14.03	9.89	100.00
1980	1.41	0.37	29.88	0.87	11.09	18.02	8.07	5.03	15.57	9.68	100.00
1985	2.48	0.26	28.48	0.75	9.78	19.16	6.85	5.11	18.63	8.51	100.00
1990	1.90	0.19	27.66	0.79	10.18	18.34	6.52	5.45	21.08	7.89	100.00
1994	1.70	0.15	26.38	0.80	10.95	17.86	6.33	5.13	23.23	7.47	100.00

GDP by kind of activity in current prices 1970 to 1994

USA

Mill US $

	Agriculture	Mining	Manufacturing	Electricity Gas and Water	Construction	Wholesale and Retail Trades	Transport and Communication	Finance Insurance and Real Estate	Community and Social Services	Government Services	Total
1970	26879	17755	254074	23264	49412	171654	62915	180902	75591	132652	995098
1975	50178	39104	360985	40350	70770	272433	96094	280711	121185	210745	1542555
1980	67330	94630	586944	65555	122744	441311	168122	537433	209755	326530	2620354
1985	85900	132100	804700	130000	181500	661100	250500	949900	366200	483000	4044900
1990	113600	104500	1032100	158300	243300	868500	325600	1423100	574100	667500	5510600
1994	109100	98600	1126200	182200	237200	1049000	379800	1699100	715900	768500	6365600

Percentage shares

	Agriculture	Mining	Manufacturing	Electricity Gas and Water	Construction	Wholesale and Retail Trades	Transport and Communication	Finance Insurance and Real Estate	Community and Social Services	Government Services	Total
1970	2.70	1.78	25.53	2.34	4.97	17.25	6.32	18.18	7.60	13.33	100
1975	3.25	2.54	23.40	2.62	4.59	17.66	6.23	18.20	7.86	13.66	100
1980	2.57	3.61	22.40	2.50	4.68	16.84	6.42	20.51	8.00	12.46	100
1985	2.12	3.27	19.89	3.21	4.49	16.34	6.19	23.48	9.05	11.94	100
1990	2.06	1.90	18.73	2.87	4.42	15.76	5.91	25.82	10.42	12.11	100
1994	1.71	1.55	17.69	2.86	3.73	16.48	5.97	26.69	11.25	12.07	100

Employment by kind of activity in current prices 1970 to 1994

USA

	Agriculture	Mining	Manufacturing	Electricity Gas and Water	Construction	Wholesale and Retail Trades	Transport Storage and Communication	Finance Insurance and Real Estate	Community and Social Services	Government Services	Total
000s											
1970	1521	627	19410	691	3624	16062	3819	6204	8027	15866	75851
1975	1660	748	18320	732	3573	18065	3818	7399	9965	16740	81020
1980	1765	1034	20337	824	4326	21445	4306	9893	12065	17914	93909
1985	1492	907	18753	890	4575	21324	4118	11902	13372	15358	92691
1990	1613	698	18679	939	5019	24061	4539	14674	16231	16831	103234
1994	1642	597	17676	929	4523	23973	4556	15374	17810	16802	103832
Percentage shares											
1970	2.01	0.83	25.59	0.91	4.78	21.18	5.03	8.18	10.58	20.92	100
1975	2.05	0.92	22.61	0.90	4.41	22.30	4.71	9.13	12.30	20.66	100
1980	1.88	1.10	21.66	0.88	4.61	22.84	4.59	10.53	12.85	19.08	100
1985	1.61	0.98	20.23	0.96	4.94	23.01	4.44	12.84	14.43	16.57	100
1990	1.56	0.68	18.09	0.91	4.86	23.30	4.39	14.21	15.71	16.30	100
1994	1.58	0.57	17.02	0.89	4.35	23.08	4.39	14.80	17.14	16.17	100

France

GDP by kind of activity in current prices 1970 to 1994

Mill FF

	Agriculture	Mining	Manufacturing	Electricity Gas and Water	Construction	Wholesale and Retail Trades	Transport Storage and Communication	Finance Insurance and Real Estate	Community and Social Services	Government Services	Total
1970	50542	6652	224957	13603	58315	83540	42766	105033	46284	78681	710373
1975	73247	12334	397391	26097	110558	161215	75722	214153	100577	162571	1333865
1980	112943	23003	722004	59215	182028	277420	154162	457451	213548	331015	2532789
1985	182310	40112	1033139	116869	243898	575507	289050	861137	231374	795561	4368957
1990	221865	29754	1394503	138739	335812	811345	378473	1390152	363473	1015534	6079650
1994	177196	31271	1415399	176232	335104	888522	427520	1704649	446240	1270319	6872452

Percentage shares

	Agriculture	Mining	Manufacturing	Electricity Gas and Water	Construction	Wholesale and Retail Trades	Transport Storage and Communication	Finance Insurance and Real Estate	Community and Social Services	Government Services	Total
1970	7.11	0.94	31.67	1.91	8.21	11.76	6.02	14.79	6.52	11.08	100
1975	5.49	0.92	29.79	1.96	8.29	12.09	5.68	16.06	7.54	12.19	100
1980	4.46	0.91	28.51	2.34	7.19	10.95	6.09	18.06	8.43	13.07	100
1985	4.17	0.92	23.65	2.67	5.58	13.17	6.62	19.71	5.30	18.21	100
1990	3.65	0.49	22.94	2.28	5.52	13.35	6.23	22.87	5.98	16.70	100
1994	2.58	0.46	20.60	2.56	4.88	12.93	6.22	24.80	6.49	18.48	100

Employment by kind of activity in current prices 1970 to 1994

France

	Agriculture	Mining	Manufacturing	Electricity Gas and Water	Construction	Wholesale and Retail Trades	Transport Storage and Communication	Finance Insurance and Real Estate	Community and Social Services	Government Services	Total
000s											
1970	588	216	5112	167	1701	5369				3431	16584
1975	454	170	5327	174	1602	2369	1205	1139	1421	3712	17573
1980	387	138	5004	189	1489	2565	1277	1357	1813	3913	18132
1985	297.1	139.7	4543.1	164.6	1262.1	2479	1184.1	1715.9	853.5	5363.8	18002.9
1990	277.3	108.7	4351.6	161.7	1351.9	2663.8	1224.8	2220.8	1035.2	5619.6	19015.4
1994	271.5	94	3990.6	160.3	1243	2570.5	1223.6	2158.2	1115.7	6011.5	18838.9
Percentage shares											
1970	3.55	1.30	30.82	1.01	10.26	32.37	0.00	0.00	0.00	20.69	100
1975	2.58	0.97	30.31	0.99	9.12	13.48	6.86	6.48	8.09	21.12	100
1980	2.13	0.76	27.60	1.04	8.21	14.15	7.04	7.48	10.00	21.58	100
1985	1.65	0.78	25.24	0.91	7.01	13.77	6.58	9.53	4.74	29.79	100
1990	1.46	0.57	22.88	0.85	7.11	14.01	6.44	11.68	5.44	29.55	100
1994	1.44	0.50	21.18	0.85	6.60	13.64	6.50	11.46	5.92	31.91	100

Germany

GDP by kind of activity in current prices 1970 to 1994

	Agriculture	Mining	Manufacturing	Electricity Gas and Water	Construction	Wholesale and Retail Trades	Transport Storage and Communication	Finance Insurance and Real Estate	Community and Social Services	Government Services	Total
Mill DM											
1970	21780	8220	259450	14500	51550	65400	38070	55590	50390	62560	627510
1975	28470	11260	354060	26410	63190	97390	59940	106670	93760	122750	963900
1980	30520	13400	490170	37860	99030	144240	83960	148330	160370	172120	1380000
1985	31920	16050	578850	50480	94810	156410	105050	231870	236840	207260	1709540
1990	36740	11390	741550	58840	127620	212550	134200	288850	386990	253200	2251930
1994	29880	12650	746310	63180	152700	246370	155280	387100	541670	301080	2636220
Percentage shares											
1970	3.47	1.31	41.35	2.31	8.22	10.42	6.07	8.86	8.03	9.97	100
1975	2.95	1.17	36.73	2.74	6.56	10.10	6.22	11.07	9.73	12.73	100
1980	2.21	0.97	35.52	2.74	7.18	10.45	6.08	10.75	11.62	12.47	100
1985	1.87	0.94	33.86	2.95	5.55	9.15	6.14	13.56	13.85	12.12	100
1990	1.63	0.51	32.93	2.61	5.67	9.44	5.96	12.83	17.18	11.24	100
1994	1.13	0.48	28.31	2.40	5.79	9.35	5.89	14.68	20.55	11.42	100

Germany

Employment by kind of activity in current prices 1970 to 1994

	Agriculture	Mining	Manufacturing	Electricity Gas and Water	Construction	Wholesale and Retail Trades	Transport Storage and Communication	Finance Insurance and Real Estate	Community and Social Services	Government Services	Total
000s											
1970	2262	310	10117	241	2319	3348	1407	597	2336	2978	25915
1975	1773	259	9106	255	1990	3360	1497	689	2521	3576	25026
1980	1436	235	9005	267	2092	3482	1467	740	2802	3911	25437
1985	248	219	8097	272	1682	2799	1410	792	2251	4118	21888
1990	231	181	8582	284	1727	3081	1502	891	2811	4305	23595
1994	226	153	7995	287	1774	3311	1541	953	3277	4335	23852
Percentage shares											
1970	8.73	1.20	39.04	0.93	8.95	12.92	5.43	2.30	9.01	11.49	100
1975	7.08	1.03	36.39	1.02	7.95	13.43	5.98	2.75	10.07	14.29	100
1980	5.65	0.92	35.40	1.05	8.22	13.69	5.77	2.91	11.02	15.38	100
1985	1.13	1.00	36.99	1.24	7.68	12.79	6.44	3.62	10.28	18.81	100
1990	0.98	0.77	36.37	1.20	7.32	13.06	6.37	3.78	11.91	18.25	100
1994	0.95	0.64	33.52	1.20	7.44	13.88	6.46	4.00	13.74	18.17	100

GDP by kind of activity in current prices 1970 to 1994

Italy

	Agriculture	Mining	Mining and Manufacturing	Electricity Gas and Water	Construction	Wholesale and Retail Trades	Transport Storage and Communication	Finance Insurance and Real Estate	Community and Social Services	Government Services	Total
Bill lira											
1970	5122		18253	3465	5250	8515	3874	10485	Included in Finance	6557	61521
1975	9644		37229	5983	9993	15875	6926	24495		14215	124360
1980	21595		103354	15635	25847	43506	20932	61585		41557	334011
1985	36327		196473	37479	50987	130048	43609	177559		96007	768489
1990	42133		293813	67008	76702	201096	74344	319071		169020	1243187
1994	46105		313383	89386	85030	237908	94751	412604		197732	1476899
Percentage shares											
1970	8.33		29.67	5.63	8.53	13.84	6.30	17.04		10.66	100
1975	7.75		29.94	4.81	8.04	12.77	5.57	19.70		11.43	100
1980	6.47		30.94	4.68	7.74	13.03	6.27	18.44		12.44	100
1985	4.73		25.57	4.88	6.63	16.92	5.67	23.10		12.49	100
1990	3.39		23.63	5.39	6.17	16.18	5.98	25.67		13.60	100
1994	3.12		21.22	6.05	5.76	16.11	6.42	27.94		13.39	100

Employment by kind of activity in current prices 1970 to 1994

Italy

	Agriculture	Mining	Mining and Manufacturing	Electricity Gas and Water	Construction	Wholesale and Retail Trades	Transport Storage and Communication	Finance Insurance and Real Estate	Community and Social Services	Government Services	Total
000s											
1970	1205		4656	171	1763	1275	740	856	Included in Finance	2333	12999
1975	1130		4893	182	1493	1407	854	979		2808	13746
1980	1075		4894	191	1452	1563	909	1247		3124	14455
1985	784		4281	193	1141	1514	1709	1879		3439	14940
1990	741		4340	197	1110	1590	1179	2101		3628	14886
1994	650		3857	184	1090	2173	1159	2196		3639	14948
Percentage shares											
1970	9.27		35.82	1.32	13.56	9.81	5.69	6.59		17.95	100
1975	8.22		35.60	1.32	10.86	10.24	6.21	7.12		20.43	100
1980	7.44		33.86	1.32	10.04	10.81	6.29	8.63		21.61	100
1985	5.25		28.65	1.29	7.64	10.13	11.44	12.58		23.02	100
1990	4.98		29.15	1.32	7.46	10.68	7.92	14.11		24.37	100
1994	4.35		25.80	1.23	7.29	14.54	7.75	14.69		24.34	100

GDP by kind of activity in current prices 1970 to 1994

UK

	Agriculture	Mining	Manufacturing	Electricity Gas and Water	Construction	Wholesale and Retail Trades	Transport Storage and Communication	Finance Insurance and Real Estate	Community and Social Services	Government Services	Total
Mill £											
1970	1266	639	14309	1385	3050	4603	3754	5465	5081	5320	44872
1975	2545	1510	26690	2707	6789	9339	7922	13127	11234	14342	96205
1980	4443	11805	49838	5963	13001	18677	15440	29344	26524	28427	203462
1985	6110	22690	76801	8204	18402	40600	24129	60347	13084	45278	315645
1990	8923	11319	111315	10583	34568	68273	40200	117414	22581	68342	493518
1994	11548	13078	121272	15458	31035	63472	49039	154550	46646	68671	574769
Percentage shares											
1970	2.82	1.42	31.89	3.09	6.80	10.26	8.37	12.18	11.32	11.86	100
1975	2.65	1.57	27.74	2.81	7.06	9.71	8.23	13.64	11.68	14.91	100
1980	2.18	5.80	24.49	2.93	6.39	9.18	7.59	14.42	13.04	13.97	100
1985	1.94	7.19	24.33	2.60	5.83	12.86	7.64	19.12	4.15	14.34	100
1990	1.81	2.29	22.56	2.14	7.00	13.83	8.15	23.79	4.58	13.85	100
1994	2.01	2.28	21.10	2.69	5.40	11.04	8.53	26.89	8.12	11.95	100

Employment by kind of activity in current prices 1970 to 1994

UK

	Agriculture	Mining	Manufacturing	Electricity Gas and Water	Construction	Wholesale and Retail Trades	Tansport Storage and Communication	Finance Insurance and Real Estate	Community and Social Services	Government Services	Total
000s											
1970	457	411	8204	366	1165		1462		6330	4433	22851
1975	392	369	7559	346	1152		1498		6407	4978	23046
1980	371	371	7024	348	1136		1530		6862	5541	23183
1985	329	244	5218	295	989	4106	1319	2122	1741	5347	21710
1990	297	172	5082	277	1087	4671	1414	2682	2267	5272	23221
1994	276	110	4357	238	834	4462	1286	2644	3349	4270	21826
Percentage shares											
1970	2.00	1.80	35.90	1.60	5.10		6.40		27.70	19.40	100
1975	1.80	1.60	33.80	1.50	5.00		6.50		27.80	22.00	100
1980	1.60	1.60	30.30	1.50	4.90		6.60		29.60	23.90	100
1985	1.42	1.12	24.04	1.36	4.56	18.91	6.08	9.77	8.02	24.63	100
1990	1.28	0.74	21.89	1.19	4.68	20.12	6.09	11.55	9.76	22.70	100
1994	1.19	0.50	19.96	1.09	3.82	20.44	5.89	12.11	15.34	19.56	100

Up to 1980 figures for Wholesale,Retail and Finance and Insurance included in the Community and Social Services total

247

GDP growth rates in constant prices (percentage change over the previous year)

	United States	Japan	France	Germany	Italy	UK	Korea	Malaysia	World
1970		9.4	5.7		5.3	2.3	8.8		3.4
1971	3.1	4.2	4.8		1.9	2	9.2	7.1	3.7
1972	4.8	8.4	4.4		2.9	3.5	5.9	9.4	4.7
1973	5.2	7.9	5.4		6.5	7.4	14.4	11.7	5.9
1974	-0.6	-1.2	3.1		4.7	-1.7	7.9	8.3	2.3
1975	-0.8	2.6	-0.3		-2.1	-0.7	7.1	0.8	1.3
1976	4.9	4.8	4.2		6.5	2.8	12.9	11.6	5.3
1977	4.5	5.3	3.2		2.9	2.4	10.1	7.8	4.4
1978	4.8	5.1	3.3		3.7	3.5	9.7	6.7	4.1
1979	2.5	5.2	3.2		5.7	2.8	7.6	9.3	4
1980	-0.5	3.6	1.6	1	3.5	-2.2	-2.2	7.4	2.6
1981	1.8	3.6	1.2	0.1	0.5	-1.3	6.7	6.9	1.6
1982	-2.2	3.2	2.5	-1	0.5	1.7	7.3	5.9	0.4
1983	3.9	2.7	0.7	1.7	1.2	3.7	11.8	6.3	2.6
1984	6.2	4.3	1.3	2.8	2.6	2.3	10.1	7.8	4.8
1985	3.2	5	1.9	2.3	2.8	3.8	6.2	-1	4
1986	2.9	2.6	2.5	2.3	2.8	4.3	11.6	1	3.4
1987	3.1	4.1	1.4	1.4	3.1	4.8	11.5	5.4	3.9
1988	3.9	6.2	3.6	3.6	3.9	5	11.3	8.8	4.5
1989	2.5	4.7	3.7	3.7	2.9	2.2	6.4	9.2	3.3
1990	1.8	4.8	5.7	5.7	2.2	0.4	9.5	9.7	2.9
1991	-1	3.8	0.8	13.2	1.1	-2	9.1	8.6	2.3
1992	2.7	1	2.2	2.2	0.6	-0.5	5.1	7.8	3.2
1993	2.2	0.3	-1.3	-1.2	-1.2	2.1	5.8	8.3	2.9
1994	3.5	0.6	2.8	2.9	2.2	4.3	8.6	9.2	4.3
1995	2	1.5	2.1	1.9	2.9	2.7	8.9	9.5	3.5
1996	2.8	3.9	1.6	1.3	0.7	2.2	7.1	8.6	3.9
1997	3.8	0.9	2.3	2	1.5	3.4	5.5	7.8	

Consumption as a percentage of GDP

	United States	Japan	France	Germany	Italy	UK	Korea	Malaysia	World
1970	82.6	59.7	72.6	70.4	73.3	79.5	84.6	78	73.2
1971	82	61.5	72.7	71.5	75.3	80.2	85.3	77.8	73.4
1972	81.3	62.2	72.6	72	76.3	81.2	83.1	79.8	73.1
1973	79.7	61.9	71.9	71.8	75.8	80.8	76.7	70.7	74.8
1974	80.9	63.4	72.9	73.6	75	84	79.4	71.3	75.4
1975	82.4	67.2	75.3	77.3	77.2	84.3	81.9	76.2	77.6
1976	81.7	67.4	75.3	76.2	75.3	83	76.8	67.7	77.1
1977	81.1	67.5	75.4	76.7	75.5	80.4	73	68.6	77.1
1978	80	67.4	75.5	76.3	75.3	79.9	71.2	67.8	76.3
1979	79.7	68.4	75.7	76	76	80.1	71.8	62.2	75.9
1980	81.2	68.7	77	77.2	77.2	81.4	76.2	67.1	76.5
1981	80.2	68.1	79.1	78.3	78.5	82.7	76.1	71.2	77.4
1982	82.8	69.3	80	78.3	79.1	82.8	75	71.4	78.6
1983	83.7	70.2	80.3	77.7	79	83	71.4	67.9	78.5
1984	82.2	69.2	80.4	77.3	79	82.9	69	64.5	77.8
1985	83.3	68.5	80.5	76.8	79.4	81.9	68.6	67.3	77.7
1986	84.2	68.3	79.3	75.2	78.7	83.8	65.2	67.9	78.3
1987	84.8	68.3	79.7	75.6	79.2	83.2	62.3	62.7	77.7
1988	84.6	67.4	78.5	74.8	79.1	83.4	60.6	63.7	76.8
1989	84	67.3	77.6	73.7	79.3	83.2	63.5	65.4	76.1
1990	84.9	67	77.6	72.6	79.5	83.6	63.8	66.6	76.7
1991	85.5	66.2	78.1	72.6	80	85	63.6	66.5	78
1992	85.3	67	79	77.1	80.9	86	64.8	64.5	78.4
1993	84.7	68	80.7	78.2	80.5	86.3	64.6	63.3	78.1
1994	83.9	69.3	79.8	76.8	80.2	85.4	64.3	61.2	79.3
1995	84.1	69.9	79.4	76.5	78.8	84.6	63.2	60.5	77.3
1996	84	69.5	80.3	77.4	78.9	84.8	64.5	57.4	77.3
1997	83.3	70.3	79.3	76.6	79.3	84.5	64.8	55.6	77.4

World exports in bill US dollars

	United States	Japan	France	Germany	Italy	UK	Korea	Malaysia	World
1970	42.66	19.32	17.88	34.23	19.30	19.43	0.84	1.69	299.70
1971	43.55	24.00	20.83	38.85	15.11	22.10	1.07	1.64	335.90
1972	49.20	29.09	26.47	46.74	18.61	23.99	1.63	1.72	399.90
1973	70.82	37.02	36.68	67.56	22.23	29.64	3.22	3.05	556.10
1974	99.44	55.47	46.48	89.37	30.47	38.20	4.46	4.24	829.10
1975	108.86	55.82	53.09	90.18	34.99	43.42	4.95	3.84	850.70
1976	116.79	67.30	56.87	102.16	37.27	45.36	7.72	5.30	958.70
1977	123.18	81.08	65.28	118.07	45.31	55.86	10.05	6.08	1086.30
1978	145.85	98.21	79.37	142.45	56.09	67.89	12.72	7.41	1257.60
1979	186.36	102.30	100.69	171.80	72.23	86.40	15.06	11.08	1625.00
1980	225.57	130.44	116.03	192.86	78.10	110.13	17.51	12.96	1940.80
1981	238.72	151.50	106.42	176.05	77.07	102.24	21.27	11.77	1924.20
1982	216.44	138.39	96.69	176.42	73.79	96.98	21.85	12.03	1765.50
1983	205.64	146.97	94.94	169.42	72.88	91.62	24.45	14.13	1734.50
1984	223.98	169.70	97.57	171.74	74.56	93.88	29.25	16.59	1840.60
1985	218.82	177.16	101.67	183.93	76.72	101.25	30.28	15.44	1872.00
1986	227.16	210.76	124.95	243.33	97.20	107.09	34.72	13.75	2046.40
1987	254.12	231.29	148.38	294.37	116.71	131.26	47.28	17.94	2401.40
1988	322.43	264.86	167.79	323.32	127.86	145.17	60.70	21.11	2742.00
1989	363.81	273.93	179.40	341.23	140.56	152.35	62.38	25.05	2981.50
1990	393.59	287.58	216.59	410.10	170.30	185.17	65.02	29.42	3395.30
1991	421.73	314.79	217.10	402.84	169.47	184.96	71.87	34.35	3489.10
1992	448.16	339.89	235.87	422.27	178.16	190.00	76.63	40.71	3730.20
1993	464.77	362.24	209.35	382.47	169.15	180.18	82.24	47.12	3730.70
1994	512.63	397.01	235.91	429.72	191.42	204.92	96.01	58.65	4244.80
1995	584.74	443.12	286.74	523.80	234.00	242.04	125.06	73.87	5079.40
1996	625.07	410.90	288.47	524.20	252.00	260.75	129.72	78.31	5286.50
1997	688.70	420.96	289.84	512.43	238.24	281.51	136.62	78.70	5546.00

Industrialized country share of world exports: USA, Japan, UK, Germany, France, Italy

Exchange rate to the US $

	Japan	France	Germany	Italy	UK
1970	357.65	5.55	3.65	623.00	2.39
1975	305.15	4.49	2.62	683.60	2.02
1980	203.00	4.52	1.96	930.50	2.39
1985	200.50	7.56	2.46	1678.50	1.44
1990	134.40	5.13	1.49	1130.20	1.93
1995	102.83	4.90	1.43	1584.70	1.55
1998 Dec	115.60	5.62	1.67	1653.10	1.65

Interest rates (money market rate) %

	Japan	France	Germany	Italy	UK	USA
1970	8.28	8.68	8.6	7.38	2	7.91
1975	10.67	7.92	4.4	10.64	6.08	7.86
1980	10.93	11.85	9.1	17.17	15.62	15.27
1985	6.46	9.93	5.2	15.25	12.41	9.93
1990	7.24	9.85	7.9	12.38	14.64	10.01
1995	1.21	6.35	4.5	10.46	5.98	8.83
1998 Dec	0.25	3.09	3.4	3.95	6	7.75

Consumer prices index

	Japan	France	Germany	Italy	UK	USA
1970	34.6	21.6	45.4	10.9	14.7	29.7
1975	59.2	32.9	61.2	18.7	27.1	41.2
1980	81.6	54.3	74.5	39.9	53	63.1
1985	93.5	85.9	90.2	75.9	75	82.4
1990	100	100	96.5	100	100	100
1995	107	111.6	114.8	127.8	118.2	116.6
1998 Dec	110	116.1	119.7	204	130.3	125.4

Share prices index

	Japan	France	Germany	Italy	UK	USA
1970	7.5	16.3	29.2	15.6	11.9	23.4
1975	14.3	16	29.1	10.1	11.3	24.7
1980	21.7	23.7	30.7	16.2	23.8	34.4
1985	45.7	43.2	67.5	49.6	57.7	53.2
1990	100	100	100	100	100	100
1995	63.3	102.5	103.3	95.4	147.3	164.1
1998 Dec	50.8	216.9	206.6	138.9	222.1	365

Sources: For the tables on national GDP by sector and employment the OECD National Accounts Volume II has been used.
For all other tables the IMF World Financial Statistics Yearbook has been used.

Addresses of Internet web pages for statistical material and business information

Organisation for Economic Co-operation and Development (OECD)
http://www.oecd.org/

International Monetary Fund (IMF)
http://www.imf.org/

IMF/World Bank Joint Library
http://jolis.worldbankimflib.org/external.htm

US Chamber of Commerce
http://www.uschamber.org/

US Department of Commerce
http://www.doc.gov/

US Bureau of Economic Analysis
http://www.bea.doc.gov/

US Bureau of the Census
http://www.census.gov/

US Federal Reserve
http://www.nttc.edu/gov/independents/frs.html

MITI (Japan)
http://www.wave.co.jp/wave/government/miti/

JETRO (Japan)
http://www.jetro.go.jp/top/index.html

Index